ASPEN PUBLISHERS

Casenote™ *Legal Briefs*

CONSTITUTIONAL LAW

Keyed to Courses Using

Stone, Seidman, Sunstein, Tushnet, and Karlan's
Constitutional Law

Sixth Edition

Wolters Kluwer

Law & Business

AUSTIN   BOSTON   CHICAGO   NEW YORK   THE NETHERLANDS

This publication is designed to provide accurate and authoritative information in regard to the subject matter covered. It is sold with the understanding that the publisher is not engaged in rendering legal, accounting, or other professional services. If legal advice or other expert assistance is required, the services of a competent professional person should be sought.

> — From a Declaration of Principles adopted jointly by a Committee of the American Bar Association and a Committee of Publishers and Associates

To contact Customer Care, e-mail customer.care@aspenpublishers.com, call 1-800-234-1660, fax 1-800-901-9075, or mail correspondence to:

Aspen Publishers
Attn: Order Department
P.O. Box 990
Frederick, MD 21705

Printed in the United States of America.

1 2 3 4 5 6 7 8 9 0

ISBN 978-0-7355-7879-1

FREEDOM OF SPEECH

TWO CONCERNS

1. Types of Protected Speech
2. Speech Regulations

DANGEROUS SPEECH

1. *Unlawful Activity:* The state may prohibit speech advocating unlawful or subversive action.
   a. *Clear and Present Danger:* Words used in a manner and specific context where they would bring about a criminal harm. *Schenck v. United States*, 249 U.S. 47 (1919).
   b. *Overthrow of Government by Force:* Words that may cause harm by influencing others to undertake harmful acts, even those taught as advocacy of a certain doctrine. *Gitlow v. New York*, 268 U.S. 652 (1925).
2. *Incitement:* The urging of a group or person to take immediate action. *Brandenburg v. Ohio*, 395 U.S. 444 (1969).
   a. Likely to cause harmful action;
   b. Speaker intends to incite or produce imminent lawless action and is likely to do so;
   c. Applies only where speaker urges illegal action in opposition to government, government policies, or private parties.
3. *Fighting Words:* Direct personal insults likely to cause a person to react violently. Other injurious insults are not prosecuted. *Chaplinsky v. New Hampshire*, 315 U.S. 568 (1942).
4. *Group Libel:* False and derogatory statements tending to produce hate or prejudice about a particular group. *Example: Statements that a certain race, creed, or religion is depraved. Beauharnais v. Illinois*, 343 U.S. 250 (1952).
5. *Defamation:* False and derogatory statements, tending to harm the reputation of the subject discussed. *New York Times v. Sullivan*, 376 U.S. 254 (1964).
   a. *Public Figures:*
      i. *Actual malice required:* statement made with knowledge of falsity or in reckless disregard for the truth. *Milkovich v. Lorain Journal*, 497 U.S. 1 (1990).
      ii. Applies to statements of fact. *Exception: where reasonable person would interpret statement of opinion as based on fact.*
   b. *Private Persons:*
      i. Malice required if private persons voluntarily place themselves into a particular controversy. Private person becomes a "public figure" for a limited range of issues.
      ii. Malice is NOT required for private persons not involved in public issue, or involuntarily involved in a public matter. *Gertz v. Robert Welch, Inc.*, 418 U.S. 323 (1974).
6. *Invasion of Privacy:* Disclosure of true facts that are private or harm to reputation based on false impression created by statement. *Exception:*
   a. Disclosure of private information that is already publicly known because it is:
      i. in public record; *Cox Broadcasting Corp. v. Cohn*, 420 U.S. 469 (1975).
      ii. otherwise publicly apparent. *Zacchini v. Scripps-Howard Broadcasting Co.*, 433 U.S. 562 (1977).

CONTENT REGULATION

First Amendment prevents regulation of speech based on its content or the viewpoint expressed by the speaker. Laws that regulate speech on the basis of content or viewpoint are unconstitutional.

1. *Content Neutral:* A law that doesn't distinguish between types of speech on the basis of what the speech is about, is constitutional.
2. *Viewpoint Neutral:* A law that regulates an entire topic or speech regardless of the opinions or views expressed about that topic is constitutional.
2. *Content-based Regulation:* Government may regulate speech on the basis of content if:
   a. The government has a compelling interest to do so and the means of regulation are necessary to achieve that interest.
   b. The law regulates conduct and not the content of the speech associated with it.

PRIOR RESTRAINT

1. Government regulation of speech before it has taken place is generally unconstitutional.
2. Prior restraint on speech is permissible where:
   a. National security interests are affected by the publication of particular subject matter. *Near v. Minnesota (ex rel. Olson)*, 283 U.S. 697 (1931).
   b. Government interest exists in securing a fair trial. *Nebraska Press Assn. v. Stuart*, 427 U.S. 539 (1976).

VAGUENESS AND OVERBREADTH

Government regulations that are vague or overbroad are unconstitutional as regulating more or less speech than they purport to proscribe.

1. *Vagueness:* A statute is vague if persons of common intelligence cannot guess what type of behavior is being regulated. *Connally v. General Construction Co.*, 269 U.S. 385 (1926).
2. *Overbreadth:* A statute is overbroad if it is worded in such a way that permits a state to regulate both matters that it may constitutionally proscribe, and those that it may not constitutionally regulate or proscribe.

OBSCENE SPEECH

Miller v. California, 413 U.S. 15 (1973)

1. To the average person applying contemporary community standards, the expression is obscene if:
   a. It appeals to the prurient interest;
   b. Work is patently offensive; and
   c. Taken as a whole, lacks serious literary, artistic, political, or scientific value.

INDECENT AND OFFENSIVE SPEECH

Government cannot prohibit the use of specific words in a public place where speech is not legitimately restricted. Words so protected are not obscene; but are merely indecent, vulgar, or offensive. Risk of censorship in specific words is the possibility of a government ban on the expression of an unpopular message. *Cohen v. California*, 403 U.S. 15 (1971).

Regulation of Conduct Associated with Speech

1. *Symbolic Speech (Expressive Conduct):* If law regulates expression based on its content, strict scrutiny will be applied to uphold regulation. If regulation incidentally affects expression, or government has important aim unrelated to the expression, balancing test is applied: government interest is weighed against the impact of the law on expression. *United States v. O'Brien*, 391 U.S. 367 (1968).
2. *Discriminatory Conduct:* First Amendment does not protect speech and attendant conduct that is motivated by bias or discrimination.
3. *Time, Place, and Manner Regulations:* The government may regulate the time, place, and manner of access to locations that may be used for expressive purposes. Laws regulating access to property on the basis of the speech that is to be made on such property are generally unconstitutional.
   a. *Public Forums:* Specific types of public property traditionally associated with the act of speech or expression. Laws regulating speech in public forums may by upheld if they are:
      i. content neutral;
      ii. narrowly tailored to serve a compelling governmental interest; and
      iii. allow for alternative channels of communication.
   b. *Nonpublic Forums:* Property that is not traditionally associated with speech, or whose primary use is not for expressive activity. Laws regulating speech in nonpublic forums may be upheld if they are:
      i. viewpoint neutral; and
      ii. reasonably related to a legitimate government purpose.
   c. *Private Forums:* Property that is not open to the public at large, or otherwise in the hands of private parties. Laws regulating speech in private forums may be upheld if states allow access to shopping centers for expression, but otherwise the Constitution does not apply to private property.

COMMERCIAL SPEECH

Any speech that is economically motivated or which does nothing more than propose a commercial transaction is protected. Commercial speech also provides information helping consumers make choices about products or services. *Exception: Government may regulate commercial speech that is likely to deceive or that is related to an illegal activity.*

FREEDOM OF THE PRESS

IN GENERAL

Press has special rights beyond those conferred by the free speech guarantee. *New York Times Co. v. United States (The Pentagon Papers Case)*, 403 U.S. 713 (1971).

1. *Government Inquiry:* Press not immune from subpoena or search warrants.
2. *Access to Information:*
   a. Government must ensure that places traditionally open to the public remain open unless government has a compelling interest in closing.
   b. Press only has same right of access as the public itself.

THE COMMERCE POWER/CLAUSE
ARTICLE I § 8

Congress has the power to regulate commerce between the states. What may Congress regulate?

1. *"Commerce":* Any activity may be regulated, even if it is not commerce in the traditional sense (the movement of persons or goods), as long as that activity:

   a. Takes place within interstate commerce.

   b. Uses the channels or instrumentalities of interstate commerce.

   c. Affects interstate commerce.

2. *Interstate v. Intrastate:* Congress may clearly regulate any activity that affects interstate commerce. Congress may regulate some activities that take place wholly intrastate, due to their effects on, or relationship to, interstate commerce. *Gibbons v. Ogden*, 22 U.S. 1 (1824).

   a. Any intrastate activity which has a substantial effect on interstate commerce. *United States v. Lopez*, 514 U.S. 549 (1995).

      i. *"Substantial effect":* Currently, an intrastate activity will have a substantial effect on interstate commerce only if the matter regulated is economic or commercial.

   b. Individual activities that have an aggregate effect on interstate commerce.

   c. All parts of an enterprise, even if only a part of the enterprise affects interstate commerce, where the nonregulated part may adversely impact the part affecting commerce.

3. *Scope of Power:* Congress's control over interstate commerce is plenary. Congress can prohibit or condition the movement of persons or goods regardless of its motive, so long as it does not violate any other constitutional provision.

   a. May do so to protect the national economy.

   b. As a means to achieve health, safety, or welfare aims.

      i. To a degree, Congress can regulate what happens after interstate commerce has taken place. *United States v. Sullivan*, 332 U.S. 689 (1948).

      ii. Congress may regulate and protect the instrumentalities of interstate commerce, such as vehicles, transportation terminals, even if the threat comes from intrastate activities. *Southern Railway Co. v. United States*, 222 U.S. 20 (1911).

      iii. Congress's conclusion that an activity affects interstate commerce need only be reasonable. *Hodel v. Virginia Surface Mining & Reclamation Assn.*, 452 U.S. 264 (1981).

      iv. Once Congress finds that a class or aggregate of activities affects commerce, that activity may be regulated regardless of whether any particular instance of that activity affects commerce. *Perez v. United States*, 402 U.S. 146 (1971).

FEDERAL EXECUTIVE POWER

DOMESTIC POWERS

Executive Power: Constitution confers the executive power on the president to administer and carry out the laws, and act in times of national, not domestic, emergencies without authorizing congressional legislation. ARTICLE II § 1

1. Presidential Pardon ARTICLE II § 2: Can pardon individuals or whole classes of persons any time after offense is committed. Effect of pardon is to preclude conviction or to mitigate or remove any penalties that result from conviction. The power to pardon cannot be limited by Congress. *United States v. Klein*, 80 U.S. 128 (1871)

2. Presidential Veto ARTICLE 1 § 7: President has power to disapprove of any legislation passed by Congress. President has power to override, Congress needs a vote of two-thirds of each house.

3. Power of Appointment ARTICLE II § 2: President has the ability to vest executive power in certain government officers through the power of appointment.

   a. *"Officers of the United States":* President can appoint officers who exercise "significant authority under the laws of the United States." Includes persons who formulate government policy, enact rulemaking and adjudication, or otherwise have broad governmental powers. *Buckley v. Valeo*, 424 U.S. 1 (1976).

   b. *Inferior Officers:* Power to appoint belongs to Congress, not President. Includes the heads of departments, or officers whose work is "directed and supervised" by persons appointed by the President. *Edmond v. United States*, 520 U.S. 651 (1997).

   c. *Removal Power:* President has power to terminate at will those officials whose exercise of discretion is essential to the functioning of the executive branch. Congress can create an "independent" executive branch for officials relatively free from presidential control, who may only be removed "for cause." *Morrison v. Olson*, 487 U.S. 654 (1988).

FOREIGN AFFAIRS POWERS

Executive branch has some ability to take action or enter into international commitments on behalf of the United States as a sovereign state among other sovereign states.

1. *Treaties:* President negotiates treaties. For treaty to be effective, Senate must still consent by ratifying it. ARTICLE II § 2

2. *Executive Agreements:* President can enter into international agreements without consent of Senate. To be valid, an executive agreement must be:

   a. Pursuant to the exercise of a presidential power;

   b. Based on authorizing legislation;

   c. Based on a prior treaty;

   d. Adopted by Congress (congressional-executive agreement).

3. *Military Powers and Foreign Affairs:* The President as Commander-in-Chief has the power to take some military actions without authorization by Congress.

PRESIDENTIAL IMMUNITIES AND PRIVILEGES

1. *Executive Liability:* President is absolutely immune from civil damages liability for his official acts. No immunity, or temporary immunity while in office, against civil litigation arising from events that took place before President took office. Criminal proceedings may be brought only after President has been impeached. No immunity from judicial process; court may order the President to comply with a subpoena. *United States v. Nixon*, 418 U.S. 683 (1974).

2. *Executive Privilege:* Communications conducted in exercise of executive function are confidential. Not in Constitution, but inferred by the Supreme Court. Exceptions:

   a. Disclosure to ensure justice. *United States v. Nixon*, 418 U.S. 683 (1974).

   b. Disclosure to ensure preservation of records.

GOVERNMENTAL RELATIONS

TWO TYPES

1. Federalism

2. Separation of Powers
(use chart on Page 4)

1. FEDERALISM—DEFINITION

Constitution balances power between dual sovereign governments; one belonging to the states, and the other to a central, federal government.

1. FEDERALISM—LIMITATIONS OF STATE POWER

1. Exclusive Federal Power ARTICLE I § 8:

   a. *Necessary and Proper Clause:* Congress has the power to make all laws "necessary and proper" for executing its powers and all others given by the Constitution to federal government. Congress has broad authority to choose the means for achieving some legitimate aim of the government. *Heart of Atlanta Motel, Inc. v. United States*, 379 U.S. 241 (1964).

   b. *Enumerated Powers:* Congress may use any of its enumerated powers to achieve any result not forbidden by the Constitution. *McCulloch v. Maryland*, 17 U.S. 316 (1819).

2. Concurrent State and Federal Power:

   a. *Supremacy Clause:* When Congress acts within its powers, it may expressly or implicitly enact laws that preempt state law. Congress acts implicitly to preempt state law if:

      i. It regulates a subject matter pervasively; or

      ii. It enacts a law that directly conflicts with a state law.

   b. *Preemption:* Where Congress has not enacted conflicting law and state action does not interfere with the federal structure, states may exercise nonexclusive federal power.

Governmental Relations
continues on page 3 ▶

Preemption questions generally involve determining Congress's intent:

i. States may not regulate if Congress has "occupied the field";

ii. *Express preemption:* if Congress has not occupied the field, state laws not consistent with the regulatory scheme may still be valid.

iii. *Implicit preemption:* Same issues as to extent of preemption must be court-determined.

iv. *Factors:* In determining the scope of preemption, courts must consider the nature of the subject matter regulated and the comprehensiveness of the regulation in addition to legislative intent and history, plain meaning, and construction.

OTHER LIMITS ON STATE REGULATION

1. *Dormant Commerce Clause:* Not expressly provided for, but implied from Constitution (dormant). Limits state regulation of interstate commerce. While Congress has plenary power over interstate commerce, in the absence of congressional action, states can regulate local matters for health, safety or welfare even if it affects interstate commerce. States may not, however, discriminate against or impose unjustifiable state burdens on interstate commerce. ARTICLE I § 8

    a. If state regulation discriminatory:
        i. *Discriminatory on face:* regulation is unconstitutional.
        ii. *Discriminatory in effect:* will be upheld where:
            a. legitimate state interest.
            b. no other nondiscriminatory alternatives.
    b. If state regulation nondiscriminatory:
        i. Benefit to state must outweigh burden.
        ii. Where substantial burden is to commerce, regulation is unconstitutional. Market Participant exception:
            a. When a state decides to regulate a particular market, it may enter that market as a participant (such as a trader or manufacturer).
            b. Dormant Commerce Clause will not apply to that state's regulatory activities.
            c. It may therefore favor its own citizens over others, subsidize the activities of its citizens and operate a business favoring state citizens. *Exception: Market participant exception only applies to state activities in a particular market, narrowly defined.*
            d. Privileges of Immunities Exception ARTICLE IV § 2: *A state cannot treat a noncitizen differently than a citizen with respect to the exercise of a privilege without substantial justification.*

. *Contract Clause:* Generally prohibits state law from impairing contracts. Financial contracts may be impaired. ARTICLE I § 10

    a. Where impairment reasonable and necessary to important public purpose.

    5th Amendment Takings: No taking of private property for public use without just compensation.

    a. *Public Purpose Nexus:*
        i. Taking is for public use if the means chosen must further a public purpose. *Pennsylvania Coal Co. v. Mahon*, 260 U.S. 393 (1922).

b. *Compensable Takings:* the government must pay compensation for a taking that involves:
    i. Physical invasion/occupation;
    ii. Denial of economically beneficial use *Lucas v. South Carolina Coastal Council*, 505 U.S. 1003 (1992); or
    iii. Public functions.

c. *Non-compensable Takings:* the government is NOT required to pay compensation for takings that involve:
    i. Public harm to be prevented; or
    ii. Economically viable use still exists *Nollan v. California Coastal Commn.*, 483 U.S. 825 (1987).

d. *Temporary Takings:* even if the property taken is returned, the government must pay damages incurred by the property returned.

1. FEDERALISM— INTERGOVERNMENTAL IMMUNITIES

1. *State Taxation/Regulation of Federal Activity:* Supremacy Clause provides that federal government and its properties are immune from state taxation and regulation. *McCulloch v. Maryland*, 17 U.S. 316 (1819). *Exceptions:*

    a. *Indirect Taxation:* Federal government does not have the direct legal obligation to pay the tax, but pays it incidental to another arrangement.
    b. Congress consents to state taxation and regulation. *Cleveland v. United States*, 323 U.S. 329 (1945).
    c. State income taxation of federal employees. *Johnson v. Maryland*, 254 U.S. 51 (1920).
    d. *State Taxation of Interstate Commerce:* A state may impose a direct tax on interstate business where:
        i. tax is on activity having a substantial nexus with the state;
        ii. tax is fairly apportioned between commerce originating in state & commerce from out of state;
        iii. tax must not discriminate against interstate commerce;
        iv. tax is related to some service the state provides (e.g., sales tax).

2. *Federal Regulation of States:* Supreme Court recognizes expansive power of Congress to influence or affect almost any state activity. *Exception: 10th Amendment limits federal power to override state laws concerning traditional governmental "functions essential to the separate and independent existence" of the states.*

3. *Federal Taxation of States:* No state immunity from federal taxation. *Exception: Federal tax which discriminates against a state or unduly interferes with essential state functions is impermissible.*

4. *Relations between States:*

    a. *Full Faith and Credit Clause:* requires that states recognize and give appropriate effect to the legal acts and proceedings of other states. ARTICLE IV § 1
    b. *Interstate Compacts:* states may enter into agreements with other states, including those involving multi-state relationships, without first obtaining the consent of Congress. ARTICLE I § 10 *Exception: Those agreements that might increase the political power of member states in a way that might encroach on the supremacy of the federal government.*

c. *Interstate Privileges and Immunities:* states must accord residents and nonresidents equal treatment with regard to certain interests Essential to a national economy and interstate harmony (i.e., "fundamental rights"). ARTICLE IV § 2

    i. Equal treatment for fundamental interests: states must give nonresidents the same rights as their own residents for "fundamental rights," including:
        a. owning, possessing, or disposing of property;
        b. engaging in employment;
        c. doing business;
        d. traveling through and within a state, including changing state residence;
        e. seeking medical care; and
        f. equal treatment by justice institutions. *Exception: States MAY treat a nonresident differently with respect to those rights that are fundamental, if:*
            • State has a substantial reason for different treatment;
            • nonresidents are the cause of the problem the state is trying to remedy; and
            • there is no alternative that would be less injurious to the exercise of the nonresident's rights. *Supreme Court of New Hampshire v. Piper*, 470 U.S. 274 (1985).

    ii. If rights infringed are nonfundamental, a state need only show that it did not act arbitrarily.
        a. *Unconstitutional discrimination:*
            • State may not impose residency requirement on nonresident women seeking abortions; *Doe v. Bolton*, 410 U.S. 179 (1973).
            • State may not require employers to give state residents preference in hiring; *Hicklin v. Orbeck*, 437 U.S. 518 (1978).
            • State may not condition bar admission on residency *Supreme Court of Virginia v. Friedman*, 487 U.S. 59 (1988).
        b. *Constitutional discrimination:* State may charge nonresident hunters higher fees for hunting licenses than residents. *Baldwin v. Fish and Game Commn. of Montana*, 436 U.S. 371 (1978).

    iii. Clause only applies to "citizens," meaning only natural persons born in or naturalized in the United States. The Clause does not apply to corporations or aliens.

1. FEDERALISM—STATE RELATIONS

1. The Constitution establishes a central federal system of government as well as independent state governments.
   All citizens are subjects of both governments. Both federal and state governments are sovereign and possess independent governmental power.

2. States' independent powers are defined by:
    a. Prohibition of exercise by the Constitution;
    b. Constitution's delegation of exclusively federal power;
    c. Reservation solely to the states by the 10th Amendment.

Governmental Relations continues on page 4 ▶

2. SEPARATION OF POWERS

	...TO LEGISLATIVE	...TO JUDICIAL	...TO EXECUTIVE
LEGISLATIVE IN RELATION...	• Delegation of Powers • Bicameralism *INS v. Chadha*, 462 U.S. 919 (1983) • Removal of Legislative Officers	• Assignment of Non-Judiciary Tasks • Article I Legislative Courts • Privilege against Congressional Arrest • Judicial Inquiry into Congressional Doings • Legislative Re-opening of Final Judgments	• Removal of Executive Officers • Presentment • Executive Inquiry into Congressional Doings • Executive Immunities and Privileges
JUDICIAL IN RELATION...	• Will not Re-open Final Judgments • Political Question	• Independence, Impartiality • Life Tenure	• Judicial, not Executive Duties *Marbury v. Madison*, 5 U.S. 137 (1803) • Executive Immunities and Privilege • Political Question
EXECUTIVE IN RELATION...	• Removal of Presidential Officers • Congress cannot override, unless for cause • Veto power (Presentment) • Cannot Inquire into Congressional Doings • Executive Immunities and Privileges	• Executive Immunities and Privileges • Political Question	• Removal of Executive Officers

DUE PROCESS

TWO TYPES

1. **Substantive Due Process**
2. **Procedural Due Process**

▼

1. SUBSTANTIVE DUE PROCESS

1. States cannot act to affect certain rights. *In re Slaughter-House Cases*, 83 U.S. 36 (1976).
2. State legislation affecting fundamental rights subject to review similar to strict scrutiny: regulation must be narrowly tailored to meet a compelling state interest. *Exception: Economic substantive due process legislation that involves governmental regulation of social and economic matters is subject to the rational basis test.*
3. Applies only to fundamental rights (some of which are not expressly stated in the Constitution).

▼

2. PROCEDURAL DUE PROCESS

No taking of life, liberty, or property without adequate procedures. What Procedures are appropriate? To determine "adequate procedures," examine several factors that must be balanced against each other:

1. What private interest is affected? The more important the affected interest, the more careful the applied procedures must be.
2. What risk of error is inherent in procedure? The higher the risk, the more careful and specific the applied procedures must be.
3. Weigh interest of government against alternatives? The greater the government interest, the greater likelihood of using a procedure that will achieve government aims and reduce administrative costs. Interests protected by procedural due process:
   a. Life—criminal procedure for death penalty cases.
   b. Liberty—liberties contained in the Bill of Rights: right to privacy, family relationships, and unlawful incarceration.
   c. Property—usually any property interest.

Fundamental Rights

1. *Right to Privacy:*
   a. Create, maintain, or change family relationships *Zablocki v. Redhail*, 434 U.S. 374 (1978);
   b. Procreate, educate and nurture children *Meyer v. Nebraska*, 262 U.S. 390 (1923);
   c. Maintain parent-child relationship;
   d. Engage in consensual sexual practices within marriage *Bowers v. Hardwick*, 478 U.S. 186 (1986); *Griswold v. Connecticut*, 381 U.S. 479 (1965);
   e. Refuse involuntary medical treatment *Washington v. Harper*, 494 U.S. 210 (1990);
   f. NOT including the right of family members to withdraw life-sustaining treatment for an incapacitated person *Cruzan v. Dir., Missouri Dept. of Health*, 497 U.S. 261 (1990);
   g. *Abortion:* fundamental right of women to terminate a pregnancy without undue state interference. Balance against state interests, formula devised to weigh woman's right against state interests and life of fetus; *Roe v. Wade*, 410 U.S. 113 (1973); *Planned Parenthood v. Casey*, 505 U.S. 833 (1992):
      i. *First trimester:* state cannot interfere; strict scrutiny applied;
      ii. *Second trimester:* state interest in health of mother is compelling; state may regulate to protect mother's health and safety;
      iii. *Third trimester:* fetus is viable and state interest in that life is compelling; may regulate to prevent abortion, except where health or life of mother is at issue.
2. *Right to Vote:*
   a. *Two-part analysis:* Court balances state restriction of voting rights against state's interest in imposing the restriction:
      i. if effect to voting rights outweighs the state's interest, regulation must be narrowly drawn to advance a compelling government interest;
      ii. if state interest outweighs restriction, regulation will be upheld if it is reasonable and nondiscriminatory, and the state interest is important.
   b. *Types of vote regulations:* Qualifying or restricting votes, vote dilution *Reynolds v. Sims*, 377 U.S. 533 (1964), and gerrymandering.

3. *Right to Travel (Interstate):* State imposition of penalties for a nonresident traveling from one state to relocate to another is subject to fundamental rights analysis. Types of travel regulations:
   a. *Deter immigration:* states may not save state funds by preventing nonresidents from receiving state benefits. Cannot deter indigent immigrants in this manner *Shapiro v. Thompson*, 394 U.S. 618 (1969).
   b. *Durational residency requirements:* denial of basic necessities of life is subject to strict scrutiny. May not apportion funds based on length of residency. May not grant preferential treatment based on date of residency. *Exceptions: (no right exists).*
4. *Right to Education:*
   a. There is no fundamental right to education *San Antonio Ind. School District v. Rodriguez*, 411 U.S. 1 (1973).
   b. States are not required to ensure that equivalent financial resources are devoted to the education of each child. *Plyler v. Doe*, 457 U.S. 202 (1982).
5. *Right to Basic Necessities of Life:* Welfare benefits are a matter of social/economic legislation, subject to rational basis review, not strict fundamental rights scrutiny. There is no fundamental constitutional right to the basic necessities of life requiring strict scrutiny review in welfare benefits legislation *Dandridge v. Williams*, 397 U.S. 471 (1970).

▶

QUICK COURSE OUTLINE
CONSTITUTIONAL LAW

FEDERAL JUDICIAL POWER

JUDICIAL REVIEW

Definition: The Supreme Court's authority to review the actions of the legislative and executive branches to determine their constitutionality. The doctrine requires courts to interpret and apply the Constitution to acts to determine their validity. The power a federal court has to adjudicate over claims brought before it. *Marbury v. Madison*, 5 U.S. 137 (1803).

1. *Original Jurisdiction* ARTICLE III § 2: Federal courts have authority to first hear or try cases involving:
   a. Ambassadors
   b. Public ministers and consuls
   c. Cases in which the state is a party
2. *Appellate Jurisdiction* ARTICLE III § 2: Federal courts may also hear other (non-original jurisdictional) cases that come to court by appeal.
3. *Supreme Court Review:*
   a. *Discretionary Review/Writ of Certiorari:* Cases may be petitioned for review by writ of certiorari. Supreme Court has discretion to hear or refuse.
   b. *State Court Review of Federal Issues:* Federal courts may only review final judgments of federal issues made by the highest court in a state.
      Exception: On Adequate Independent State Grounds, Federal court will not review state decision, that is independent of that state's separate ruling on federal law that may otherwise be incorrect.
   c. *State Court Refusal to Hear Federal Claims:* States are generally required to hear appropriately presented federal claims, but the state may refuse. Federal courts may review state court's refusal to hear such claims.

JUDICIAL LIMITS ON JUDICIAL REVIEW

1. *Abstention:* Federal courts will abstain from hearing a case involving an unsettled or unclear state statute on whose construction a federal constitutional issue depends, until a state court interprets it. *Railroad Commn. of Texas v. Pullman Co.*, 312 U.S. 496 (1941).
2. *Equitable Restraint:* Federal courts may enjoin state criminal actions to protect constitutional rights. *Ex parte Young*, 209 U.S. 123 (1908).
3. *Constitutional Question:* A case issue involves the constitutionality of statute. Court will apply rules of statutory construction to avoid passing on constitutional questions:
   a. Alternative (nonconstitutional) ground exists to dispose of case.
   b. Between several possible interpretations, one exists that permits a finding of constitutionality.
   c. Courts will otherwise construe a statute reasonably.
   d. *Racial Challenges:* Challenger must show there is no circumstance under which the legislative act or administrative regulation would be valid.

CONSTITUTIONAL LIMITS ON JUDICIAL REVIEW ARTICLE III § 2

1. *Cases and Controversies: Aetna Life Ins. Co. v. Haworth*, 300 U.S. 227 (1937).
   a. *Justiciability:* A case is justiciable if there is standing to sue, the Constitution permits the issue to be judicially resolvable, and there is no cause for judicial restraint.
   b. *Standing:* To have standing to bring a suit, a plaintiff must meet three criteria:
      i. *Injury:* Plaintiff must show facts demonstrating any injury in fact. Injury can be small or trifling, but must be real. *Sierra Club v. Morton*, 405 U.S. 727 (1972).
      ii. *Causation:* Injury must be proximately and directly traceable to defendant's conduct. *Lujan v. Defenders of Wildlife*, 504 U.S. 555 (1992).
      iii. *Redressibility:* Plaintiff must show facts that demonstrate the relief she is entitled to will substantially eliminate or redress the injury. *Warth v. Seldin*, 422 U.S. 490 (1975).
   c. *Ripeness:* Case must involve concrete disputes between genuine adversaries or will not be heard. A court will not give advisory opinions.
   d. *Mootness:* If underlying controversy is not real or has been resolved/dissolved prior to the adjudication, case is moot and will not be adjudicated. *Exceptions: cases that appear moot but are not.*
      i. Cases involving continuing harm.
      ii. Harms that have ended but may recur.
      iii. Cases capable of repetition but evading review. *Roe v. Wade*, 410 U.S. 113 (1973).
2. *Political Question:* Even if plaintiff has standing, courts may refuse to decide a "political" question.
   a. Constitutionally committed or need exists for deference to another branch of government.
   b. There is a lack of judicially discoverable and manageable standards for resolving it.
3. *11th Amendment:* State sovereign immunity prevents citizens of a state from suing that state in federal court without that state's consent. *Hans v. Louisiana*, 134 U.S. 1 (1890).

STRUCTURE OF THE GOVERNMENT

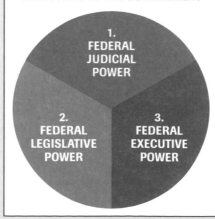

1. FEDERAL JUDICIAL POWER
2. FEDERAL LEGISLATIVE POWER
3. FEDERAL EXECUTIVE POWER

FEDERAL LEGISLATIVE POWER

THE SPENDING POWER ARTICLE I § 8

Congress has the power to spend for the common defense and general welfare. This includes spending done in order to exercise its other powers or for proper public purpose. Congress by conditioning receipt of funds on compliance with federal regulations is able to indirectly regulate what it cannot regulate directly.

TREATY POWER ARTICLE I § 10

Power co-exists with the President's power to make treaties pursuant to the advice and consent of the Senate. Treaties, once ratified, become the law of the land.

1. Treaties take precedent over conflicting state and federal law but are not equal in authority to the Constitution.
2. Treaties pertaining to matters of international concern are binding in the states even if they regulate an area normally under state control. *Missouri v. Holland*, 252 U.S. 416 (1920).

THE TAXING POWER ARTICLE I § 8

Congress can regulate or limit activities by imposing taxes on them, effectively prohibiting them where the tax is substantial. As long as the tax produces revenue, it may be enacted for any motive, even purely regulatory ones that have no genuine money-raising purpose at all.

THE IMMIGRATION POWER ARTICLE I § 8

Congress has exclusive control over immigration.

1. May admit, expel, exclude, or deport noncitizens of the United States.
2. May not treat naturalized citizens differently from native-born citizens.

WAR AND MILITARY AFFAIRS POWER ARTICLE I § 8

1. *Domestic War Power:* Congress has broad power to enact economic or other regulations during wartime or after war to restore the economy.
2. *Draft:* Congress can enlist men for war and use state militias to fight foreign enemies.
3. *Military Justice/Courts Martial:* Congress may establish a system of military courts and justice. Courts are legislatively created and located in the legislative branch; therefore, the Bill of Rights is inapplicable. Jurisdiction extends to all offenses committed by service personnel while in service.

Federal Legislative Power continues on page 2

EQUAL PROTECTION

Fourteenth Amendment requires that no state shall deny any person the equal protection of the laws. Equal protection analysis determines whether a state is constitutionally permitted to differentiate between persons.

▼

TYPES OF JUDICIAL REVIEW

To determine whether state legislation affecting certain rights in constitutional, a court must examine that state's goals and the means used to achieve its goal.

1. *Rational Basis:* State regulation will be upheld if it is rationally related to achieving a legitimate state purpose. Applies primarily to social and economic regulations. *Dandridge v. Williams*, 397 U.S. 471 (1970).

    a. *Taxation:* States have great latitude in creating taxation schemes as long as the schemes bear a rational relationship to a plausible policy justification. *Williams v. Vermont*, 472 U.S. 14 (1985).

    b. Over-inclusive and under-inclusive classifications are not per se unconstitutional in violation of equal protection. *Williamson v. Lee Optical Co.*, 348 U.S. 483 (1955).

    c. Prohibits arbitrary, unreasonable, and irrational classifications:

        i. Unlikely to lead to any discernable and understandable legitimate purpose.

        ii. Regulates similarly-situated parties differently, without legitimate reason. *City of Cleburne v. Cleburne Living Center*, 473 U.S. 432 (1985).

2. *Intermediate Review (Heightened Scrutiny):* State regulation will be upheld if it is substantially related to an important government purpose. Applies primarily to gender, alienage, and illegitimacy cases.

    a. Gender classifications must fairly and substantially relate to the achievement of an important and articulated government objective. Government must provide an "exceedingly persuasive justification." *United States v. Virginia*, 518 U.S. 515 (1996); *J.E.B. v. Alabama ex rel. T.B.*, 511 U.S. 127 (1994); *Mississippi University for Women v. Hogan*, 458 U.S. 718 (1982). Unconstitutional types of gender-based classifications:

        i. Statutes presuming greater male competency. *Reed v. Reed*, 404 U.S. 71 (1971).

        ii. Statutes presuming women are dependent.

        iii. Statutes presuming gender bias (peremptory challenges). *J.E.B. v. Alabama ex rel. T.B.*, 511 U.S. 127 (1994).

    b. *Alienage Classifications:*

        i. Congress has plenary power to regulate immigration and naturalization and its decisions are subject to rational basis review.

        ii. States do not have constitutional authority to regulate immigration and nationalization; state classifications based on alienage are inherently suspect and subject to strict scrutiny review.

▶

c. *Illegitimacy Classifications:* Classifications of children based on nonmarital status of parents; intermediate scrutiny applies. These include:

    i. Qualification for awards or benefits (wrongful death, workers' compensation, social security survivor's benefits, parental support, paternity suit statutes of limitations).

    ii. Interstate inheritance.

3. *Strict Scrutiny:* State regulation will be upheld if it is necessary to achieve a compelling government interest. Strict scrutiny is applied to:

    a. *Suspect Classifications:*

        i. Suspect Classes—race, national origin, ethnicity. *Katzenbach v. Morgan*, 384 U.S. 641 (1966).

        ii. Proving Discrimination—must show discriminatory intent or purpose. If disproportionate impact, intent to maintain activity is sufficient. *Washington v. Davis*, 426 U.S. 229 (1976).

        iii. Benign Racial Classifications— Affirmative Action:
            a. subject to strict scrutiny;
            b. race is only one factor to show compelling state interest.

    b. *Fundamental Rights:* Strict scrutiny used to uphold laws infringing on rights.

FREEDOM OF ASSOCIATION

IN GENERAL

Definition: The First Amendment provides for the right to associate with others for the advancement of beliefs, ideas and opinions, to communicate and to engage in all activities protected by the First Amendment. *NAACP v. Alabama*, 357 U.S. 449 (1958).

1. *Compelled Disclosure:*

    a. *Lawful associations:* law is unconstitutional if it compels disclosure of membership in a lawful association where disclosure subjects members of the organizations to sanctions, reprisals, or public embarrassment. *NAACP v. Alabama*, 357 U.S. 449 (1958).

    b. *Exception:* If there is a compelling state interest implicated. *Buckley v. Valeo*, 424 U.S. 1 (1976).

2. *Public Employees:*

    a. Inquiry into fitness or competence: inquiry into fitness or competence of applicants for public employment may be unconstitutional because it chills freedom of association.

    b. *Exception:* if inquiry is narrowly tailored to the government interest in fitness or competence.

3. *Freedom not to Associate:* The freedom of association also entails a freedom not to associate.

    a. State cannot require persons to provide for support of organizations or causes with which they disagree. *Abood v. Detroit Board of Educ.*, 431 U.S. 209 (1977); *Keller v. State Bar of California*, 496 U.S. 1 (1990).

    b. *Limitation:* application of rule is limited to political or ideological associations.

FREEDOM OF RELIGION

ESTABLISHMENT CLAUSE

States should not provide aid to religion, favoring any one religion over and above the others. If state statute aids religion, may still be upheld if:

1. It has a secular purpose.

2. Its principal or primary effect neither advances nor inhibits religion.

3. It doesn't promote excessive state entanglement with religion. *Lemon v. Kurtzman*, 403 U.S. 602 (1971). Aid to sectarian or religious schools:

    a. *Impermissible aid:* tuition, building funds.

    b. *Permissible aid:* bus transportation, secular book loans.

▼

FREE EXERCISE CLAUSE

State must permit people to believe and practice their religious beliefs without interference. State may not deny benefits to or burden persons based on their beliefs. *Empl. Div., Dept. of Human Resources of Oregon v. Smith*, 494 U.S. 872 (1990). *Exceptions:*

1. *Unemployment compensation:* denial of compensation following discharge for refusing to work on Sabbath or resigning because of religious beliefs violates strict scrutiny, compelling state interest test, and is an unconstitutional burden. *Sherbert v. Verner*, 374 U.S. 398 (1963).

2. *Religious Freedom Restoration Act [RFRA]:* Congress's attempt to restore the compelling state interest test.

CONSTITUTIONAL ACTION AGAINST PRIVATE PARTIES

STATE ACTION

Cannot bring action against private individuals for constitutional violations unless state action is shown.

A private party will be treated as a state actor, and thus subject to constitutional restrictions, in the following circumstances: *The Civil Rights Cases*, 109 U.S. 3 (1883).

1. *Public Functions:* private party exercises powers traditionally reserved to the state. *Marsh v. Alabama*, 326 U.S. 501 (1946).

2. *State Involvement:* private party has a "close nexus" to state activity that injured plaintiff, such as the use of state courts to enforce a private action, or use of state funds. *Burton v. Wilmington Parking Authority*, 365 U.S. 715 (1961).

    a. Private party's use of state enforcement of racially restrictive covenants constitutes state action. *Shelley v. Kraemer*, 334 U.S. 1 (1948).

3. *State Authorization or Encouragement:* private action pursuant to an affirmative state act designed to encourage private violations of civil rights.

About Wolters Kluwer Law & Business

Wolters Kluwer Law & Business is a leading provider of research information and workflow solutions in key specialty areas. The strengths of the individual brands of Aspen Publishers, CCH, Kluwer Law International and Loislaw are aligned within Wolters Kluwer Law & Business to provide comprehensive, in-depth solutions and expert-authored content for the legal, professional and education markets.

CCH was founded in 1913 and has served more than four generations of business professionals and their clients. The CCH products in the Wolters Kluwer Law & Business group are highly regarded electronic and print resources for legal, securities, antitrust and trade regulation, government contracting, banking, pension, payroll, employment and labor, and health-care reimbursement and compliance professionals.

Aspen Publishers is a leading information provider for attorneys, business professionals and law students. Written by preeminent authorities, Aspen products offer analytical and practical information in a range of specialty practice areas from securities law and intellectual property to mergers and acquisitions and pension/benefits. Aspen's trusted legal education resources provide professors and students with high-quality, up-to-date and effective resources for successful instruction and study in all areas of the law.

Kluwer Law International supplies the global business community with comprehensive English-language international legal information. Legal practitioners, corporate counsel and business executives around the world rely on the Kluwer Law International journals, loose-leafs, books and electronic products for authoritative information in many areas of international legal practice.

Loislaw is a premier provider of digitized legal content to small law firm practitioners of various specializations. Loislaw provides attorneys with the ability to quickly and efficiently find the necessary legal information they need, when and where they need it, by facilitating access to primary law as well as state-specific law, records, forms and treatises.

Wolters Kluwer Law & Business, a unit of Wolters Kluwer, is headquartered in New York and Riverwoods, Illinois. Wolters Kluwer is a leading multinational publisher and information services company.

Format for the Casenote Legal Brief

Nature of Case: This section identifies the form of action (e.g., breach of contract, negligence, battery), the type of proceeding (e.g., demurrer, appeal from trial court's jury instructions) or the relief sought (e.g., damages, injunction, criminal sanctions).

Fact Summary: This is included to refresh your memory and can be used as a quick reminder of the facts.

Rule of Law: Summarizes the general principle of law that the case illustrates. It may be used for instant recall of the court's holding and for classroom discussion or home review.

Facts: This section contains all relevant facts of the case, including the contentions of the parties and the lower court holdings. It is written in a logical order to give the student a clear understanding of the case. The plaintiff and defendant are identified by their proper names throughout and are always labeled with a (P) or (D).

Palsgraf v. Long Island R.R. Co.

Injured bystander (P) v. Railroad company (D)

N.Y. Ct. App., 248 N.Y. 339, 162 N.E. 99 (1928).

NATURE OF CASE: Appeal from judgment affirming verdict for plaintiff seeking damages for personal injury.

FACT SUMMARY: Helen Palsgraf (P) was injured on R.R.'s (D) train platform when R.R.'s (D) guard helped a passenger aboard a moving train, causing his package to fall on the tracks. The package contained fireworks which exploded, creating a shock that tipped a scale onto Palsgraf (P).

🏛 RULE OF LAW
The risk reasonably to be perceived defines the duty to be obeyed.

FACTS: Helen Palsgraf (P) purchased a ticket to Rockaway Beach from R.R. (D) and was waiting on the train platform. As she waited, two men ran to catch a train that was pulling out from the platform. The first man jumped aboard, but the second man, who appeared as if he might fall, was helped aboard by the guard on the train who had kept the door open so they could jump aboard. A guard on the platform also helped by pushing him onto the train. The man was carrying a package wrapped in newspaper. In the process, the man dropped his package, which fell on the tracks. The package contained fireworks and exploded. The shock of the explosion was apparently of great enough strength to tip over some scales at the other end of the platform, which fell on Palsgraf (P) and injured her. A jury awarded her damages, and R.R. (D) appealed.

ISSUE: Does the risk reasonably to be perceived define the duty to be obeyed?

HOLDING AND DECISION: (Cardozo, C.J.) Yes. The risk reasonably to be perceived defines the duty to be obeyed. If there is no foreseeable hazard to the injured party as the result of a seemingly innocent act, the act does not become a tort because it happened to be a wrong as to another. If the wrong was not willful, the plaintiff must show that the act as to her had such great and apparent possibilities of danger as to entitle her to protection. Negligence in the abstract is not enough upon which to base liability. Negligence is a relative concept, evolving out of the common law doctrine of trespass on the case. To establish liability, the defendant must owe a legal duty of reasonable care to the injured party. A cause of action in tort will lie where harm,

though unintended, could have been averted or avoided by observance of such a duty. The scope of the duty is limited by the range of danger that a reasonable person could foresee. In this case, there was nothing to suggest from the appearance of the parcel or otherwise that the parcel contained fireworks. The guard could not reasonably have had any warning of a threat to Palsgraf (P), and R.R. (D) therefore cannot be held liable. Judgment is reversed in favor of R.R. (D).

DISSENT: (Andrews, J.) The concept that there is no negligence unless R.R. (D) owes a legal duty to take care as to Palsgraf (P) herself is too narrow. Everyone owes to the world at large the duty of refraining from those acts that may unreasonably threaten the safety of others. If the guard's action was negligent as to those nearby, it was also negligent as to those outside what might be termed the "danger zone." For Palsgraf (P) to recover, R.R.'s (D) negligence must have been the proximate cause of her injury, a question of fact for the jury.

▶ ANALYSIS

The majority defined the limit of the defendant's liability in terms of the danger that a reasonable person in defendant's situation would have perceived. The dissent argued that the limitation should not be placed on liability, but rather on damages. Judge Andrews suggested that only injuries that would not have happened but for R.R.'s (D) negligence should be compensable. Both the majority and dissent recognized the policy-driven need to limit liability for negligent acts, seeking, in the words of Judge Andrews, to define a framework "that will be practical and in keeping with the general understanding of mankind." The Restatement (Second) of Torts has accepted Judge Cardozo's view.

▬

Quicknotes

FORESEEABILITY A reasonable expectation that change is the probable result of certain acts or omissions.

NEGLIGENCE Conduct falling below the standard of care that a reasonable person would demonstrate under similar conditions.

PROXIMATE CAUSE The natural sequence of events without which an injury would not have been sustained.

▬

Party ID: Quick identification of the relationship between the parties.

Concurrence/Dissent: All concurrences and dissents are briefed whenever they are included by the casebook editor.

Analysis: This last paragraph gives you a broad understanding of where the case "fits in" with other cases in the section of the book and with the entire course. It is a hornbook-style discussion indicating whether the case is a majority or minority opinion and comparing the principal case with other cases in the casebook. It may also provide analysis from restatements, uniform codes, and law review articles. The analysis will prove to be invaluable to classroom discussion.

Issue: The issue is a concise question that brings out the essence of the opinion as it relates to the section of the casebook in which the case appears. Both substantive and procedural issues are included if relevant to the decision.

Holding and Decision: This section offers a clear and in-depth discussion of the rule of the case and the court's rationale. It is written in easy-to-understand language and answers the issue presented by applying the law to the facts of the case. When relevant, it includes a thorough discussion of the exceptions to the case as listed by the court, any major cites to the other cases on point, and the names of the judges who wrote the decisions.

Quicknotes: Conveniently defines legal terms found in the case and summarizes the nature of any statutes, codes, or rules referred to in the text.

Note to Students

Aspen Publishers is proud to offer *Casenote Legal Briefs*—continuing thirty years of publishing America's best-selling legal briefs.

Casenote Legal Briefs are designed to help you save time when briefing assigned cases. Organized under convenient headings, they show you how to abstract the basic facts and holdings from the text of the actual opinions handed down by the courts. Used as part of a rigorous study regimen, they can help you spend more time analyzing and critiquing points of law than on copying bits and pieces of judicial opinions into your notebook or outline.

Casenote Legal Briefs should never be used as a substitute for assigned casebook readings. They work best when read as a follow-up to reviewing the underlying opinions themselves. Students who try to avoid reading and digesting the judicial opinions in their casebooks or online sources will end up shortchanging themselves in the long run. The ability to absorb, critique, and restate the dynamic and complex elements of case law decisions is crucial to your success in law school and beyond. It cannot be developed vicariously.

Casenote Legal Briefs represents but one of the many offerings in Aspen's Study Aid Timeline, which includes:

- *Casenote Legal Briefs*
- *Emanuel Law Outlines*
- *Examples & Explanations* Series
- *Introduction to Law* Series
- Emanuel *Law in a Flash* Flashcards
- Emanuel *CrunchTime* Series

Each of these series is designed to provide you with easy-to-understand explanations of complex points of law. Each volume offers guidance on the principles of legal analysis and, consulted regularly, will hone your ability to spot relevant issues. We have titles that will help you prepare for class, prepare for your exams, and enhance your general comprehension of the law along the way.

To find out more about Aspen Study Aid publications, visit us online at *http://lawschool.aspenpublishers.com* or email us at *legaledu@wolterskluwer.com*. We'll be happy to assist you.

Get this Casenote Legal Brief as an AspenLaw Studydesk eBook today!

By returning this form to Aspen Publishers, you will receive a complimentary eBook download of this Casenote Legal Brief in the AspenLaw Studydesk digital format.* Learn more about AspenLaw Studydesk today at *www.AspenLaw.com*.

Name	Phone ( )
Address	**Apt. No.**
City	**State**	**ZIP Code**

Law School	**Year** (check one)
	☐ 1st ☐ 2nd ☐ 3rd

Cut out the UPC found on the lower left corner of the back cover of this book. Staple the UPC inside this box. Only the original UPC from the book cover will be accepted. (No photocopies or store stickers are allowed.)

Attach UPC inside this box.

Email (Print legibly or you may not get access!)

Title of this book (course subject)

ISBN of this book (10- or 13-digit number on the UPC)

Used with which casebook (provide author's name)

Mail the completed form to: Aspen Publishers, Inc.
Legal Education Division
130 Turner Street, Bldg 3, 4th Floor
Waltham, MA 02453-8901

* Upon receipt of this completed form, you will be emailed a code for the digital download of this book in AspenLaw Studydesk format. The AspenLaw Studydesk application is available as a 60-day free trial at *www.AspenLaw.com*.

For a full list of print titles by Aspen Publishers, visit *lawschool.aspenpublishers.com*.
For a full list of digital eBook titles by Aspen Publishers, visit *www.AspenLaw.com*.

Make a photocopy of this form and your UPC for your records.

For detailed information on the use of the information you provide on this form, please see the PRIVACY POLICY at www.aspenpublishers.com.

How to Brief a Case

A. Decide on a Format and Stick to It

Structure is essential to a good brief. It enables you to arrange systematically the related parts that are scattered throughout most cases, thus making manageable and understandable what might otherwise seem to be an endless and unfathomable sea of information. There are, of course, an unlimited number of formats that can be utilized. However, it is best to find one that suits your needs and stick to it. Consistency breeds both efficiency and the security that when called upon you will know where to look in your brief for the information you are asked to give.

Any format, as long as it presents the essential elements of a case in an organized fashion, can be used. Experience, however, has led *Casenotes* to develop and utilize the following format because of its logical flow and universal applicability.

NATURE OF CASE: This is a brief statement of the legal character and procedural status of the case (e.g., "Appeal of a burglary conviction").

There are many different alternatives open to a litigant dissatisfied with a court ruling. The key to determining which one has been used is to discover *who is asking this court for what.*

This first entry in the brief should be kept as *short as possible.* Use the court's terminology if you understand it. But since jurisdictions vary as to the titles of pleadings, the best entry is the one that addresses who wants what in this proceeding, not the one that sounds most like the court's language.

RULE OF LAW: A statement of the general principle of law that the case illustrates (e.g., "An acceptance that varies any term of the offer is considered a rejection and counteroffer").

Determining the rule of law of a case is a procedure similar to determining the issue of the case. Avoid being fooled by red herrings; there may be a few rules of law mentioned in the case excerpt, but usually only one is *the* rule with which the casebook editor is concerned. The techniques used to locate the issue, described below, may also be utilized to find the rule of law. Generally, your best guide is simply the chapter heading. It is a clue to the point the casebook editor seeks to make and should be kept in mind when reading every case in the respective section.

FACTS: A synopsis of only the essential facts of the case, i.e., those bearing upon or leading up to the issue.

The facts entry should be a short statement of the events and transactions that led one party to initiate legal proceedings against another in the first place. While some cases conveniently state the salient facts at the beginning of the decision, in other instances they will have to be culled from hiding places throughout the text, even from concurring and dissenting opinions. Some of the "facts" will often be in dispute and should be so noted. Conflicting evidence may be briefly pointed up. "Hard" facts must be included. Both must be *relevant* in order to be listed in the facts entry. It is impossible to tell what is relevant until the entire case is read, as the ultimate determination of the rights and liabilities of the parties may turn on something buried deep in the opinion.

Generally, the facts entry should not be longer than three to five *short* sentences.

It is often helpful to identify the role played by a party in a given context. For example, in a construction contract case the identification of a party as the "contractor" or "builder" alleviates the need to tell that that party was the one who was supposed to have built the house.

It is always helpful, and a good general practice, to identify the "plaintiff" and the "defendant." This may seem elementary and uncomplicated, but, especially in view of the creative editing practiced by some casebook editors, it is sometimes a difficult or even impossible task. Bear in mind that the *party presently* seeking something from this court may not be the plaintiff, and that sometimes only the cross-claim of a defendant is treated in the excerpt. Confusing or misaligning the parties can ruin your analysis and understanding of the case.

ISSUE: A statement of the general legal question answered by or illustrated in the case. For clarity, the issue is best put in the form of a question capable of a "yes" or "no" answer. In reality, the issue is simply the Rule of Law put in the form of a question (e.g., "May an offer be accepted by performance?").

The major problem presented in discerning what is *the* issue in the case is that an opinion usually purports to raise and answer several questions. However, except for rare cases, only one such question is really the issue in the case. Collateral issues not necessary to the resolution of the matter in controversy are handled by the court by language known as *"obiter dictum"* or merely *"dictum."* While dicta may be included later in the brief, they have no place under the issue heading.

To find the issue, ask *who wants what* and then go on to ask *why did that party succeed or fail in getting it.* Once this is determined, the "why" should be turned into a question.

The complexity of the issues in the cases will vary, but in all cases a single-sentence question should sum up the issue. *In a few cases,* there will be two, or even more rarely, three issues of equal importance to the resolution of the case. Each should be expressed in a single-sentence question.

Since many issues are resolved by a court in coming to a final disposition of a case, the casebook editor will reproduce the portion of the opinion containing the issue or issues most relevant to the area of law under scrutiny. A noted law professor gave this advice: "Close the book; look at the title on the cover." Chances are, if it is Property, you need not concern yourself with whether, for example, the federal government's treatment of the plaintiff's land really raises a federal question sufficient to support jurisdiction on this ground in federal court.

The same rule applies to chapter headings designating sub-areas within the subjects. They tip you off as to what the text is designed to teach. The cases are arranged in a casebook to show a progression or development of the law, so that the preceding cases may also help.

It is also most important to remember to *read the notes and questions* at the end of a case to determine what the editors wanted you to have gleaned from it.

HOLDING AND DECISION: This section should succinctly explain the rationale of the court in arriving at its decision. In capsulizing the "reasoning" of the court, it should always include an application of the general rule or rules of law to the specific facts of the case. Hidden justifications come to light in this entry; the reasons for the state of the law, the public policies, the biases and prejudices, those considerations that influence the justices' thinking and, ultimately, the outcome of the case. At the end, there should be a short indication of the disposition or procedural resolution of the case (e.g., "Decision of the trial court for Mr. Smith (P) reversed").

The foregoing format is designed to help you "digest" the reams of case material with which you will be faced in your law school career. Once mastered by practice, it will place at your fingertips the information the authors of your casebooks have sought to impart to you in case-by-case illustration and analysis.

B. Be as Economical as Possible in Briefing Cases

Once armed with a format that encourages succinctness, it is as important to be economical with regard to the time spent on the actual reading of the case as it is to be economical in the writing of the brief itself. This does not mean "skimming" a case. Rather, it means reading the case with an "eye" trained to recognize into which "section" of your brief a particular passage or line fits and having a system for quickly and precisely marking the case so that the passages fitting any one particular part of

the brief can be easily identified and brought together in a concise and accurate manner when the brief is actually written.

It is of no use to simply repeat everything in the opinion of the court; record only enough information to trigger your recollection of what the court said. Nevertheless, an accurate statement of the "law of the case," i.e., the legal principle applied to the facts, is absolutely essential to class preparation and to learning the law under the case method.

To that end, it is important to develop a "shorthand" that you can use to make margin notations. These notations will tell you at a glance in which section of the brief you will be placing that particular passage or portion of the opinion.

Some students prefer to underline all the salient portions of the opinion (with a pencil or colored underliner marker), making marginal notations as they go along. Others prefer the color-coded method of underlining, utilizing different colors of markers to underline the salient portions of the case, each separate color being used to represent a different section of the brief. For example, blue underlining could be used for passages relating to the rule of law, yellow for those relating to the issue, and green for those relating to the holding and decision, etc. While it has its advocates, the color-coded method can be confusing and time-consuming (all that time spent on changing colored markers). Furthermore, it can interfere with the continuity and concentration many students deem essential to the reading of a case for maximum comprehension. In the end, however, it is a matter of personal preference and style. Just remember, whatever method you use, underlining must be used sparingly or its value is lost.

If you take the marginal notation route, an efficient and easy method is to go along underlining the key portions of the case and placing in the margin alongside them the following "markers" to indicate where a particular passage or line "belongs" in the brief you will write:

N (NATURE OF CASE)
RL (RULE OF LAW)
I (ISSUE)
HL (HOLDING AND DECISION, relates to the RULE OF LAW behind the decision)
HR (HOLDING AND DECISION, gives the RATIONALE or reasoning behind the decision)
HA (HOLDING AND DECISION, APPLIES the general principle(s) of law to the facts of the case to arrive at the decision)

Remember that a particular passage may well contain information necessary to more than one part of your brief, in which case you simply note that in the margin. If you are using the color-coded underlining method instead of margin notation, simply make asterisks or checks in the margin next to the passage in question in the colors that indicate the additional sections of the brief where it might be utilized.

The economy of utilizing "shorthand" in marking cases for briefing can be maintained in the actual brief writing process itself by utilizing "law student shorthand" within the brief. There are many commonly used words and phrases for which abbreviations can be substituted in your briefs (and in your class notes also). You can develop abbreviations that are personal to you and which will save you a lot of time. A reference list of briefing abbreviations can be found on page xii of this book.

C. Use Both the Briefing Process and the Brief as a Learning Tool

Now that you have a format and the tools for briefing cases efficiently, the most important thing is to make the time spent in briefing profitable to you and to make the most advantageous use of the briefs you create. Of course, the briefs are invaluable for classroom reference when you are called upon to explain or analyze a particular

case. However, they are also useful in reviewing for exams. A quick glance at the fact summary should bring the case to mind, and a rereading of the rule of law should enable you to go over the underlying legal concept in your mind, how it was applied in that particular case, and how it might apply in other factual settings.

As to the value to be derived from engaging in the briefing process itself, there is an immediate benefit that arises from being forced to sift through the essential facts and reasoning from the court's opinion and to succinctly express them in your own words in your brief. The process ensures that you understand the case and the point that it illustrates, and that means you will be ready to absorb further analysis and information brought forth in class. It also ensures you will have something to say when called upon in class. The briefing process helps develop a mental agility for getting to the *gist* of a case and for identifying, expounding on, and applying the legal concepts and issues found there. The briefing process is the mental process on which you must rely in taking law school examinations; it is also the mental process upon which a lawyer relies in serving his clients and in making his living.

Abbreviations for Briefs

acceptance	acp		offer	O
affirmed	aff		offeree	OE
answer	ans		offeror	OR
assumption of risk	a/r		ordinance	ord
attorney	atty		pain and suffering	p/s
beyond a reasonable doubt	b/r/d		parol evidence	p/e
bona fide purchaser	BFP		plaintiff	P
breach of contract	br/k		prima facie	p/f
cause of action	c/a		probable cause	p/c
common law	c/l		proximate cause	px/c
Constitution	Con		real property	r/p
constitutional	con		reasonable doubt	r/d
contract	K		reasonable man	r/m
contributory negligence	c/n		rebuttable presumption	rb/p
cross	x		remanded	rem
cross-complaint	x/c		res ipsa loquitur	RIL
cross-examination	x/ex		respondeat superior	r/s
cruel and unusual punishment	c/u/p		Restatement	RS
defendant	D		reversed	rev
dismissed	dis		Rule Against Perpetuities	RAP
double jeopardy	d/j		search and seizure	s/s
due process	d/p		search warrant	s/w
equal protection	e/p		self-defense	s/d
equity	eq		specific performance	s/p
evidence	ev		statute of limitations	S/L
exclude	exc		statute of frauds	S/F
exclusionary rule	exc/r		statute	S
felony	f/n		summary judgment	s/j
freedom of speech	f/s		tenancy in common	t/c
good faith	g/f		tenancy at will	t/w
habeas corpus	h/c		tenant	t
hearsay	hr		third party	TP
husband	H		third party beneficiary	TPB
in loco parentis	ILP		transferred intent	TI
injunction	inj		unconscionable	uncon
inter vivos	I/v		unconstitutional	unconst
joint tenancy	j/t		undue influence	u/e
judgment	judgt		Uniform Commercial Code	UCC
jurisdiction	jur		unilateral	uni
last clear chance	LCC		vendee	VE
long-arm statute	LAS		vendor	VR
majority view	maj		versus	v
meeting of minds	MOM		void for vagueness	VFV
minority view	min		weight of the evidence	w/e
Miranda warnings	Mir/w		weight of authority	w/a
Miranda rule	Mir/r		wife	W
negligence	neg		with	w/
notice	ntc		within	w/i
nuisance	nus		without prejudice	w/o/p
obligation	ob		without	w/o
obscene	obs		wrongful death	wr/d

Table of Cases

A Abrams v. United States 112
Adarand Constructors, Inc. v. Pena 62
Adderley v. Florida 138
Allen v. Wright 8

B Baker v. Carr 11
Beauharnais v. Illinois 134
Board of Trustees v. Garrett 33
Bowsher v. Synar 46
Brandenburg v. Ohio 118
Branzburg v. Hayes 144
Brown v. Board of Education of Topeka
      (Brown I) 54
Brown v. Board of Education of Topeka
      (Brown II) 55
Buckley v. Valeo 142
Burton v. Wilmington Parking Authority 159
Bush v. Gore 12
Butler, United States v. 30

C C & A Carbone, Inc. v. Clarkstown 24
Cantwell v. Connecticut 119
Chaplinsky v. New Hampshire 121
City of Boerne v. Flores 32
City of Mobile v. Bolden 82
City of Philadelphia v. New Jersey 23
Cleveland Board of Education v. Loudermill 96
Cohen v. California 133
Corporation of Presiding Bishop of the
      Church of Jesus Christ of Latter-Day
      Saints v. Amos 152
Cox Broadcasting Corp. v. Cohn 129
Craig v. Boren 67
Cruzan v. Director, Missouri Department
      of Health 94
Curtiss-Wright Corp., United States v. 39

D Dames & Moore v. Regan 40
Dennis v. United States 116
Dred Scott v. Sandford 52

E Employment Division, Department of
      Human Resources v. Smith 151
Exxon Corp. v. Governor of Maryland 27

F Feiner v. New York 120
Flagg Brothers v. Brooks 156

G Gibbons v. Ogden 16
Gitlow v. New York 113
Gonzales v. Carhart 92
Gooding v. Wilson 124
Griswold v. Connecticut 87
Grutter v. Bollinger 63

H Hamdi v. Rumsfeld 41
Hammer v. Dagenhart
      (The Child Labor Case) 17
Harper v. Virginia State Board of
      Elections 79
Home Building & Loan Association v.
      Blaisdell 98
Hunt v. Washington State Apple Advertising
      Commission 26

I INS v. Chadha 44

J Jackson v. Metropolitan Edison Co. 162

K Kassel v. Consolidated Freightways Corp. 28
Korematsu v. United States 58
Kramer v. Union Free School District 80

L Lawrence v. Texas 93
Lee v. Weisman 148
Lehman v. City of Shaker Heights 140
Lochner v. New York 76
Lopez, United States v. 21
Lovell v. Griffin 125
Loving v. Virginia 59
Lucas v. South Carolina Coastal Council 103
Lujan v. Defenders of Wildlife 9
Lynch v. Donnelly 149

M Marbury v. Madison 2
Marsh v. Alabama 163
Martin v. Hunter's Lessee 4
Massachusetts v. EPA 10
Masses Publishing Co. v. Patten 110
Mathews v. Eldridge 97
McCardle, Ex parte 7
McCleskey v. Kemp 61
McCulloch v. Maryland 5
Miller v. California 131
Miller v. Schoene 101
Missouri v. Holland 34
Moose Lodge No. 107 v. Irvis 161
Morrison v. Olson 47
Mueller v. Allen 150

N Near v. Minnesota 126
New York v. United States 35
New York Times Co. v. United States;
      United States v. Washington Post Co. 122
New York Times v. Sullivan 127
New York City Transit Authority v. Beazer 56
Nixon, United States v. 43
NLRB v. Jones & Laughlin Steel Corp. 19

O O'Brien, United States v. 141

P   Palazzolo v. Rhode Island *104*
         Parents Involved in Community Schools v.
              Seattle School Dist. No. 1 .... *65*
         Paris Adult Theatre I v. Slaton *132*
         Penn Central Transportation Co. v.
              New York City *102*
         Pennsylvania Coal Co. v. Mahon *99*
         Planned Parenthood of Southeastern
              Pennsylvania v. Casey *90*
         Plessy v. Ferguson *53*
         Plyler v. Doe *86*
         Police Department of Chicago v. Mosley *139*

R   R.A.V. v. City of St. Paul *135*
         Red Lion Broadcasting Co. v. FCC *145*
         Reynolds v. Sims *81*
         Roe v. Wade *88*
         Romer v. Evans *70*

S   San Antonio Independent School
              District v. Rodriguez *85*
         Schenck v. United States *111*

         Shapiro v. Thompson *83*
         Shelley v. Kraemer *157*
         Skinner v. Oklahoma *78*
         Slaughter-House Cases, The *75*
         State v. Post *51*
         Steward Machine Co. v. Davis *31*
         Strauder v. West Virginia *57*
         Sugarman v. Dougall *71*

V   Virginia, United States v. *69*
         Virginia v. Black *137*
         Virginia State Board of Pharmacy v.
              Virginia Citizens Consumer Council *130*

W   Washington v. Davis *60*
         Washington v. Glucksberg *95*
         West Lynn Creamery, Inc. v. Healy *25*
         Whitney v. California *114*
         Wickard v. Filburn *18*

Y   Youngstown Sheet & Tube Co. v. Sawyer
              (The Steel Seizure Case) *38*

CHAPTER 1

The Supreme Court in the Constitutional Order

Quick Reference Rules of Law

PAGE

1. **Basic Framework.** The Supreme Court has the power, implied from Article VI, § 2 of the   *2*
Constitution, to review acts of Congress and if they are found repugnant to the
Constitution, to declare them void. (Marbury v. Madison)

2. **Basic Framework.** The U.S. Supreme Court has jurisdiction over issues of federal law in   *4*
state courts. (Martin v. Hunter's Lessee)

3. **Sources of Judicial Decisions.** (1) Certain federal powers giving Congress the discretion   *5*
and power to choose and enact the means to perform the duties imposed upon it are to be
implied from the Necessary and Proper Clause. (2) The federal Constitution and the laws
made pursuant to it are supreme and control the constitutions and the laws of the states.
(McCulloch v. Maryland)

4. **Power of Political Control over the Supreme Court.** Although the Supreme Court   *7*
derives its appellate jurisdiction from the Constitution, the Constitution also gives Congress
the express power to make exceptions to that appellate jurisdiction. (Ex parte McCardle)

5. **Standing.** One does not have standing to sue in federal court unless he can allege the   *8*
violation of a right personal to him. (Allen v. Wright)

6. **Standing.** Only individuals who have suffered concrete harm have standing to seek judicial   *9*
review of agency rules. (Lujan v. Defenders of Wildlife)

7. **Standing.** A plaintiff has standing if it demonstrates a concrete injury that is both fairly   *10*
traceable to the defendant and redressable by judicial relief. (Massachusetts v. EPA)

8. **Political Questions.** Reapportionment issues present justiciable questions. (Baker v. Carr)   *11*

9. **Political Questions.** Having once granted the right to vote on equal terms, the state may   *12*
not, by later arbitrary and disparate treatment, value one person's vote over that of
another. (Bush v. Gore)

Marbury v. Madison

Justice (P) v. Secretary of State (D)

5 U.S. (1 Cranch) 137 (1803).

NATURE OF CASE: Writ of mandamus to compel delivery of commission.

FACT SUMMARY: President Jefferson's Secretary of State, Madison (D), refused to deliver a commission granted to Marbury (P) by former President Adams.

🏛 RULE OF LAW
The Supreme Court has the power, implied from Article VI, § 2 of the Constitution, to review acts of Congress and if they are found repugnant to the Constitution, to declare them void.

FACTS: On March 2, 1801, the outgoing President of the United States, John Adams, named forty-two justices of the peace for the District of Columbia under the Organic Act passed the same day by Congress. William Marbury (P) was one of the justices named. The commissions of Marbury (P) and other named justices were signed by Adams on his last day in office, March 3, and signed and sealed by the Acting Secretary of State, John Marshall. However, the formal commissions were not delivered by the end of the day. The new President, Thomas Jefferson, treated those appointments that were not formalized by delivery of the papers of commission prior to Adams leaving office as a nullity. Marbury (P) and other affected colleagues brought this writ of mandamus to the Supreme Court to compel Jefferson's Secretary of State, James Madison (D), to deliver the commissions. John Marshall, the current Chief Justice of the Supreme Court, delivered the opinion.

ISSUE: Does the Constitution give the Supreme Court the authority to review acts of Congress and declare them, if repugnant to the Constitution, to be void?

HOLDING AND DECISION: (Marshall, C.J.) Yes. The Supreme Court has the power, implied from Article VI, § 2 of the Constitution, to review acts of Congress and if they are found repugnant to the Constitution, to declare them void. The government of the United States is a government of laws, not of men. The President, bound by these laws, is given certain political powers by the Constitution that he may use at his discretion. To aid him in his duties, he is authorized to appoint certain officers to carry out his orders. Their acts as officers are his acts and are never subject to examination by the courts. However, where these officers are given by law specific duties on which individual rights depend, any individual injured by breach of such duty may resort to his country's laws for a remedy. Here, Marbury (P) had a right to the commission, and Madison's (D) refusal to deliver it violated that right. The present case is clearly one for mandamus.

However, should the Supreme Court be the court to issue it? The Judiciary Act of 1789 established and authorized United States courts to issue writs of mandamus to courts or persons holding office under U.S. authority. Secretary of State Madison (D) comes within the Act. If the Supreme Court is powerless to issue the writ of mandamus to him, it must be because the Act is unconstitutional. Article III of the Constitution provides that the Supreme Court shall have original jurisdiction in all cases affecting ambassadors, other public ministers and consuls, and where a state is a party. In all other cases, the Supreme Court shall have appellate jurisdiction. Marbury (P) urged that since Article III contains no restrictive words, the power to assign original jurisdiction to the courts remains in the legislature. But if Congress is allowed to distribute the original and appellate jurisdiction of the Supreme Court, as in the Judiciary Act, then the constitutional grant of Article III is form without substance. But no clause in the Constitution is presumed to be without effect. For the Court to issue a mandamus, it must be an exercise of appellate jurisdiction. The grant of appellate jurisdiction is the power to revise and correct proceedings already instituted; it does not create the cause. To issue a writ of mandamus ordering an executive officer to deliver a paper is to create the original action for that paper. This would be an unconstitutional exercise of original jurisdiction beyond the power of the Court. It is the province and duty of the judicial department to say what the law is. And any law, including acts of the legislature, which is repugnant to the Constitution, is void. Mandamus denied.

▌ ANALYSIS

Judicial review of legislative acts was a controversial subject even before the Constitution was ratified and adopted. Alexander Hamilton upheld the theory of judicial review in the Federalist Papers. He argued that the judiciary, being the most vulnerable branch of the government, was designed to be an intermediary between the people and the legislature. Since the interpretation of laws was the responsibility of the judiciary, and the Constitution the supreme law of the land, any conflict between legislative acts and the Constitution were to be resolved by the court in favor of the Constitution. But other authorities have attacked this position. In the case of *Eakin v. Raub*, 12 Serg. & Rawle 330, 353 (Pa. 1825), Justice Gibson dissented, stating that the judiciary's function was limited to interpreting the laws and should not extend to scrutinizing the legislature's authority to enact them. Judge Learned Hand felt that judicial review was inconsistent with the separation of powers. But history has supported the

Continued on next page.

authority of judicial review of legislative acts. The United States survives on a tripartite government. Theoretically, the three branches should be strong enough to check and balance the others. To limit the judiciary to the passive task of interpretation would be to limit its strength in the tripartite structure. *Marbury* served to buttress the judiciary branch making it equal to the executive and legislative branches.

■■■

Quicknotes

APPELLATE JURISDICTION The power of a higher court to review the decisions of lower courts.

JUDICIAL REVIEW The authority of the courts to review decisions, actions or omissions committed by another agency or branch of government.

ORIGINAL JURISDICTION The power of a court to hear an action upon its commencement.

WRIT OF MANDAMUS A court order issued commanding a public or private entity, or an official thereof, to perform a duty required by law.

■■■

Martin v. Hunter's Lessee

British citizen (P) v. U.S. citizen (D)

14 U.S. (1 Wheat.) 304 (1816).

NATURE OF CASE: Appeal of land title dispute in state court involving issues of federal law.

FACT SUMMARY: The Virginia Court of Appeals held that the U.S. Supreme Court did not have jurisdiction to decide matters of federal law in state courts.

RULE OF LAW
The U.S. Supreme Court has jurisdiction over issues of federal law in state courts.

FACTS: Martin (P), a British subject, claimed certain land. Hunter (D) claimed the land under a grant from the state. Martin (P) claimed that certain treaties between the United States and England gave him the land. The state trial court found for Martin (P); the state appellate court reversed. The U.S. Supreme Court reversed on the basis of the treaties and matters of federal law, and directed the state court to enter judgment for Martin (P). The state court refused. The U.S. Supreme Court reached the issue of its jurisdiction in the matter.

ISSUE: Does the U.S. Supreme Court have jurisdiction over issues of federal law in state courts?

HOLDING AND DECISION: (Story, J.) Yes. The U.S. Supreme Court has jurisdiction over issues of federal law in state courts. The Constitution grants power to the Court in all cases arising under the Constitution or federal laws, irrespective of the tribunal of origin. It cannot be said that U.S. Supreme Court review of state court decisions is overly intrusive on state power, since it is accepted that Congress can supersede state laws, and this is equally intrusive. Finally, the laws of the United States require national uniformity, and only by having one final arbiter of federal law may this be achieved. Reversed.

ANALYSIS

This action was a landmark in American judicial history. It is difficult to envision what the American legal system would be like today if this decision had gone the other way. It would seem that the federal system in that case would have been little different than the state systems.

Quicknotes

APPELLATE JURISDICTION The power of a higher court to review the decisions of lower courts.

JURISDICTION The authority of a court to hear and declare judgment in respect to a particular matter.

McCulloch v. Maryland

Bank cashier (D) v. State (P)

17 U.S. (4 Wheat.) 316 (1819).

NATURE OF CASE: Action arising out of violation of a state statute.

FACT SUMMARY: McCulloch (D), the cashier of the Baltimore branch of the U.S. Bank, issued bank notes in violation of a Maryland (P) statute providing that no bank, without authority from the state, could issue bank notes except on stamped paper issued by the state.

🏛 RULE OF LAW
(1) Certain federal powers giving Congress the discretion and power to choose and enact the means to perform the duties imposed upon it are to be implied from the Necessary and Proper Clause.
(2) The federal Constitution and the laws made pursuant to it are supreme and control the constitutions and the laws of the states.

FACTS: A Maryland (P) statute prohibited any bank operating in the state without state authority from issuing bank notes except upon stamped paper issued by the state. The law specifies the fees payable for the paper, and provides for penalties for violators. An Act of Congress established a U.S. Bank. McCulloch (D), the U.S. Bank's cashier for its Baltimore branch, issued bank notes without complying with the Maryland (P) law.

ISSUE:
(1) Does Congress have the power to incorporate a bank?
(2) Does a state have the power to impose fees on the operation of an institution created by Congress pursuant to its constitutional powers?

HOLDING AND DECISION: (Marshall, C.J.)
(1) Yes. Certain federal powers giving Congress the discretion and power to choose and enact the means to perform the duties imposed upon it are to be implied from the Necessary and Proper Clause. It's true that this government is one of enumerated powers. However, the Constitution does not exclude incidental or implied powers. It does not require that everything be granted expressly and minutely described. To have so required would have entirely changed the character of the Constitution and made it into a legal code. The enumerated powers given to the government imply the ordinary means of execution. The power of creating a corporation may be implied as incidental to other powers, or used as a means of executing them. The Necessary and Proper Clause gives Congress the power to make "all laws which shall be necessary and proper for carrying into execution" the powers vested by the Constitution in the U.S. Government. Maryland (P) argues that the word "necessary" limits the right to pass laws for the execution of the granted powers to those that are indispensable. However, in common usage "necessary" frequently means convenient, useful, and essential. Considering the word's common usage, its usage in another part of the Constitution (Article 1, Section 10), and its inclusion among the powers given to Congress, rather than among the limitations upon Congress, it cannot be held to restrain Congress. The sound construction of the Constitution must allow Congress the discretion to choose the means to perform the duties imposed upon it. So long as the end is legitimate and within the scope of the Constitution, any means that are appropriate, that are plainly adapted to that end, and that are not prohibited by the Constitution, but are consistent with its spirit, are constitutional. A bank is a convenient, useful, and essential instrument for handling national finances. Hence, it is within Congress's power to enact a law incorporating a U.S. bank.
(2) No. The Federal Constitution and the laws made pursuant to it are supreme and control the constitutions and the laws of the states. Maryland (P) was incorrect in its contention that the powers of the federal government are delegated by the states, which alone are truly sovereign. The Constitution derives its authority from the people, not from the states. Here, Maryland's (P) statute in effect taxes the operation of the U.S. Bank, a bank properly created within Congress's power. The power to tax involves the power to destroy. Here it is in opposition to the supreme congressional power to create a bank. Also, when a state taxes an organization created by the U.S. Government, it acts upon an institution created by people over whom it claims no control. The states have no power, by taxation or otherwise, to impede, burden, or in any manner control the operations of constitutional laws enacted by Congress. The Maryland (P) statute is, therefore, unconstitutional and void.

▌ANALYSIS

Federalism is the basis of the Constitution's response to the problem of governing large geographical areas with diverse local needs. The success of federalism depends upon maintaining the balance between the need for the supremacy and sovereignty of the federal government and the interest in maintaining independent state government and curtailing national intrusion into intrastate affairs. The

Continued on next page.

U.S. federal structure allocates powers between the nation and the states by enumerating the powers delegated to the national government and acknowledging the retention by the states of the remainder. The Articles of Confederation followed a similar scheme. The Constitution expanded the enumerated national powers to remedy weaknesses of the Articles. The move from the Articles to the Constitution was a shift from a central government with fewer powers to one with more powers.

■≡■

Quicknotes

ENUMERATED POWERS Those powers expressly delegated by the Constitution to a particular branch of government.

FEDERALISM A scheme of government whereby the power to govern is divided between a central and localized governments.

IMPLIED POWERS Powers impliedly delegated to the various branches of government that, while not expressly stated in the Constitution, are necessary to effectuate the enumerated powers.

■≡■

Ex parte McCardle

Federal government (P) v. Newspaper editor (D)

74 U.S. (7 Wall.) 506 (1869).

NATURE OF CASE: Appeal from denial of habeas corpus.

FACT SUMMARY: McCardle (D) appealed from a denial of habeas corpus to the Supreme Court, but Congress passed an act forbidding the Court jurisdiction.

🏛 **RULE OF LAW**
Although the Supreme Court derives its appellate jurisdiction from the Constitution, the Constitution also gives Congress the express power to make exceptions to that appellate jurisdiction.

FACTS: After the Civil War, Congress imposed military government on many former Confederate states under authority of the Civil War Reconstruction Acts. McCardle (D), a Mississippi newspaper editor, was held in military custody on charges of publishing libelous and incendiary articles. McCardle (D) brought a habeas corpus writ based on a Congressional Act passed on February 5, 1867. The Act authorized federal courts to grant habeas corpus to persons held in violation of Constitutional rights, and also gave authority for appeals to the Supreme Court. The circuit court denied McCardle's (D) habeas corpus writ, but the Supreme Court sustained jurisdiction for an appeal on the merits. However, after arguments were heard, Congress passed an act on March 27, 1868, that repealed that much of the 1867 Act that allowed an appeal to the Supreme Court from the circuit court and the exercise by the Supreme Court by jurisdiction on any such appeals, past or present.

ISSUE: Does Congress have the power, under the Constitution, to make exceptions to the appellate jurisdiction of the Supreme Court?

HOLDING AND DECISION: (Marshall, C.J.) Yes. Although the Supreme Court derives its appellate jurisdiction from the Constitution, the Constitution also gives Congress the express power to make exceptions to that appellate jurisdiction. The appellate jurisdiction of the Supreme Court is not derived from acts of Congress, but is conferred by the Constitution with such exceptions and regulations as Congress shall make. And though Congress has affirmatively described in the Act of 1789 the regulations governing the exercise of the Supreme Court's appellate jurisdiction, with the implication that any exercise of that jurisdiction not within the purview of the Act would be negated, the exception to the appellate jurisdiction in the present case is not to be inferred from such affirmations. The exceptions in this case are express. That part of the 1867 Act giving the Court appellate jurisdiction in habeas corpus cases is expressly repealed. The effect is to take away the court's jurisdiction, dismissing the cause. When a legislative act is repealed, it is as if it had never existed except to transactions past and closed. Thus, no judgment can be rendered in a suit after repeal of the act under which it was brought. But this does not deny forever the Court's appellate power in habeas corpus cases. The Act of 1868 affects only such appeals from circuit courts brought under the Act of 1867. Dismissed.

▶ ANALYSIS

McCardle is clearly an example of judicial restraint. The authority of Congress to control the jurisdiction of the Supreme Court is not unlimited. This was proved in *Marbury v. Madison* where the Court, faced with an extension by Congress of its original jurisdiction as granted under the Constitution, refused to accept the constitutionality of the congressional act. While this specifically limited the Supreme Court's original jurisdiction, it provided Marshall with the ideal arena to assert the doctrine of judicial review. But in *McCardle*, the Court backed away from confrontation with Congress due to current-day political crises that followed the Civil War. Thereafter, the Court sought to limit congressional power by the power of judicial review announced in *Marbury*. The Court held on several occasions that certain congressional attempts to delimit its jurisdiction were unconstitutional attempts to invade the judicial province. Such congressional actions were considered a violation of the separation of powers. Today, it is doubtful that *McCardle* would be sustained.

■▬■

Quicknotes

APPELLATE JURISDICTION The power of a higher court to review the decisions of lower courts.

ORIGINAL JURISDICTION The power of a court to hear an action upon its commencement.

■▬■

Allen v. Wright

Parents (P) v. IRS (D)

468 U.S. 737 (1984).

NATURE OF CASE: Appeal of order denying tax-exempt status to racially discriminatory private schools.

FACT SUMMARY: Certain parents (P) of black schoolchildren filed an action to compel the Internal Revenue Serivce (IRS) (D) to deny tax-exempt status to racially discriminatory private schools, in conformity with the law.

🏛 RULE OF LAW
One does not have standing to sue in federal court unless he can allege the violation of a right personal to him.

FACTS: Certain parents of black schoolchildren brought an action to compel the Internal Revenue Service (IRS) (D) to deny tax-exempt status to private schools that discriminate, an illegal practice. It was alleged that the practice promoted segregated schools and made desegregation more difficult. The court of appeals held in favor of the parents (P).

ISSUE: Does one have standing to sue in federal court if he cannot allege a violation of a right personal to him?

HOLDING AND DECISION: (O'Connor, J.) No. One does not have standing to sue in federal court if he cannot allege a violation of a right personal to him. Federal courts are not designed to air generalized grievances. A plaintiff must allege injury traceable to a defendant's conduct likely to be redressed by the requested relief. It has long been held that the "right" to have the government act in accordance with the law will not confer standing; something more personal is required. To do this would constitute an excessive intrusion of the Judiciary into the Executive branch of government. In the area in question, a plaintiff must show that he himself has been denied equal treatment in order to have standing. This has not been shown here. The allegation that the conduct of the IRS (D) promotes segregation is purely speculative. No allegation is made that withdrawal of the funds would make a difference in public school integration. Since no personal injury traceable to the IRS's (D) conduct has been alleged, no standing exists. Reversed.

DISSENT: (Brennan, J.) Alleging that the IRS's (D) conduct hinders black schoolchildren's rights to a desegregated education is alleging a concrete injury.

DISSENT: (Stevens, J.) The plaintiffs basically allege that the conduct of the IRS (D) promotes the exodus of white children who would otherwise attend integrated schools. This is a sufficient concrete injury to confer standing. When a subsidy makes a given activity more or less expensive, injury can be fairly traced to the subsidy for purposes of standing analysis because of the resulting increase or decrease in the ability to engage in the activity. Here, the action of the IRS will cause the process of desegregation to be advanced since the withdrawal of the subsidy for segregated schools means the incentive structure facing white parents who seek such schools for their children will be altered.

▌ANALYSIS

The requirements of standing are based on both textual and non-textual concerns. The "case or controversy" requirement is a basis for standing requirements. Also forming a basis are prudential concerns such as not interfering with other branches unnecessarily.

■≡■

Quicknotes

GENERALIZED GRIEVANCE Refers to a class of actions that does not have standing because it does not represent a controversy for the particular plaintiff, but is something that affects the general public.

REDRESSABILITY Requirement that in order for a court to hear a case there must be an injury that is redressable or capable of being remedied.

STANDING Whether a party possesses the right to commence suit against another party by having a personal stake in the resolution of the controversy.

■≡■

Lujan v. Defenders of Wildlife

Federal government (D) v. Members (P)

504 U.S. 555 (1992).

NATURE OF CASE: Appeal from denial of motion to dismiss action seeking declaratory judgment and injunction against administrative rule.

FACT SUMMARY: Defenders of Wildlife (P) sought a declaratory judgment and injunction to extend application of the Endangered Species Act to government actions taken in foreign nations.

🏛 RULE OF LAW
Only individuals who have suffered concrete harm have standing to seek judicial review of agency rules.

FACTS: The U.S. Interior Department (D) reinterpreted the Endangered Species Act (ESA) to apply only to government actions taken in the United States or on the high seas, and not in foreign nations. Two Defenders of Wildlife members (P) had visited separate sites abroad and claimed harm by such reinterpretation. The members (P) planned to return sometime to observe endangered animals in the sites they had previously visited, but the Interior Department's (D) new interpretation would probably increase the extinction rate of the endangered species they planned to study. The members (P) sought a declaratory judgment and an injunction requiring the Interior Department (D) to apply the ESA to actions taken in foreign nations.

ISSUE: Do individuals who have suffered no concrete harm have standing to seek judicial review of agency rules?

HOLDING AND DECISION: (Scalia, J.) No. Only individuals who have suffered concrete harm have standing to seek judicial review of agency rules. That Defenders of Wildlife members (P) intend to return "someday" to wildlife sites does not constitute "actual or imminent" injury caused by the Interior Department's (D) reinterpretation of the ESA. Further, it is unclear that applying the ESA to actions in foreign nations will effect the redress sought by Defenders (P). Reversed.

CONCURRENCE: (Kennedy, J.) While the ESA permits citizen suits, it fails to establish injury in "any person" by virtue of any "violation." Since standing is not established, the redressability issue should not be reached.

CONCURRENCE: (Stevens, J.) While the Interior Department's (D) reinterpretation of the ESA is correct, an injury is suffered whenever action is taken that harms the interest in studying animals in natural habitats.

DISSENT: (Blackmun, J.) The professional backgrounds of the Defenders of Wildlife members (P) make it reasonable to assume the members (P) will soon return to the foreign sites, thus satisfying the "actual or imminent" injury requirement for standing. Requiring a specific return date in the future is an empty formality. Such rigid principles as enunciated by the plurality are likely to apply only in environmental claims. Environmental plaintiffs should not be held to have special standing disabilities.

▶ ANALYSIS

Minimally, showing "standing" requires three elements: (1) plaintiff suffers an injury; (2) the injury is caused by the conduct complained of; and (3) a favorable decision is likely to redress the injury. In *Northeastern Fla. Chapter of Assoc. Gen. Contractors v. Jacksonville*, 508 U.S. 656 (1993), the Supreme Court held a nonminority group had standing to challenge a city's minority set-aside program. The Court held the group need only show it was ready and able to bid on contracts, but was prevented from doing so on an equal basis; no actual loss of contract need be shown.

Quicknotes

DECLARATORY JUDGMENT A judgment of the court establish the rights of the parties.

INJUNCTION A court order requiring a person to do or prohibiting that person from doing a specific act.

Massachusetts v. EPA

State (P) v. Federal agency (D)

549 U.S. 497, 127 S. Ct. 1438 (2007).

NATURE OF CASE: Appeal challenging a federal agency's alleged refusal to enforce the federal Clean Air Act against motor-vehicle emissions.

FACT SUMMARY: A state and several other parties challenged the Environmental Protection Agency's (D) failure to enforce the Clean Air Act against motor-vehicle emissions.

🏛 RULE OF LAW
A plaintiff has standing if it demonstrates a concrete injury that is both fairly traceable to the defendant and redressable by judicial relief.

FACTS: The Environmental Protection Agency (EPA) (D) refused to enforce the Clean Air Act against motor-vehicle emissions. Massachusetts (P) and several other parties appealed the EPA's (D) refusal [by petitioning the Court of Appeals for the District of Columbia Circuit to review the Agency's (D) decision. The appellate court did not affirmatively hold that Massachusetts (P) had standing, but a majority of that court did uphold the EPA's (D) decision. Massachusetts (P) petitioned the U.S. Supreme Court for further review.]

ISSUE: Does a plaintiff have standing if it demonstrates a concrete injury that is both fairly traceable to the defendant and redressable by judicial relief?

HOLDING AND DECISION: (Stevens, J.) Yes. A plaintiff has standing if it demonstrates a concrete injury that is both fairly traceable to the defendant and redressable by judicial relief. The jurisdiction of federal courts is limited to "cases" and "controversies," and Massachusetts (P) has satisfied that threshold hurdle here. As a State, Massachusetts (P) proceeds in its quasi-sovereign capacity, and caselaw supports applying different standards of justiciability for such litigants. The particularized injury for Massachusetts (P) in this case is the damage to the State's (P) coastline that will, and will continue to, occur. Further, the injury to that coastline is fairly traceable to the EPA's (D) inaction; even small effects on an injury in fact satisfy the causation requirement in federal standing analysis. Finally, Massachusetts' (P) injury can be redressed judicially, even though the outcome of a judicial remedy might be delayed while new motor-vehicle emissions are implemented. Accordingly, Massachusetts (P) has standing. [Reversed and remanded.]

DISSENT: (Roberts, C.J.) Any redress of the injuries in this case should be left to the political branches. Relaxing standing requirements for a state exists nowhere in this Court's precedents. Under normal standing analysis, Massachusetts' (P) injury fails to satisfy the requirement of a "concrete and particularized" injury; injuries to "humanity at large" do not suffice. Also, any causal connection between the EPA's (D) inaction and damage to the coastlines is so tenuous and speculative that it cannot support a finding of standing. Further, Massachusetts (P) cannot satisfy the redressability factor because emissions from other countries are likely to dwarf any reduction in emissions that might result from the EPA's (D) enforcement of the Clean Air Act. Diluting the appropriate standing requirements only permits courts to encroach upon authority that is properly committed to Congress and the President.

▶ ANALYSIS

The three factors in the standing analysis announced by *Lujan v. Defenders of Wildlife,* 504 U.S. 555 (1992), are very clear: the complaining party must have suffered (1) an injury in fact (2) that is fairly traceable to the defendant and (3) that can be redressed by judicial relief. As the Court's 5-4 decision in this case shows, however, what is not so clear is how those three factors should apply to any specific dispute. The fundamental importance of justiciability, as Chief Justice Roberts notes in dissent, resides in the most basic questions about the kinds of disputes that courts should—and should not—hear.

■■■

Quicknotes

REDRESSABILITY Requirement that in order for a court to hear a case there must be an injury that is redressable or capable of being remedied.

■■■

Baker v. Carr

Voters (P) v. State (D)

369 U.S. 186 (1962).

NATURE OF CASE: Appeal from denial of challenge to state apportionment system.

FACT SUMMARY: A 60-year-old Tennessee apportionment system was attacked as obsolete.

 RULE OF LAW
Reapportionment issues present justiciable questions.

FACTS: A 1901 statute apportioned members of the Tennessee Assembly among the state's counties. By 1961, the population had experienced substantial redistribution. Certain individuals (P) filed a district court action challenging the apportionment system as arbitrary and capricious, seeking reapportionment. The court of appeals held that the issue was nonjusticiable.

ISSUE: Do reapportionment issues present justiciable questions?

HOLDING AND DECISION: (Brennan, J.) Yes. Reapportionment issues present justiciable questions. Nonjusticiable or "political" questions are those properly left to other branches of government, either because courts do not have the resources to handle them or because they are best decided through the political process. Examples include foreign relations and the validity of enactments (other than the constitutionality thereto). The issue here, however, is whether the guarantees of equal protection found in the Constitution are being met. Thus, in this issue, the Court is being called upon to judge the constitutionality of the system under attack, something squarely within the Court's power and duty. Reversed.

DISSENT: (Frankfurter, J.) The Court should not interject itself into political disagreements, as it has done here. Also, it is doubtful that the Court is adequately equipped to handle the subtleties of reapportionment issues. Finally, the structure of state institutions should be given great respect.

▶ *ANALYSIS*

It is important to understand the difference between a nonjusticiable political question and a political issue. Political issues with constitutional dimensions generally are fair game for judicial review. Political questions are issues that may have constitutional dimensions but are of a nature that they should be resolved in the political arena. The classic example is foreign relations.

Quicknotes

JUSTICIABILITY An actual controversy that is capable of determination by the court.

Bush v. Gore

Candidate (D) v. Candidate (P)

531 U.S. 98 (2000).

NATURE OF CASE: Suit seeking stay of state supreme court order.

FACT SUMMARY: Bush (D) sought a stay of the Florida Supreme Court's order permitting a manual recount of ballots in the 2000 presidential election.

🏛 RULE OF LAW
Having once granted the right to vote on equal terms, the state may not, by later arbitrary and disparate treatment, value one person's vote over that of another.

FACTS: After a machine count and recount of ballots in the 2000 Florida presidential election, Gore (P) trailed Bush (D) by less than 1,000 votes. Gore (P) sought further recounts in certain Florida counties. The U.S. Supreme Court vacated a decision of the Florida Supreme Court extending the deadline for the completion of recounts. The Florida Supreme Court ordered a manual recount of all "undervotes"—those ballots on which the machine did not record any presidential choice. Bush (D) sought a stay of the Florida Supreme Court ruling. The U.S. Supreme Court stayed the Florida Supreme Court's order three days before the statutory deadline for the completion of proceedings bearing on the final certification of the state's electors.

ISSUE: Having once granted the right to vote on equal terms, may the state, by later arbitrary and disparate treatment, value one person's vote over that of another?

HOLDING AND DECISION: (Per curiam) No. Having once granted the right to vote on equal terms, the state may not, by later arbitrary and disparate treatment, value one person's vote over that of another. The right to vote is protected both in its allocation as well as its exercise. The recount mechanism implemented here does not satisfy the minimum requirement for non-arbitrary treatment of voters necessary to secure the fundamental right. The standards for accepting or rejecting contested ballots vary not only from county to county but within the county from team to team of recounters. Because any recount seeking to meet the December 12 date will be unconstitutional without substantial additional work, the decision of the Florida Supreme Court ordering the recount to proceed is reversed and the case is remanded.

CONCURRENCE: (Rehnquist, C.J.) There are grounds for reversal in addition to those in the per curiam opinion. I. Where the election of the President is involved, and the Constitution imposes a duty on a branch of state government, the text of the state's election law, and not just its interpretation by the state courts, takes on independent significance. Therefore, 3 U.S.C. § 5 informs the application of the Constitution's mandate in Art. II, § 1, cl. 2 that the state legislature shall appoint electors to the electoral college in a manner of its choosing to the state's electoral scheme. Section 5 provides that the state's selection of electors will be conclusive if the selection is accomplished pursuant to laws enacted prior to the election and is complete six days prior to the meeting of the electoral college. To respect the legislature's powers, postelection state-court actions must not be allowed to frustrate the legislative desire to attain the "safe harbor" provided by § 5, and, to determine whether a state court has infringed upon the legislature's Article II authority, the Court must examine the state's election law. II. Here, the Florida court's interpretation of "legal vote" and, therefore, its decision to order a contest-period recount, plainly departed from the legislative scheme. The election code does not require the counting of improperly marked ballots, and for the court to reject this established practice, prescribed by the Secretary of State, was also a departure from the legislative scheme. III. The Florida Supreme Court's order jeopardizes the "legislative wish" to take advantage of the safe harbor provided by 3 U.S.C. § 5. The state court ordered a massive recount four days before the last date for a final determination that will satisfy § 5. However, no one claims that the ballots the court seeks to have recounted were not previously tabulated. Those ballots were initially read by voting machines at the time of the election, and then reread pursuant to the state's automatic recount provision. There is also no claim of fraud.

DISSENT: (Stevens, J.) While the use of differing substandards for determining voter intent in different counties employing similar voting systems may raise serious concerns, those concerns are alleviated by the fact that a single impartial magistrate will ultimately adjudicate all objections arising from the recount process. The loser in this Presidential election is the Nation's confidence in the judge as an impartial guardian of the rule of law.

DISSENT: (Souter, J.) The case should be remanded to the Florida courts with instructions to establish uniform standards in any further recounting.

DISSENT: (Ginsburg, J.) The Court contradicts the basic principle that a State may organize itself as it sees fit. Article II does not call for the scrutiny taken by this Court.

DISSENT: (Breyer, J.) This Court should resist the temptation to resolve tangential legal disputes, where doing so threatens to determine the outcome of the election.

Continued on next page.

▶ *ANALYSIS*

The Court here does not challenge the Florida Supreme Court's authority to resolve election disputes or to define a legal vote or order a manual recount. The Court rejects the standard employed, which was the "intent of the voter," and the absence of specific standards to ensure its equal application.

■≡■

Quicknotes

DUE PROCESS CLAUSE Clauses found in the Fifth and Fourteenth Amendments to the United States Constitution providing that no person shall be deprived of "life, liberty, or property, without due process of law."

EQUAL PROTECTION A constitutional guarantee that no person shall be denied the same protection of the laws enjoyed by other persons in like circumstances.

■≡■

CHAPTER 2

Federalism: Congress and the National Economy

Quick Reference Rules of Law

PAGE

1. **Federalism and Judicial Review.**   If a state law conflicts with a congressional act regulating commerce, the congressional act is controlling. (Gibbons v. Ogden)   *16*

2. **Federalism and Judicial Review.**   The making of goods and the mining of coal are not commerce, nor does the fact that these things are to be afterwards shipped or used in interstate commerce make their production a part of such commerce. (Hammer v. Dagenhart (The Child Labor Case))   *17*

3. **Federalism and Judicial Review.**   Farm production that is intended for consumption on the farm is subject to Congress's commerce power, since it may have a substantial economic effect on interstate commerce. (Wickard v. Filburn)   *18*

4. **The Evolution of Commerce Clause Doctrine.**   Under the Commerce Clause, Congress has the power to regulate any activity, even intrastate production, if the activity has an appreciable effect, either direct or indirect, on interstate commerce. (NLRB v. Jones & Laughlin Steel Corp.)   *19*

5. **The Evolution of Commerce Clause Doctrine.**   Congress has the authority to regulate through its commerce power only those activities that have a substantial effect upon interstate commerce. (United States v. Lopez)   *21*

6. **State Regulation of Interstate Commerce.**   A state may not enact bans on articles of commerce absent legitimate public welfare concerns. (City of Philadelphia v. New Jersey)   *23*

7. **State Regulation of Interstate Commerce.**   Discrimination against interstate commerce in favor of local businesses is per se invalid unless the municipality can demonstrate that it has no other means to advance a legitimate local interest. (C & A Carbone, Inc. v. Clarkstown)   *24*

8. **State Regulation of Interstate Commerce.**   An assessment scheme that levies a tax on all distribution of a good but disburses its assets only to local producers is unconstitutional. (West Lynn Creamery, Inc. v. Healy)   *25*

9. **Facially Neutral Statutes with Significant Effects on Interstate Commerce.**   Facially neutral statutes that discriminate against certain out-of-state products violate the Commerce Clause. (Hunt v. Washington State Apple Advertising Commission)   *26*

10. **Facially Neutral Statutes with Significant Effects on Interstate Commerce.**   A state may prohibit the retailing of petroleum products by producers. (Exxon Corp. v. Governor of Maryland)   *27*

11. **Facially Neutral Statutes with Significant Effects on Interstate Commerce.**   A state safety regulation will be unconstitutional if its asserted safety purpose is outweighed by its degree of interference with interstate commerce. (Kassel v. Consolidated Freightways Corp.)   *28*

Gibbons v. Ogden

Ship operator (D) v. Ship operator (P)

22 U.S. (9 Wheat.) 1 (1824).

NATURE OF CASE: Action seeking an injunction to protect an exclusive right to operate ships between New York City and New Jersey.

FACT SUMMARY: Ogden (P), after acquiring a monopoly right from the State of New York to operate ships between New York City and New Jersey, sought to enjoin Gibbons (D) from operating his ships, licensed by the federal government, between the same points.

🏛 RULE OF LAW
If a state law conflicts with a congressional act regulating commerce, the congressional act is controlling.

FACTS: In 1803, the New York legislature granted an exclusive right to Robert Livingston and Robert Fulton to operate ships powered by fire or steam in New York waters for twenty years. The right was subsequently extended for another ten years. Ogden (P) obtained an assignment from Livingston and Fulton to operate his ships between Elizabethtown, New Jersey, and New York City. Gibbons (D) was also running two boats between these points and his boats had been enrolled and licensed under the laws of the United States for carrying on the coasting trade. Ogden (P) obtained an injunction stopping Gibbons (D) from operating his ships between the points for which Ogden (P) had received an exclusive right to operate his own ships. The case was appealed to the Supreme Court. Ogden (P) claimed that the federal government did not have exclusive jurisdiction over commerce but that the states had retained power by which they could regulate commerce within their own states and that the exclusive right to operate his ships only concerned intrastate commerce. Gibbons (D) contended that Congress had exclusive power to regulate interstate commerce and that New York had attempted to regulate interstate commerce by granting the exclusive right and enforcing it with the injunction.

ISSUE: If a state law conflicts with a congressional act regulating commerce, is the congressional act controlling?

HOLDING AND DECISION: (Marshall, C.J.) Yes. If a state law conflicts with a congressional act regulating commerce, the congressional act is controlling. Congress has the power to regulate navigation within the limits of every state and, therefore, the regulations that Congress passed controlling navigation within the boundaries of New York were valid. Ogden (P) argued that the states through the Tenth Amendment have the power to regulate commerce with foreign nations and among the states because the power that the states gave up to Congress to regulate commerce wasn't absolute and the residue of that power remained with the states. But Congress was given all the power to regulate interstate commerce, although it is possible for the states to pass regulations that may affect some activity associated with interstate commerce. In that case, states must base such regulations on some other source of power than the commerce power (such as the police power of the state). Regardless of the source of the state power, anytime a state regulation conflicts with a federal regulation, the state regulation must yield to the federal law. Since in this case the law of New York conflicted with a federal regulation dealing with interstate commerce, the New York law is not valid. Accordingly, the Court dismissed Ogden's (P) suit to obtain an injunction against Gibbons (D).

▶ ANALYSIS

The federal commerce power is concurrent with state power over commerce within the state. Hence, the Court has been asked many times to define the line between federal and state power to regulate commerce. During the early history of the United States, the court was not often called upon to determine the scope of federal power under the Commerce Clause. Instead, the early cases generally involved some state action that was claimed to discriminate against or burden interstate commerce. Hence, the Commerce Clause operated as a restraint upon state powers. Most of these cases did not involve any exercise of the commerce power by Congress at all. Large-scale regulatory action by Congress began with the Interstate Commerce Act in 1887 and the Sherman Antitrust Act in 1890. Challenges to these statutes initiated the major modern confrontations between the Court and congressional authority regarding commerce.

■=■

Quicknotes

INJUNCTION A court order requiring a person to do, or prohibiting that person from doing, a specific act.

RESIDUUM The leftover balance; surplus or residue.

■=■

Hammer v. Dagenhart (The Child Labor Case)

U.S. Attorney General (D) v. Parent (P)

247 U.S. 251 (1918).

NATURE OF CASE: Appeal from a decree enjoining enforcement of the Child Labor Act.

FACT SUMMARY: Congress passed a law prohibiting the shipment in interstate commerce of any products of any mills, mines, or factories that employed children.

🏛 RULE OF LAW
The making of goods and the mining of coal are not commerce, nor does the fact that these things are to be afterwards shipped or used in interstate commerce make their production a part of such commerce.

FACTS: A congressional act prohibited the shipment in interstate commerce of the product of any mine or quarry that employed children under the age of 16. It prohibited the shipment in such commerce of the product of any mill, cannery, workshop, or factory that employed children under the age of 14 or employed children between the ages of 14 and 16 for more than eight hours a day or more than six days a week or before 6 a.m. or after 7 p.m. Dagenhart (P) brought this action on behalf of his two minor children after being informed by the company where they worked of their impending discharge on the effective date of the Act. Hammer (D), the U.S. Attorney General, and the company that had employed Dagenhart's (P) children were named as defendants.

ISSUE: Can Congress, under its commerce power, pass a law prohibiting the transportation in interstate commerce of products of companies that employed children as laborers in violation of the terms of the law?

HOLDING AND DECISION: (Day, J.) No. It is argued that the power of Congress to regulate commerce includes the power to prohibit the transportation of ordinary products in commerce. However, in cases such as the Lottery Case, 188 U.S. 321 (1903), the power to prohibit the carrying of lottery tickets is to those particular objects the same as the exertion of the power to regulate. In those cases, the use of interstate commerce was necessary to the accomplishment of harmful results. Regulation over commerce could only be accomplished by prohibiting the use of interstate commerce to affect the evil intended. Here, the thing intended to be accomplished by this Act is the denial of interstate commerce facilities to those employing children within the prohibited ages. The goods shipped are of themselves harmless. The production of articles intended for interstate commerce is a matter of local regulation. The making of goods and the mining of coal are not commerce, nor does the fact that these things are to be afterwards shipped or used in interstate commerce make their production a part thereof. It is also argued that congressional regulation is necessary because of the unfair advantage possessed by manufacturers in states that have less stringent child labor laws. However, Congress has no power to require states to exercise their police powers to prevent possible unfair competition. The act is unconstitutional, and the decree enjoining its enforcement is affirmed.

DISSENT: (Holmes, J.) The Lottery Case and others following it establish that a law is not beyond Congress's commerce power merely because it prohibits certain transportation. There is no legal distinction between the evils sought to be controlled in those cases and the evil of premature and excessive child labor. The Court has no right to substitute its judgment of which evils may be controlled.

▌ ANALYSIS

After the *Hammer* decision, Congress sought to regulate child labor through the taxing power. That law was invalidated in *Bailey v. Drexel Furnishing Co.*, 259 U.S. 20 (1922). Subsequently, Congress submitted a proposed constitutional amendment to the states that authorized a national child labor law. The amendment has not been ratified, but the need for it has largely disappeared in view of *U.S. v. Darby*, 312 U.S. 100 (1941), which overruled Hammer.

■■■■

Quicknotes

COMMERCE POWER The power delegated to Congress by the Constitution to regulate interstate commerce.

■■■■

Wickard v. Filburn

Department of Agriculture (P) v. Farmer (D)

317 U.S. 111 (1942).

NATURE OF CASE: Action to enjoin enforcement of penalty provisions of the Agricultural Adjustment Act.

FACT SUMMARY: Filburn (D) was ordered to pay a penalty imposed by the Agriculture Adjustment Act for producing wheat in excess of his assigned quota. He argued that the federal regulations could not be constitutionally applied to his crops because part of his crop was intended for his own consumption, not for interstate commerce.

🏛 RULE OF LAW
Farm production that is intended for consumption on the farm is subject to Congress's commerce power, since it may have a substantial economic effect on interstate commerce.

FACTS: The purpose of the Agriculture Adjustment Act was to control the volume of wheat moving in interstate commerce to avoid surpluses and shortages that would result in abnormally high or low prices and thereby obstruct commerce. Under the Act, the Secretary of Agriculture would set a national acreage allotment for wheat production, which would be divided into allotments for individual farms. Filburn (D) was the owner and operator of a small farm. In the past he had grown a small amount of wheat of which he sold part, fed part to poultry and livestock (some of the livestock were later sold), used part in making flour for home consumption, and kept the rest for seeding the next year. In 1940, his wheat production exceeded the maximum he was allowed under the Agriculture Adjustment Act and he was assessed a penalty for the excess. Filburn (D) refused to pay on the ground that the Act was unconstitutional in that it attempted to regulate purely local production and consumption which, at most, had an indirect effect on interstate commerce. The government argued that the Act regulated not production and consumption, but only marketing (which was defined in the Act to include the feeding of the wheat to livestock that was later sold), and even if interpreted to include production and consumption, it was a legitimate exercise of the Commerce Clause and the Necessary and Proper Clause.

ISSUE: Does Congress, under the Commerce Clause, have the power to regulate the production of wheat that is grown for home consumption purposes rather than for sale in interstate commerce?

HOLDING AND DECISION: (Jackson, J.) Yes. Farm production that is intended for consumption on the farm is subject to Congress's commerce power, since it may have a substantial economic effect on interstate commerce. A local activity, such as production, may be reached under the Commerce Clause if it exerts a substantial economic effect on interstate commerce. The Act was enacted because of the problems of the wheat market: there had been a decrease in export in recent years, causing surpluses that in turn caused congestion in the market and lower prices. It has been repeatedly held that the commerce power of Congress includes the power to regulate prices and practices affecting prices. Wheat destined for home consumption has an effect on the interstate price of wheat and is, therefore, subject to regulation. As the market price of wheat climbs, farmers will sell more of their crop that was intended for home consumption on the market causing a decrease in prices. Even if the wheat is never sold, there still is a substantial effect on interstate commerce because it reduces demand for wheat; that wheat which Filburn (D) produces for his own use means that he will buy less wheat on the market. Although the actual effect of Filburn's (D) overproduction will be small, the combination of all such producers does cause a substantial effect on commerce. Reversed.

▶ ANALYSIS

Wickard is yet another application of the "affectation doctrine." The Court focuses not on the nature of the regulated activity (e.g., whether it is local) but on the final economic effect of that activity. Here, although the effect of Filburn's (D) excess wheat production was insignificant on the national market, there still was some effect, at least in theory, so regulation was allowed. The Court in *Wickard* expressly rejected the old formulas for determining the extent of the commerce power such as direct/indirect and production/commerce.

◼▬◼

Quicknotes

LOCAL ACTIVITY An activity such as mining or manufacturing that has only an indirect effect in interstate commerce because it can be conducted entirely within the boundaries of the state.

NECESSARY AND PROPER CLAUSE, ACT I, § 8 OF THE CONSTITUTION Enables Congress to make all laws that may be "necessary and proper" to execute its other, enumerated powers.

◼▬◼

NLRB v. Jones & Laughlin Steel Corp.

Labor board (P) v. Steel company (D)

301 U.S. 1 (1937).

NATURE OF CASE: Action alleging unfair labor practice under the National Labor Relations Act.

FACT SUMMARY: Jones & Laughlin Steel Corp. (D), a manufacturing company with subsidiaries in several states and nationwide sales, was charged with an unfair labor practice under the National Labor Relations Act. In defense, Jones & Laughlin (D) claimed that the Act was an unconstitutional attempt to regulate intrastate production.

RULE OF LAW
Under the Commerce Clause, Congress has the power to regulate any activity, even intrastate production, if the activity has an appreciable effect, either direct or indirect, on interstate commerce.

FACTS: Pursuant to a complaint filed by a labor union, the National Labor Relations Board (NLRB) (P) found that Jones & Laughlin Steel (D) had engaged in "unfair labor practices." The Board (P) issued a cease and desist order to Jones & Laughlin (D) to stop using discriminatory and coercive practices to prevent union organization at two steel plants in and around Pittsburgh. The company refused to comply and the Board (P) went to court for judicial enforcement of its order under the authority of the National Labor Relations Act of 1935. Jones and Laughlin (D) contended that the order was an unconstitutional exercise of the Board's (P) authority since the plants were not engaged in interstate commerce, being totally manufacturing facilities. The court of appeals upheld the company's position and refused enforcement of the order on the ground the order "lay beyond the range of federal power."

ISSUE: Does Congress have the power to regulate any activity, even intrastate production, under the Commerce Clause if the activity has an appreciable effect, either direct or indirect, on interstate commerce?

HOLDING AND DECISION: (Hughes, C.J.) Yes. Under the Commerce Clause, Congress has the power to regulate any activity, even intrastate production, if the activity has an appreciable effect, either direct or indirect, on interstate commerce. The act of the Board (P), in ordering Jones & Laughlin (D) to cease interfering with its employees' rights of self-organization and collective bargaining, is an exercise of the congressional power to regulate interstate commerce. The definitions in the Act restrict the Board's (P) actions to protecting interstate commerce in the constitutional sense, and the Board (P) is given the power to determine if the practice in question affects commerce in such a way as to be subject to federal control. Congress has the power to protect interstate commerce by all appropriate types of legislation, and the controlling question is the effect on interstate commerce, not the source of the interference. Although such legislation may result in the regulation of acts that are intrastate in character, Congress still has the power to regulate if the intrastate acts bear such a close and substantial relation to interstate commerce that control is appropriate for the protection of commerce. Congress is forbidden only from regulating acts that have a remote and indirect effect on interstate commerce. Here, even though the application of the National Labor Relations Act results in the regulation of labor practices at Jones & Laughlin's (D) manufacturing plants, the circumstances indicate the required substantial effect on interstate commerce. If production were interrupted at one of the plants due to a labor dispute, the extensive nationwide operations of Jones & Laughlin (D) indicate that there would necessarily be an immediate effect on interstate commerce. Therefore, the National Labor Relations Act as applied to the facts of this case is a proper exercise of Congress's power to regulate interstate commerce. Reversed.

ANALYSIS

With this case the Supreme Court retreated from its strict geographical definition of interstate commerce and the direct/indirect approach that it used in *A.L.A. Schechter Poultry Corp. v. United States*, 295 U.S. 495 (1935), and *Carter v. Carter Coal Co.*, 298 U.S. 238 (1936). *Jones & Laughlin* states that under the Commerce Clause Congress has the power to regulate any activity that has a significant effect on interstate commerce, regardless of whether that effect is direct or indirect. This new concept is often called the "affectation doctrine." Although the court cited prior cases in its opinion and said it was not creating new law, *Jones & Laughlin* is, in effect, a reversal of the *Schechter* line of cases. The Court now bases its opinions on a combination of the Commerce Clause and the Necessary and Proper Clause—power to regulate interstate commerce extends to control over intrastate activities when necessary and appropriate to make regulation of interstate commerce effective.

■=■

Quicknotes

COLLECTIVE BARGAINING Negotiations between an employer and employee that are mediated by a specified third party.

Continued on next page.

COMMERCE CLAUSE Article 1, section 8, clause 3 of the United States Constitution, granting Congress the power to regulate commerce with foreign countries and between the states.

NATIONAL LABOR RELATIONS ACT Guarantees employees the right to engage in collective bargaining, and regulates labor unions.

■■■■

United States v. Lopez

Federal government (P) v. Handgun possessor (D)

514 U.S. 549 (1995).

NATURE OF CASE: Certiorari from reversal of conviction for violation of the Gun-Free School Zones Act.

FACT SUMMARY: Lopez (D) was arrested for carrying a handgun in school in violation of state and federal law.

RULE OF LAW

Congress has the authority to regulate through its commerce power only those activities that have a substantial effect upon interstate commerce.

FACTS: Lopez (D) was a twelfth-grade student at Edison High School in San Antonio, Texas. He arrived at school with a .38 caliber handgun and five bullets. He was arrested and charged under Texas law for firearm possession on school premises. State charges were dropped after federal agents charged Lopez (D) with violating the Gun-Free School Zones Act of 1990. The district court convicted Lopez (D). The Fifth Circuit Court of Appeals reversed because it held that the Act was beyond the power of Congress under the Commerce Clause.

ISSUE: Does the Gun-Free School Zones Act exceed the powers of Congress under the Commerce Clause?

HOLDING AND DECISION: (Rehnquist, C.J.) Yes. Congress has the authority to regulate through its commerce power only those activities that have a substantial effect upon interstate commerce. The Constitution creates a federal government of enumerated powers that are listed in Article 1, § 8. That power expanded dramatically under later court decisions but has always retained some outer limits. There are three broad categories of activity that Congress may regulate under its commerce power: (1) Congress may regulate the use of the channels of interstate commerce; (2) Congress may regulate and protect the instrumentalities of interstate commerce even if the threat is only from intrastate activities; and (3) Congress may regulate those activities having a substantial relation to interstate commerce. The activities addressed by the Gun-Free School Zones Act definitely do not fall into either of the first two categories. Moreover, there is nothing in the statute itself or in its legislative history that expresses congressional findings regarding the effects upon interstate commerce of gun possession in a school zone. It would be imprudent to convert congressional authority under the Commerce Clause into a general police power of the sort retained by the states. Affirmed.

CONCURRENCE: (Kennedy, J.) There are two lessons to be learned from reviewing prior decisions about the Commerce Clause. The first is that there is imprecision of content-based boundaries involved, such as distinction between "commerce" and "manufacture." The second is that there is an immense stake in the stability of the Commerce Clause jurisprudence. Stare decisis counsels not to call into question the essential principles of Commerce Clause analysis. That does not mean, however, that courts lack the authority and responsibility to review congressional attempts to alter the federal balance. Therefore, the political branches must not forget their sworn obligation to preserve and protect the Constitution. The Gun-Free School Zones Act upsets the federal balance and is an unconstitutional assertion of the commerce power.

CONCURRENCE: (Thomas, J.) The power that we have accorded to Congress through the Commerce Clause has swallowed Article I, § 8. The "substantial effects" test has eviscerated any notion of federalism. Without boundaries that limit use of the Commerce Clause to truly commercial activity, we give the federal government a blank check to regulate anything under the guise of the Commerce Clause.

DISSENT: (Stevens, J.) Guns are articles of commerce and can be used to restrain commerce. The national interest justifies prohibiting the possession of guns by school-age children.

DISSENT: (Souter, J.) The Court should only look into whether the legislative judgment is within the realm of reason. Congress should have plenary power to legislate under the Commerce Clause as long as the law passes the rational basis test.

DISSENT: (Breyer, J.) Violence in the schools interferes with the quality of education. Education is inextricably tied to the economy. Therefore, Congress could have rationally concluded that the possession of guns in school zones is related to interstate commerce. Furthermore, the majority decision contradicts well-settled precedent that allows Congress to regulate non-commercial activity that affects interstate commerce.

ANALYSIS

The *Lopez* decision generated some discussion about whether there was going to be a serious modification of the "1937 Revolution" and therefore a major restriction on the powers of Congress through the Commerce Clause. Immediately after the *Lopez* decision came down, the Supreme Court decided *United States v. Robertson*, 514 U.S. 669 (1995), a per curiam reversal of the Ninth Circuit's reversal of a RICO (Racketeer Influenced and Corrupt Organizations Act) conviction because the defendant's investment in an

Continued on next page.

Alaskan gold mine may not have been engaged in or affecting interstate commerce. The Supreme Court noted that the defendant purchased $100,000 of equipment and supplies, some of which were purchased in California. Similarly, the defendant also sought workers from out of state and took some of the profits out of state.

■══■

Quicknotes

CERTIORARI   A discretionary writ issued by a superior court to an inferior court in order to review the lower court's decisions; the Supreme Court's writ ordering such review.

■══■

City of Philadelphia v. New Jersey

Municipality (P) v. State (D)

437 U.S. 617 (1978).

NATURE OF CASE: Appeal of state court decision upholding state-imposed limitations on waste importation.

FACT SUMMARY: New Jersey (D) enacted a statute banning the importation of waste products for disposal.

🏛 **RULE OF LAW**
A state may not enact bans on articles of commerce absent legitimate public welfare concerns.

FACTS: The State of New Jersey (D) enacted a ban on the importation of refuse into the state for disposal. The law was couched in environmentalist terms. Philadelphia (P) and other entities interested in disposing in New Jersey (D) challenged the constitutionality of the law. The New Jersey Supreme Court upheld the measure, and Philadelphia (P) appealed.

ISSUE: May a state enact bans on articles of commerce absent legitimate public welfare concerns?

HOLDING AND DECISION: (Stewart, J.) No. A state may not enact bans on articles of commerce absent legitimate public welfare concerns. Only when there is something apart from the external status of an article giving the reason for the prohibition of importation may the prohibition be legitimate. When the focus is on the out-of-state character of the article, the measure is protectionist. Whether the article is desirable or undesirable is irrelevant. Here, the only distinction made is between in-state and out-of-state waste. The public health is an issue, but public health cannot be advanced in a way that unnecessarily burdens interstate commerce. While New Jersey (D) could attack this problem by regulating more closely all waste, it cannot do so by enacting protectionist measures. Reversed.

DISSENT: (Rehnquist, J.) There is no difference between a state enacting legitimate quarantine laws and doing what New Jersey (D) did here.

▶ **ANALYSIS**

Generally speaking, health measures restricting interstate commerce fall into two categories. One is protectionism in health and safety clothing. This is illegitimate. The other is legitimate safety legislation incidentally affecting commerce, which are valid enactments. The law here was something different, a legitimate health measure that was accomplished by protectionist means.

■=■

Quicknotes

COMMERCE CLAUSE Article 1, section 8, clause 3 of the United States Constitution, granting Congress the power to regulate commerce with foreign countries and among the states.

■=■

C & A Carbone, Inc. v. Clarkstown

Recycling center (D) v. Town (P)

511 U.S. 383 (1994).

NATURE OF CASE: Review of municipal ordinance regulating solid waste disposal.

FACT SUMMARY: The Town of Clarkstown (P) mandated that all solid waste leaving the city be processed through a particular transfer station.

🏛 RULE OF LAW
Discrimination against interstate commerce in favor of local businesses is per se invalid unless the municipality can demonstrate that it has no other means to advance a legitimate local interest.

FACTS: The Town of Clarkstown (P) entered an arrangement with a local contractor that the latter would build and operate a solid waste transfer station. In order to amortize the cost of the facility, the Town (P), by ordinance, mandated that all solid waste leaving the Town (P) be processed through that station. When C & A Carbone, Inc. (D), a recycling center in town, attempted to ship its nonrecyclable waste to another state in order to save money, the Town (P) sought an injunction to force Carbone (D) to comply with the ordinance. Carbone (D) challenged the ordinance as contrary to the Commerce Clause. The state courts rejected the challenge, and the Supreme Court granted review.

ISSUE: Is discrimination against interstate commerce per se invalid?

HOLDING AND DECISION: (Kennedy, J.) Yes. Discrimination against interstate commerce is per se invalid unless the municipality can demonstrate that it has no other means to advance a legitimate local interest. Any ordinance that deprives nonlocal businesses from access to local markets discriminates against interstate commerce and is invalid under the dormant Commerce Clause. With respect to waste, the commodity at issue is not the waste itself but rather the service of processing it and/or transporting it. When a city designates a particular commercial entity as the sole provider of such services, nonlocal providers of the service are effectively shut out. Local governments may not use their regulatory power to favor local businesses by prohibiting patronage of out-of-state competitors. Here, the City (P) has shut out nonlocal solid waste operators, although it has a number of nondiscriminatory alternatives that would satisfy its environmental and fiscal concerns, and thus its ordinance is unconstitutional. Reversed and remanded.

CONCURRENCE: (O'Connor, J.) The proper analysis here is that of benefits versus burdens, not of actual discrimination.

DISSENT: (Souter, J.) The instant ordinance falls outside that class of tariff or protectionist measures that the Commerce Clause has traditionally thought to bar states from enacting against each other. By subsuming the ordinance within the class of laws that have been struck down as facially discriminatory, the majority is here in fact greatly extending the Clause's dormant reach.

▶ ANALYSIS

The essential vice in discriminatory ordinances that mandate local processing is that they bar the import of the processing service. These laws hoard a local resource—be it shrimp, milk, or solid waste—for the benefit of local businesses that treat it. Clarkstown's (P) ordinance was even more egregiously protectionist than most such laws since it favored a single local proprietor.

■━■

Quicknotes

INTERSTATE COMMERCE Commercial dealings between two parties located in different states or located in one state and accomplished through a point in another state or a foreign country; commercial dealings transacted between two states.

■━■

West Lynn Creamery, Inc. v. Healy

Milk dealer (P) v. State (D)

512 U.S. 186 (1994).

NATURE OF CASE: Review of judicial rejection of legal challenge to agricultural assessment.

FACT SUMMARY: A law assessing a fee on all milk sold in Massachusetts (D), the funds of which were disbursed solely to local producers, was challenged as unconstitutional.

🏛 RULE OF LAW
An assessment scheme that levies a tax on all distribution of a good but disburses its assets only to local producers is unconstitutional.

FACTS: The legislature of the Commonwealth of Massachusetts (D), perceiving a need to protect local dairy producers, enacted an assessment system wherein a certain levy was placed on all dairy products sold in Massachusetts, the proceeds of which were disbursed only to Massachusetts producers. The system was challenged by West Lynn Creamery (P), a milk dealer who purchased out-of-state milk, as unconstitutional. The state courts rejected the challenge, and the Supreme Court granted review.

ISSUE: Is an assessment scheme that levies on all distribution of a good but disburses its assets to local producers unconstitutional?

HOLDING AND DECISION: (Stevens, J.) Yes. An assessment scheme that levies on all distribution of a good but disburses its assets only to local producers of the distributed goods is unconstitutional. A state may not enact a tariff on out-of-state goods; to do so is a clear violation of the Commerce Clause. The system at issue here, although taking two steps to achieve its goal, is a de facto tariff. While all producers pay equally into the fund, the assets go only to local producers. This is, in effect, a tariff. The fact that Massachusetts (D) could validly enact either a local subsidy or a nondiscriminatory tax is irrelevant; coupled, the two measures constitute a tariff and cannot stand, as the assessment is clear discrimination against interstate commerce. Reversed.

CONCURRENCE: (Scalia, J.) The Court's opinion unnecessarily broadens the scope of the dormant Commerce Clause. Unless a law facially discriminates against interstate commerce or falls within a precedent of this Court, it should survive Commerce Clause scrutiny. The Massachusetts law should be invalidated because it is indistinguishable from an otherwise nondiscriminatory tax from which in-state members are exempted, a method of taxation that has been held unconstitutional by this Court.

DISSENT: (Rehnquist, C.J.) The Massachusetts law represents this sort of subsidy of a domestic industry that has heretofore been approved under the Commerce Clause.

▶ ANALYSIS

The Commerce Clause, in its dormant expression, operates on two levels. If a law directly discriminates against commerce from another state, it is per se invalid. If it only incidentally burdens interstate commerce, a court must look to the benefits of the law versus its burdens. The law at issue here was of the former type.

━━■

Quicknotes

COMMERCE CLAUSE Article 1, section 8, clause 3 of the United States Constitution, granting Congress the power to regulate commerce with foreign countries and between the states.

DORMANT COMMERCE CLAUSE The regulatory effect of the Commerce Clause on state activity affecting interstate commerce, where Congress itself has not acted to control the activity; a provision inferred from, but not expressly present in, the language of the Commerce Clause.

TARIFF Duty or tax imposed on articles imported into the United States.

━━■

Hunt v. Washington State Apple Advertising Commission

Apple growers (D) v. State agency (P)

432 U.S. 333 (1977).

NATURE OF CASE: Review of constitutional challenge to state statute.

FACT SUMMARY: The Washington State Apple Advertising Commission (P) alleged that a new North Carolina statute unlawfully discriminated against Washington apples.

🏛 RULE OF LAW
Facially neutral statutes that discriminate against certain out-of-state products violate the Commerce Clause.

FACTS: Washington State Apple Advertising Commission (P) claimed that a new North Carolina statute requiring that all apples sold or shipped into the state bear only the U.S. or standard grade had the practical effect of burdening interstate sales of Washington apples. North Carolina agreed that the statute placed substantial financial burdens on Washington apple producers (P), and the court held that the statute was unconstitutional. Hunt (D) appealed. The Supreme Court granted certiorari.

ISSUE: Do facially neutral statutes that discriminate against certain out-of-state products violate the Commerce Clause?

HOLDING AND DECISION: (Burger, C.J.) Yes. Facially neutral statutes that discriminate against certain out-of-state products violate the Commerce Clause. The Washington apple producers (P) are put at a financial disadvantage by the new North Carolina requirements. The statute discriminates against the Washington growers (P) because it serves to protect the interests of local North Carolina growers who cannot compete with the higher quality standards set by Washington producers. Nondiscriminatory alternatives to the outright ban of Washington State grades appear to be readily available to protect consumers from the deception and confusion resulting from the multiplicity of different state grades of apples. Affirmed.

▌ ANALYSIS

This case involved the application of Commerce Clause jurisprudence. State legislation conflicts with the Commerce Clause when it deliberately discriminates against interstate goods. But such legislation also conflicts with the Commerce Clause when, as here, a facially neutral statute has the effect of discrimination against out-of-state business.

Quicknotes

COMMERCE CLAUSE Article 1, section 8, clause 3 of the United States Constitution, granting Congress the power to regulate commerce with foreign countries and between the states.

Exxon Corp. v. Governor of Maryland

Petroleum producers (P) v. State (D)

437 U.S. 117 (1978).

NATURE OF CASE: Appeal of ruling upholding a petroleum retailing statute.

FACT SUMMARY: Maryland (D) enacted a statute prohibiting petroleum producers from operating at the retail level.

RULE OF LAW
A state may prohibit the retailing of petroleum products by producers.

FACTS: Maryland (D) enacted a statute prohibiting producers or refiners of gasoline from entering the retail market. The effect of this was to force producers to sell to independent distributors or leave the state. All gasoline sold in Maryland (D) was shipped in interstate commerce. Exxon Corp. (P) and other producers sought to have the statute declared a violation of the Commerce Clause. The lower courts upheld the law.

ISSUE: May a state prohibit the retailing of petroleum products by producers?

HOLDING AND DECISION: (Stevens, J.) Yes. A state may prohibit the retailing of petroleum products by producers. To do this is not protectionism, because out-of-state independent retailers are not prohibited from entering the market. The law in no way affects the interstate flow of petroleum products. The fact that the burden of regulations falls on some companies that participate in interstate commerce does not make a law unconstitutional. It is only when the interstate market itself is burdened that a law comes under Commerce Clause scrutiny. This has not happened here. Affirmed.

DISSENT: (Blackmun, J.) Here, no facial inequality exists. The state's ban will preclude the major gasoline companies from enhancing brand recognition and consumer acceptance through retail outlets with company-controlled standards, thus inflicting significant hardship on Maryland's major brand gasoline companies, all of which are out-of-state firms. The protectionist discrimination employed by Maryland (D) is not justified by any legitimate state interest that cannot be vindicated by more evenhanded regulation.

ANALYSIS

A side issue raised by *Exxon* was that due to the inherent interstate nature of the petroleum trade, the Commerce Clause by itself pre-empted the field of retail gas marketing. This only occurs when national uniformity is necessary, and the Court did not believe this to be the case here.

Quicknotes

COMMERCE CLAUSE Article 1, section 8, clause 3 of the United States Constitution, granting Congress the power to regulate commerce with foreign countries and among the states.

Kassel v. Consolidated Freightways Corp.

State (D) v. Common carrier (P)

450 U.S. 662 (1981).

NATURE OF CASE: Appeal from decision holding that an Iowa statute unconstitutionally burdens interstate commerce.

FACT SUMMARY: Consolidated Freightways Corp. (P) challenged the constitutionality of an Iowa statute that prohibited the use of certain large trucks within the state boundaries.

🏛 RULE OF LAW
A state safety regulation will be unconstitutional if its asserted safety purpose is outweighed by its degree of interference with interstate commerce.

FACTS: The State of Iowa (D) passed a statute restricting the length of vehicles that may use its highways. The state law sets a general length limit of 55 feet for most vehicles, and 60 feet for trucks pulling two trailers ("doubles"). Iowa (D) was the only state in the western or midwestern United States to outlaw the use of 65-foot doubles. Consolidated Freightways Corp. (P), one of the largest common carriers in the country, alleged that the Iowa statute unconstitutionally burdened interstate commerce. The district court and the court of appeals found the statute unconstitutional and Kassel (D), on behalf of the State, appealed.

ISSUE: Will a state safety regulation be held to be unconstitutional if its asserted safety purpose is outweighed by the degree of interference with interstate commerce?

HOLDING AND DECISION: (Powell, J.) Yes. A state safety regulation will be unconstitutional if its asserted safety purpose is outweighed by its degree of interference with interstate commerce. While bona fide state safety regulations are entitled to a strong presumption of validity, the asserted safety purpose must be weighed against the degree of interference with interstate commerce. Less deference will be given to the findings of state legislators where the local regulation has a disproportionate effect on out-of-state residents and businesses. Here, Iowa (D) failed to present any persuasive evidence that 65-foot doubles were less safe than 55-foot single trailers. Consolidated Freightways (P) demonstrated that Iowa's law substantially burdened interstate commerce by compelling trucking companies either to route 65-foot doubles around Iowa or use the smaller trucks allowed by the state statute. Thus, the Iowa statute was in violation of the Commerce Clause. Affirmed.

CONCURRENCE: (Brennan, J.) In ruling on the constitutionality of state safety regulations, the burdens imposed on commerce must be balanced against the regulatory purposes identified by the state legislators. Protectionist legislation is unconstitutional under the Commerce Clause, even if its purpose is to promote safety, rather than economic purposes.

DISSENT: (Rehnquist, J.) A sensitive consideration must be made when weighing the safety purposes of a statute against the burden on interstate commerce. A state safety regulation is invalid if its asserted safety justification is merely a pretext for discrimination against interstate commerce. The Iowa statute is a valid highway safety regulation and is entitled to the strongest presumption of validity.

▶ ANALYSIS

Traditionally, states have been free to pass public safety regulations restricting the use of highways and railway facilities. However, state safety regulations have been struck down when only a marginal increase in safety causes a substantial burden on interstate commerce. This case simply follows this rationale.

■■■

Quicknotes

COMMERCE CLAUSE Article 1, section 8, clause 3 of the United States Constitution, granting Congress the power to regulate commerce with foreign countries and between the states.

DORMANT COMMERCE CLAUSE The regulatory effect of the Commerce Clause on state activity affecting interstate commerce, where Congress itself has not acted to control the activity; a provision inferred from, but not expressly present in, the language of the Commerce Clause.

■■■

CHAPTER 3

Congress's Powers: Taxing and Spending, War Powers, Individual Rights, and State Autonomy

Quick Reference Rules of Law

	PAGE
1. **Spending Power.** Congress may not tax in an area of local concern. (United States v. Butler)	*30*
2. **Spending Power.** A federal unemployment insurance tax statute that provides for credit for contributions made to state unemployment funds is valid since: (1) Congress enacted it primarily to safeguard its own treasury; (2) the proceeds of the tax are not earmarked for a special group but go into the General Treasury; and (3) the Act is directed to an end for which Congress and the states may lawfully cooperate. (Steward Machine Co. v. Davis)	*31*
3. **Congress's Enforcement Power under the Reconstruction Amendments.** The RFRA unconstitutionally exceeds Congress's enforcement power under the Due Process Clause of the Fourteenth Amendment. (City of Boerne v. Flores)	*32*
4. **Congress's Enforcement Power under the Reconstruction Amendments.** The ADA provision requiring employers to make "reasonable accommodations" for disabled workers is unconstitutional as applied to state employers. (Board of Trustees v. Garrett)	*33*
5. **The Tenth Amendment as a Federalism-Based Limitation on Congressional Power.** Congress can constitutionally enact a statute under Article 1, Section 8 to enforce a treaty created under Article 2, Section 2, even if the statute by itself is unconstitutional. (Missouri v. Holland)	*34*
6. **The Tenth Amendment as a Federalism-Based Limitation on Congressional Power.** The federal government may not order a state government to enact particular legislation. (New York v. United States)	*35*

United States v. Butler

Federal government (P) v. Taxpayers (D)

297 U.S. 1 (1936).

NATURE OF CASE: Appeal of decision invalidating portions of the Agricultural Adjustment Act of 1933.

FACT SUMMARY: Congress instituted a tax on certain agricultural processors to subsidize farmers in order to reduce acreage and stabilize farm prices.

 RULE OF LAW
Congress may not tax in an area of local concern.

FACTS: In response to collapsed farm prices, Congress passed the Agricultural Adjustment Act of 1933 in which a tax was levied on certain agricultural processors to pay for a subsidy of farmers who voluntarily reduced their crop output, the goal being acreage reduction. The power invoked for this Act was the taxing and spending power. The tax was challenged in court, and the lower court held the tax unconstitutional.

ISSUE: May Congress tax in an area of local concern?

HOLDING AND DECISION: (Roberts, J.) No. Congress may not tax in an area of local concern. The federal government is one of limited, enumerated powers, and can only act on those enumerated powers. While Congress does have the power to tax and spend for the general welfare, it only has this right in areas within the sphere of federal power. Just as Congress cannot regulate a local business, it may not tax it, as the power to tax is a form of regulation. Here, the businesses taxed are local. Congress may neither regulate nor tax them; to do so would usurp the power of the states. Also, to try to induce certain practices by farmers via subsidies infringes on state powers. Affirmed.

DISSENT: (Stone, J.) Attempting to influence behavior by offering subsidies is not the same as regulation and is a proper exercise of the taxing and spending power.

▶ *ANALYSIS*

The opinion was internally inconsistent. On the one hand, it rejected the view that "general welfare" spending included only specifically enumerated areas (the so-called Madisonian view). On the other hand, the Court held that Congress could not tax and spend on areas of "local" concern. It seems that the Court both broadened and narrowed the spending power at once.

Quicknotes

TAXING POWER The authority delegated to Congress by the Constitution to impose taxes.

Steward Machine Co. v. Davis

Taxpayer (P) v. Federal government (D)

301 U.S. 548 (1937).

NATURE OF CASE: Action challenging the constitutionality of the Social Security Act as applied to employers.

FACT SUMMARY: The Social Security Act levies an excise tax on employers and the proceeds go into the General Treasury; however, if a taxpayer has made contributions to a state unemployment fund, such contributions can be credited against the federal tax.

🏛 RULE OF LAW

A federal unemployment insurance tax statute that provides for credit for contributions made to state unemployment funds is valid since: (1) Congress enacted it primarily to safeguard its own treasury; (2) the proceeds of the tax are not earmarked for a special group but go into the General Treasury; and (3) the Act is directed to an end for which Congress and the states may lawfully cooperate.

FACTS: The Social Security Act imposes an excise tax on employers based on the wages paid. The proceeds go into the General Treasury. However if a taxpayer has made contributions to a state unemployment fund, such contributions can be credited against the federal tax provided that the state law has been certified by the Social Security Board as satisfying certain minimum criteria. Between 1929 and 1936, there was an unprecedented number of unemployed in the United State, and the states were unable to give the requisite relief to the needy. Steward Machine Co. (P) paid a tax in accordance with the statute and filed a claim to recover the payment, asserting that the statute is unconstitutional.

ISSUE: Is a federal unemployment insurance tax that provides for credit for contributions made to a state unemployment fund constitutional?

HOLDING AND DECISION: (Cardozo, J.) Yes. The presence of this urgent need for some remedial expedient does not overstep the bounds of congressional power. Operation of this legislation does not constitute a constraint, but rather the creation of a larger freedom, the states and the nation joining in a cooperative endeavor to avert a common evil: lack of unemployment insurance. Every tax is in some way regulatory and to some extent imposes an economic impediment to the activity taxed as compared with others not taxed. However, to hold that motive or temptation is equivalent to coercion is to plunge the law in endless difficulties. The instant legislation does not call for the states' surrender of powers essential to their quasi-sovereign existence. Furthermore, a wide range of judgment is given to the states as to the particular type of statute and conditions that they may see fit to enact. Even if opinion may differ as to the fundamental quality of one or more of the conditions, the difference will not vitiate the statute. In determining essentials, Congress must have the benefit of a fair margin of discretion. Affirmed.

▶ ANALYSIS

Policy guidance via the spending power goes back to the beginning of the nation, as is pointed out in the majority opinion in *Steward*. The programs have increased considerably over the years, and there has been increasing opposition to narrow categorical grants-in-aid and advocacy of broader unrestricted grants to state and local governments. The Advisory Commission on Intergovernmental Relations was established in 1959. One of its major functions is the examination of the impact of national spending on the federal system. In its Annual Report for 1969, it stated that "unless state and local governments are permitted 'free,' albeit limited, access to the prime power source—the federal income tax—their positions within our federal systems are bound to deteriorate."

■━■

Quicknotes

TAXING POWER The authority delegated to Congress by the Constitution to impose taxes.

■━■

City of Boerne v. Flores

Zoning authority (D) v. Church (P)

521 U.S. 507 (1997).

NATURE OF CASE: Review of judgment sustaining the constitutionality of the Religious Freedom Restoration Act of 1993.

FACT SUMMARY: A decision by zoning authorities in Boerne (D) to deny a church (P) a building permit was challenged under the Religious Freedom Restoration Act.

> ## 🏛 RULE OF LAW
> The Religious Freedom Restoration Act unconstitutionally exceeds Congress's enforcement power under the Due Process Clause of the Fourteenth Amendment.

FACTS: The Religious Freedom Restoration Act (RFRA) prohibited the government from substantially burdening a person's exercise of religion, even if the burden is the result of a generally applicable law, unless the government has a compelling interest and is using the least restrictive means. Flores (P) sought a building permit to expand his church, a historic landmark. The city of Boerne (D) denied the permit and Flores (P) sued, invoking the RFRA. The district court determined that the RFRA exceeded congressional power, but the Fifth Circuit reversed, holding the Act constitutional. Boerne (D) appealed.

ISSUE: Does the RFRA unconstitutionally exceed Congress's enforcement power under the Due Process Clause of the Fourteenth Amendment?

HOLDING AND DECISION: (Kennedy, J.) Yes. The RFRA unconstitutionally exceeds Congress's enforcement power under the Due Process Clause of the Fourteenth Amendment. Here, Congress, with the RFRA, attempts to replace, with the compelling interest test, this Court's decision in *Employment Div., Dept. of Human Resources of Ore. v. Smith*, 494 U.S. 872 (1990). *Smith* held that the compelling interest test is inappropriate in cases where general prohibitions are opposed by free exercise challenges. But the RFRA violates the long tradition of separation of powers established by the Constitution. The judiciary is to determine the constitutionality of laws, and the powers of the legislature are defined and limited. While Congress can enact remedial, preventive legislation that deters violations, the RFRA is not a preventive law. Instead, the RFRA redefines the scope of the Free Exercise Clause and nothing in our history extends to Congress the ability to take such action. The RFRA is so out of proportion to a supposed remedial or preventive object that it cannot be regarded as a response to unconstitutional behavior. Reversed.

▶ ANALYSIS

The Religious Freedom Restoration Act was one of the four federal laws overturned by the Supreme Court during its 1997 term. Although the Court has endorsed judicial restraint in recent years, it has not hesitated to quash improper intrusions on its authority to set unconstitutional standards. The Court, however, chose not to revisit the religious freedom issue in its *Boerne* decision, leaving intact the ruling in *Smith* that inspired Congress to pass the RFRA. In *Smith*, the Court approved Oregon's use of its ban on peyote to prohibit the drug's use in Native American religious rituals. The RFRA was intended to guarantee religious observance a higher degree of statutory protection than the *Smith* court thought necessary.

Quicknotes

FREE EXERCISE CLAUSE The guarantee of the First Amendment to the United States Constitution prohibiting Congress from enacting laws regarding the establishment of religion or prohibiting the free exercise thereof.

Board of Trustees v. Garrett

State employer (D) v. ADA claimant (P)

531 U.S. 356 (2001).

NATURE OF CASE: [Procedural posture of case not set forth in textbook excerpt.]

FACT SUMMARY: When Garrett (P) and Ash (P), both partially physically disabled state employees, were refused their requests under the Americans with Disabilities Act for reasonable accommodations, they sued the state (D) for money damages.

> **RULE OF LAW**
> The American with Diabilities Act provision requiring employers to make "reasonable accommodations" for disabled workers is unconstitutional as applied to state employers.

FACTS: Garrett (P), a registered nurse, and Ash (P), a security officer, both employed by departments of the State of Alabama (D), were refused their requests for reasonable accommodations under the Americans with Disabilities Act (ADA) for their medical conditions. When they were transferred to lower paying positions because of their medical conditions, they sued the State of Alabama (D) for money damages for violation of the ADA reasonable accommodation provision.

ISSUE: Is the ADA provision requiring employers to make "reasonable accommodations" for disabled workers unconstitutional as applied to state employers?

HOLDING AND DECISION: (Rehnquist, C.J.) Yes. The ADA provision requiring employers to make "reasonable accommodations" for disabled workers is unconstitutional as applied to state employers. Under rational-basis review, where a group possesses distinguishing characteristics relevant to interests the state has authority to implement, a state's decision to act on the basis of those differences does not give rise to a constitutional violation. Thus, states are not required by the Fourteenth Amendment to make special accommodations for the disabled, so long as their actions toward such individuals are rational. If special accommodations for the disabled are to be required, they have to come from positive law and not through the Fourteenth Amendment. Here, the legislative record of the ADA simply fails to show that Congress did in fact identify a pattern of irrational state discrimination in employment against the disabled. While historically there are indeed many instances of such employment discrimination, the great majority of these incidents do not deal with the activities of states. Even were it possible to squeeze out a pattern of such unconstitutional discrimination by the states, the rights and remedies created by the ADA against the states would raise concerns as to congruence and proportionality.

CONCURRENCE: (Kennedy, J.) Here, an equal protection violation has not been shown with respect to the states. What is in question is not whether Congress can compel the states to act. What is involved is only the question whether the states can be subjected to liability in suits brought, not by the federal government, but by private persons seeking to collect money damages from the state treasury without the consent of the state.

DISSENT: (Breyer, J.) Since Congress has the power to enforce, by appropriate legislation, the Fourteenth Amendment's equal protection guarantee, Congress reasonably could have concluded that the money damages remedy for ADA violation constitutes an appropriate way to enforce this basic equal protection requirement. The majority's decision serves no constitutionally based federalism interest.

▍ ANALYSIS

As the *Garrett* decision makes clear, Congress is the final authority as to desirable public policy, but in order to authorize private individuals to recover money damages against the states, there must be a pattern of discrimination by the states that violates the Fourteenth Amendment, and the remedy imposed by Congress must be congruent and proportional to the targeted violation.

■■■■

Quicknotes

EQUAL PROTECTION CLAUSE A constitutional provision that each person be guaranteed the same protection of the laws enjoyed by other persons in like circumstances.

FOURTEENTH AMENDMENT Declares that no state shall make or enforce any law that shall abridge the privileges and immunities of citizens of the United States. No state shall deny to any person within its jurisdiction the equal protection of the laws.

■■■■

Missouri v. Holland

State (P) v. Federal game warden (D)

252 U.S. 416 (1920).

NATURE OF CASE: An action in equity to enjoin the enforcement of the Migratory Bird Treaty Act.

FACT SUMMARY: Missouri (P) claims that the Bird Treaty Act was an unconstitutional interference with the rights reserved to the states by the Tenth Amendment.

🏛 RULE OF LAW
Congress can constitutionally enact a statute under Article 1, section 8 to enforce a treaty created under Article 2, section 2, even if the statute by itself is unconstitutional.

FACTS: On December 8, 1916, the United States entered into a treaty with Great Britain to protect birds that migrated between Canada and the United States. Congress passed a statute to enforce the Migratory Bird Treaty that allowed the Secretary of Agriculture to formulate regulations to enforce the treaty. The State of Missouri (P) filed a bill in equity to prevent Holland (D), the game warden of the United States, from enforcing the treaty. Missouri (P) claimed that the statute was an unconstitutional interference with the rights reserved to the states by the Tenth Amendment and that it had a pecuniary interest as owner of the wild birds being affected. Before the treaty had been entered into, Congress had attempted to regulate the killing of migratory birds within the states and that statute, standing by itself, had been declared unconstitutional. The United States contended that Congress had the power to enact the statute to enforce the treaty and that the statute and treaty were the supreme law of the land.

ISSUE: Can Congress validly enact a statute to enforce a treaty if the statute standing by itself would be unconstitutional because it interfered with the rights reserved to the states by the tenth amendment?

HOLDING AND DECISION: (Holmes, J.) Yes. Congress can constitutionally enact a statute under Article 1, Section 8 to enforce a treaty created under Article 2, section 2, even if the statute by itself is unconstitutional. Article 11, section 2 grants the President the power to make treaties and Article VI, section 2 declares that treaties shall be part of the supreme law of the land. If a treaty is a valid one, Article 1, section 8 gives Congress the power to enact legislation that is a necessary and proper means to enforce the treaty. While acts of Congress are the supreme law of the land only when they are made in pursuance of the Constitution, treaties are valid when made under the authority of the United States. The Court stated that there were qualifications to the treaty-making power, but felt that the qualifications must be determined by looking at the facts of each case.

There are situations that require national action that an act of Congress could not deal with, but that a treaty enforced with a congressional act could. Because Missouri (P) did not have the power to adequately control the problem connected with the migratory birds (nor did any other state acting alone), this was a situation that required national action. Therefore, even though Missouri (P) would have been able to establish regulations pertaining to the birds if Congress had not already done so, Congress could establish regulations in conjunction with the treaty without infringing on the rights reserved to the states by the Tenth Amendment. The court rejected Missouri's (P) claim that it had a pecuniary interest as an owner when the birds were in the state. There is no ownership until there is possession and the birds never came into the possession of the State of Missouri (P). Congress can, therefore, constitutionally enact a statute under Article 1, section 8 to enforce a treaty even if the statute by itself would be unconstitutional. Affirmed.

▌ ANALYSIS

Many people were upset with the decision in this case because they feared that the Court had interpreted the treaty power so broadly that all constitutional limitations could be overridden by the use of treaties and accompanying congressional legislation. In 1954, the Bricker Amendment, which was narrowly defeated, required that a treaty could only become effective as internal law in the United States through legislation which would be valid in the absence of the treaty. This would have, in effect, overruled the decision in this case, because the congressional act was not valid when standing by itself. Several other similar proposals were made during the following three years, which also failed.

■■■

Quicknotes

PECUNIARY INTEREST A monetary interest.

TENTH AMENDMENT The Tenth Amendment to the United States Constitution reserving those powers therein, not expressly delegated to the federal government or prohibited to the states, to the states or to the people.

TREATY POWER The power delegated to the President by the Constitution to enter into treaties upon the approval of two-thirds of the Senate that is present.

■■■

New York v. United States

State (P) v. Federal government (D)

505 U.S. 144 (1992).

NATURE OF CASE: Appeal of dismissal of suit for declaratory judgment.

FACT SUMMARY: New York (P) sought a declaration that the Low-Level Radioactive Waste Policy Amendments Act (1985 Act) was unconstitutional.

🏛 RULE OF LAW
The federal government may not order a state government to enact particular legislation.

FACTS: Three states had disposal sites for radioactive waste. After study and negotiation, the National Governors' Association (NGA) devised a plan that became the 1985 Act. The 1985 Act set deadlines for every state to join a regional waste compact, develop in-state disposal, or find another way to dispose of its own waste. The 1985 Act assured the sited states they would not have the entire nation's waste burden, and gave the other 47 states seven more years of access to active sites. The 1985 Act provided three incentives for state compliance: (1) Congress authorized sited states to impose a surcharge, part of which would go into federal escrow, with funds to be returned to complying states; (2) Congress empowered sited states to deny access to states not in compliance; and (3) any state not in compliance by 1992 had to either take title to all waste generated in their state or else become liable to in-state waste generators for all damages. As of 1990 New York (P) had not joined a regional waste compact. Unable to settle on an in-state site, New York (P) sought to invalidate the 1985 Act as violative of state sovereignty principles of the Tenth Amendment. The sited states intervened as defendants. The district court dismissed, the court of appeals affirmed, and New York (P) appealed.

ISSUE: May the federal government order a state government to enact particular legislation?

HOLDING AND DECISION: (O'Connor, J.) No. The federal government may not order a state government to enact particular legislation. The federal government may provide incentives for states to regulate in a certain way by tying funding to acceptance of a federal plan or by giving states a choice between enacting a federal plan or having state law preempted by federal law. Here, the first incentive is a congressional exercise of Commerce Clause power (allowing sited states to impose a surcharge on interstate commerce and imposing a federal tax on that surcharge) combined with an exercise of Spending Clause power (making return of surcharges contingent on compliance with the federal plan). The second incentive is a routine exercise of the commerce power. If a state chooses not to follow the federal plan, generators of waste within that state become subject to federal regulation authorizing states with waste sites to deny access. The burden would fall on the waste generators, not on the state, and the state would not be forced to spend funds or accede to federal direction. The third incentive, however, crossed the line to coercion. Whether a state "chooses" to take title to waste or to accept liability for disposal, the burden of not enacting the federal plan falls on the state. The strength of the federal interest is irrelevant. Federal courts may issue directives to state officials, but the Constitution expressly grants that authority. Such authority is outside Congress's enumerated powers and, for that reason, also infringes on state sovereignty reserved by the Tenth Amendment. While the 1985 Act was a creation of and compromise among the states, the states may not constitutionally consent to give up their sovereignty. Affirmed as to the first two incentives; reversed as to the third.

DISSENT: (White, J.) The Acts were the product of cooperative federalism. The states bargained among themselves to solve an imminent crisis and achieve compromises for Congress to sanction. New York (P) reaped the benefits of the 1985 Act, an agreement that it helped formulate, and should not be able to sue now. The majority wrongly finds that states cannot consent to relinquish some sovereignty. Tenth Amendment restrictions on the commerce power are procedural limits, designed to prevent federal destruction of state governments, not to protect substantive areas of state autonomy.

▶ ANALYSIS

Under the Articles of Confederation, the federal government could only act by ordering states to enact legislation. The Framers decided that the federal government needed power to regulate citizens directly and so drafted the Constitution. The Court interpreted the Framers' decision as a rejection of federal power to order states to enact legislation.

━━■

Quicknotes

ENUMERATED POWERS Specific powers mentioned in, and granted by, the Constitution, e.g., the taxing power.

STATE SOVEREIGNTY The absolute power of self-government possessed by a state.

━━■

CHAPTER 4

The Distribution of National Powers

Quick Reference Rules of Law

PAGE

1. **Presidential Seizure.** The President may not effect the seizure of private property absent congressional approval. (Youngstown Sheet & Tube Co. v. Sawyer (The Steel Seizure Case)) — *38*

2. **Foreign Affairs: Executive Authority.** Presidential proclamations that pertain to foreign affairs are valid and enforceable. (United States v. Curtiss-Wright Corp.) — *39*

3. **Foreign Affairs: Executive Authority.** A President may issue an order setting legal claims when the order is ancillary to major foreign policy issues and Congress acquiesces. (Dames & Moore v. Regan) — *40*

4. **Foreign Affairs: Executive Authority.** Due process requires that a citizen held in the United States as an enemy combatant be given a meaningful opportunity to contest the factual basis for that detention before a neutral decisionmaker. (Hamdi v. Rumsfeld) — *41*

5. **Domestic Affairs: Executive Authority.** Absent a claim of need to protect military, diplomatic, or sensitive national security secrets, an absolute, unqualified presidential privilege of immunity from judicial process under all circumstances does not exist. (United States v. Nixon) — *43*

6. **Domestic Affairs: Legislative Authority.** Because it constitutes an exercise of legislative power and is thus subject to the bicameralism and presentment requirements of Article I of the Constitution, the federal statute purporting to authorize a one-house veto of the Attorney General's decision to allow a particular deportable alien to remain in the United States is unconstitutional. (INS v. Chadha) — *44*

7. **Domestic Affairs: Legislative Authority.** When Congress elects to exercise its legislative power, it may not authorize a lesser representative of the legislative branch to act on its behalf. (Bowsher v. Synar) — *46*

8. **Domestic Affairs: Legislative Authority.** The independent counsel provisions of the Ethics in Government Act are constitutional. (Morrison v. Olson) — *47*

Youngstown Sheet & Tube Co. v. Sawyer
(The Steel Seizure Case)

Steel company (P) v. Federal government (D)

343 U.S. 579 (1952).

NATURE OF CASE: Appeal of decision upholding presidentially ordered seizure of steel mills.

FACT SUMMARY: President Truman ordered the seizure of the nation's strike-plagued steel mills absent congressional approval.

🏛 RULE OF LAW
The President may not effect the seizure of private property absent congressional approval.

FACTS: A strike in the steel industry was called by labor leaders. Fearful of the effect a steel shortage might have on national defense and facing nonaction by Congress, President Truman ordered the nation's mills seized so that they would resume production. Youngstown Sheet & Tube Co. (P) complied with the order, but filed suit to have the action enjoined. The district court held the order unconstitutional, but the court of appeals reversed.

ISSUE: May the President effect the seizure of private property absent congressional approval?

HOLDING AND DECISION: (Black, J.) No. The President may not effect the seizure of private property absent congressional approval. Without such approval, such a power could only stem from the Constitution. No such power is expressly granted. The power to do this cannot be implied either. The President's duty to see that the laws are faithfully executed is inapplicable, as no law exists that is being executed. The President's role as Commander-in-Chief does not grant the power, for the theater of war is not so broad as to encompass domestic private property. As only Congress can pass a law taking private property, the President's action was in excess of his powers. Reversed.

CONCURRENCE: (Frankfurter, J.) By not granting the President power to seize the steel mills, Congress has withheld from him authority to do so.

CONCURRENCE: (Jackson, J.) The President's powers are at a maximum when his acts are authorized by Congress. In the absence of congressional input, the President has some areas of action independent of Congress. When Congress specifically disapproves of the President's action, he can rely on only his powers as enumerated in the Constitution. This action falls into the second category, and the President has overstepped his ability to move independent of Congress.

CONCURRENCE: (Douglas, J.) The Fifth Amendment can only be read to give condemnation power to Congress.

DISSENT: (Vinson, C.J.) A work stoppage in the steel mills would put the nation's defense in such jeopardy that the President's military authority legitimized his actions.

▶ ANALYSIS

Of all the opinions here, the most influential was that of Justice Jackson. While only a concurring opinion, it has taken the status as an important authority on the extent and source of presidential power. If is often cited when such power is under debate.

━■━■

Quicknotes

FIFTH AMENDMENT Provides that no person shall be compelled to serve as a witness against himself, or be subject to trial for the same offense twice, or be deprived of life, liberty, or property without due process of law.

━■━■

United States v. Curtiss-Wright Corp.

Federal government (P) v. Arms dealer (D)

299 U.S. 304 (1936).

NATURE OF CASE: Indictment charging a conspiracy to sell guns illegally.

FACT SUMMARY: Curtiss-Wright (D) planned to sell machine guns to Bolivia contrary to a presidential proclamation that declared such sales to be illegal.

 RULE OF LAW
Presidential proclamations that pertain to foreign affairs are valid and enforceable.

FACTS: A joint resolution of Congress expressly authorized the President to declare it illegal to sell weaponry in the United States (P) to countries engaged in armed conflict in the Chaco region. Violators of any presidential proclamation to that effect were to be subject to a fine of $10,000 or less and/or a prison sentence of up to two years. Pursuant to the joint resolution, the President did issue a proclamation declaring it illegal to sell weapons to countries at war in the Chaco. Curtiss-Wright Corp. (D) was indicted for allegedly conspiring to sell 15 machine guns to Bolivia, which was then involved in the conflict in the Chaco. Curtiss-Wright (D) demurred to the indictment, contending that the joint resolution was an unconstitutional delegation of legislative powers from Congress to the President. The trial court sustained the demurrer, but on appeal the United States (P) argued that the proclamation was effective and enjoyed the force of law.

ISSUE: Does the President have the power to issue proclamations relating to international affairs?

HOLDING AND DECISION: (Sutherland, J.) Yes. Presidential proclamations that pertain to foreign affairs are valid and enforceable. It is unnecessary to consider whether a proclamation issued under these circumstances would have been valid had it related to domestic matters. The federal government has always had exclusive authority in the area of foreign affairs. This power does not derive from the states, but has instead always belonged to the national government. It is exercisable by the President, not always with the aid of Congress. The President alone possesses complete knowledge of often sensitive information concerning foreign governments, and it would be unwise to require him to share his knowledge with Congress so that it might participate in the decision-making process. In fact, information pertaining to foreign affairs is much more jealously protected from disclosure than is domestic information. The President's unique knowledge concerning confidential information makes it appropriate for him to issue occasional proclamations concerning foreign affairs, with or without congressional approval. Clearly, the proclamation in dispute was not the result of an improper delegation of power. Thus, the lower court should not have sustained Curtiss-Wright's (D) demurrer.

▶ ANALYSIS

In colonial times, states occasionally enacted laws that frustrated or were inconsistent with treaties entered into by the national government. As a result, the Framers of the Constitution took some care to clarify the respective roles of the state and federal governments in matters relating to foreign affairs. Their simple solution was to confer all powers relating to international relations upon the federal government. It was assumed that individual states had never had any powers with respect to foreign matters, and the Constitution invested them with no such powers. By granting to the President the power to enter into treaties with foreign nations, subject only to the counsel and assent of the Congress, the Framers virtually guaranteed that primary responsibility for foreign affairs would devolve upon the nation's highest-ranking executive officer.

Quicknotes

EXECUTIVE ORDER An order issued by the President, or another executive of government, which has the force of law.

Dames & Moore v. Regan

Creditor (P) v. Federal government (D)

453 U.S. 654 (1981).

NATURE OF CASE: Appeal of court order upholding an executive agreement barring claims against Iran or its citizens.

FACT SUMMARY: President Carter, in exchange for release of U.S. hostages, issued an order barring court action against Iran or its citizens.

RULE OF LAW
A President may issue an order setting legal claims when the order is ancillary to major foreign policy issues and Congress acquiesces.

FACTS: President Carter worked out the following deal in exchange for release of U.S. hostages held in Iran: all existing legal claims against Iran or its citizens were to be dismissed from court and referred to a special claims tribunal. All Iranian assets held in the United States were to be unfrozen. Dames & Moore (P), asserting a contractual claim against several Iranian banks, brought an action to have the executive order declared unconstitutional. Congress had neither approved nor disapproved of the action. The lower courts upheld the order.

ISSUE: May a President issue an order settling legal claims when the order is ancillary to major foreign policy issues and Congress acquiesces?

HOLDING AND DECISION: (Rehnquist, J.) Yes. A President may issue an order settling claims when the order is ancillary to major foreign policy issues and Congress acquiesces. Congress has passed the International Emergency Economic Powers Act, which, while not covering the exact issue at hand, gives the President similar powers for similar situations. Congress cannot be expected to legislate for every contingency, and it can be inferred that if Congress authorizes certain presidential actions similar action is also authorized. Since the President acted with congressional approval, his powers were at high tide. While extinguishing claims by presidential order is an extreme exercise of power, the fact that Congress had at least tacitly approved it and the President was exercising his constitutional foreign policy role, the action was legitimate. Affirmed.

ANALYSIS

Supreme Court cases cannot be considered in a vacuum. Political reality has a way of intruding on legal niceties. The present decision was made in a political climate that would have been very adverse to a contrary decision and would have left the United States looking foolish to the international community. What precedential effect this decision will have only time will tell. The Court itself, in the opinion, underscored the narrowness of the decision.

Quicknotes

EXECUTIVE ORDER An order issued by the President, or another executive need of government, which has the force of law.

Hamdi v. Rumsfeld

Alleged enemy combatant (P) v. Secretary of Defense (D)

542 U.S. 507 (2004).

NATURE OF CASE: Appeal from the denial of right to challenge enemy-combatant status.

FACT SUMMARY: Hamdi (P), an American citizen designated as an enemy-combatant, argued that he was entitled to contest such designation in court.

🏛 RULE OF LAW
Due process requires that a citizen held in the United States as an enemy combatant be given a meaningful opportunity to contest the factual basis for that detention before a neutral decisionmaker.

FACTS: Hamdi (P), an American citizen, was designated by the Government (D) an "enemy combatant" and placed into indefinite detainment. The Federal Court of Appeals held the detention to be legally authorized and that Hamdi (P) was entitled to no further opportunity to challenge his enemy-combatant label. Hamdi (P) appealed to the United States Supreme Court.

ISSUE: Does due process require that a citizen held in the United States as an enemy combatant be given a meaningful opportunity to contest the factual basis for that detention before a neutral decisionmaker?

HOLDING AND DECISION: (O'Connor, J.) Yes. Due process requires that a citizen held in the United States as an enemy combatant be given a meaningful opportunity to contest the factual basis for that detention before a neutral decisionmaker. It is vital not to give short shrift to the values that this country holds dear or to the privilege that is American citizenship. At the same time, the exigencies of the circumstances may demand that, as here, aside from certain core elements, enemy combatant proceedings may be tailored to alleviate their uncommon potential to burden the executive branch at a time of ongoing military conflict. Hearsay, for example, may need to be accepted as the most reliable available evidence from the government in such a proceeding. Furthermore, even a burden-shifting scheme in which credible government evidence is presumed true would not offend the Constitution so long as such presumption remains a rebuttable one and fair opportunity for rebuttal is provided. The parties agree that initial captures on the battlefield need not receive the full range of constitutional guarantees. While the Court accords the greatest respect and consideration to the judgments of military authorities in matters relating to the actual prosecution of a war, and recognizes that the scope of that discretion is necessarily wide, it does not infringe on the core role of the military for the courts to exercise their own time-honored and constitutionally mandated roles of

reviewing and resolving claims such as those present here. A state of war is not a blank check for the President when it comes to the rights of the Nation's citizens. Reversed and remanded.

CONCURRING IN PART AND DISSENTING IN PART: (Souter, J.) The Government (D) has failed to demonstrate that the Force Resolution authorizes the detention complained of here, even on the facts the Government (D) claims. If the Government (D) raises nothing further than the record now shows, the Non-Detention Act entitles Hamdi (P) to be released. The branch of government asked to counter a serious threat is not the branch on which to rest the nation's entire reliance in striking the balance between the will to win and "the cost in liberty on the way to victory."

DISSENT: (Scalia, J.) If civil rights are to be curtailed during wartime, it must be done openly and democratically, as the Constitution requires, rather than by silent erosion through an opinion of the Court. Whatever the merits of the view that war silences law or modulates its voice, such view has no place in the interpretation and application of a Constitution designed precisely to confront war and, in a manner that accords with democratic principles, to accommodate it.

DISSENT: (Thomas, J.) The executive branch, acting pursuant to powers vested in the President by the Constitution and by explicit congressional approval, has determined that Hamdi (P) is an enemy combatant and should be detained. This detention falls squarely within the war powers of the federal government, and the Court lacks the expertise and capacity to second-guess such decision. Accordingly, Hamdi's (P) habeas challenge should fail, and there is no reason to remand the case.

▶ ANALYSIS

As made clear in the *Hamdi* decision, in cases of this type the court must balance two vital yet competing interests: on the one hand, respect for separation of powers and the fundamental importance of the Nation to be able to protect itself during time of war; on the other hand, the critical and deep-seated individual constitutional interests at stake.

■=■

Quicknotes

DUE PROCESS CLAUSE Clauses found in the Fifth and Fourteenth Amendments to the United States Constitution

Continued on next page.

providing that no person shall be deprived of "life, liberty, or property, without due process of law."

SEPARATION OF POWERS The system of checks and balances preventing one branch of government from infringing upon exercising the powers of another branch of government.

■══■

United States v. Nixon

Federal government (P) v. President (D)

418 U.S. 683 (1974).

NATURE OF CASE: Certiorari granted after denial of a motion to quash a third-party subpoena duces tecum.

FACT SUMMARY: Nixon (D) challenges a subpoena served on him as a third party requiring the production of tapes and documents for use in a criminal prosecution.

🏛 RULE OF LAW
Absent a claim of need to protect military, diplomatic, or sensitive national security secrets, an absolute, unqualified presidential privilege of immunity from judicial process under all circumstances does not exist.

FACTS: After the grand jury returned an indictment charging seven defendants with various offenses relating to Watergate, Special Prosecutor Jaworski moved for the issuance of a subpoena duces tecum to obtain Watergate-related tapes and documents from Nixon (D). Jaworski claimed that the materials were important to the government's proof at the criminal proceeding against the seven defendants. The subpoena was issued, and Nixon (D) turned over some materials. His lawyer then moved to quash the subpoena. Nixon (D) contended that the separation of powers doctrine precludes judicial review of a presidential claim of privilege and that the need for confidentiality of high-level communication requires an absolute privilege as against a subpoena.

ISSUE: Does the President possess an absolute executive privilege that is immune from judicial review?

HOLDING AND DECISION: (Burger, C.J.) No. Absent a claim of need to protect military, diplomatic, or sensitive national security secrets, an absolute, unqualified presidential privilege of immunity from judicial process under all circumstances does not exist. First of all, Nixon (D) claimed the court lacks jurisdiction to issue the subpoena because the matter was an intrabranch dispute within the executive branch. However, courts must look behind names that symbolize the parties to determine whether a justiciable case or controversy exists. Here, the Special Prosecutor, with his asserted need for the subpoenaed material, was opposed by the President with his assertion of privilege against disclosure. This setting assures that there is the necessary concreteness and adversity to sharpen the presentation of the issues. Against Nixon's (D) claim of absolute privilege immune from judicial review, this Court reaffirms the holding of *Marbury v. Madison*, 5 U.S. (1 Cranch) 137 (1803), that "it is emphatically the province of the Judicial Department to say what the law is," and this is true with respect to a claim of executive privilege. Absent a claim of need to protect military, diplomatic, or sensitive national security secrets, neither the doctrine of the separation of

powers nor the generalized need for the confidentiality of high-level communications, without more, can sustain an absolute unqualified presidential privilege. Now that the court has decided that legitimate needs of judicial process may outweigh presidential privilege, it is necessary to resolve those competing interests in this case. It is true that the need for confidentiality justifies a presumptive privilege for presidential communications. However, our criminal justice system depends on a complete presentation of all relevant facts. To ensure this presentation, compulsory process must be available. Here, Jaworski has demonstrated a specific need at a criminal trial for the material sought. Nixon (D) has not based his claim of privilege on the military or diplomatic content of the materials but rather on a generalized interest in confidentiality. The allowance of this privilege based on only a generalized interest in confidentiality to withhold relevant evidence in a criminal trial would cut deeply into the guarantee of due process and cannot prevail. Affirmed.

▶ ANALYSIS

On July 16, 1973, Alexander Butterfield testified before the Senate Select Committee on presidential campaign activities that conversations in President Nixon's offices had been recorded automatically at Nixon's direction. Nixon declined to comply with requests for the tapes from Special Prosecutor Cox and the Senate Select Committee. Nixon maintained that the tapes would remain under his personal control. When a subpoena for the tapes was issued, Nixon replied that he asserted executive privilege and that the President is not subject to compulsory process from the courts. The grand jury then instructed the Special Prosecutor to seek an order for the production of the tapes. It was that enforcement proceeding that produced the first ruling in the case. Judge Sirica ordered the President to produce the items for in-camera inspection. The D.C. Circuit Court of Appeals affirmed. *Nixon v. Sirica*, 487 F.2d 700 (1973).

Quicknotes

ABSOLUTE PRIVILEGE Unconditional or unqualified immunity enjoyed by a person.

SUBPOENA DUCES TECUM A court mandate compelling the production of documents under a witness's control.

INS v. Chadha

Federal agency (D) v. Illegal immigrant (P)

462 U.S. 919 (1983).

NATURE OF CASE: Consolidated actions challenging the constitutionality of a federal statute.

FACT SUMMARY: Chadha (P) and others challenged the constitutionality of a federal statute that purported to authorize one House of Congress, by resolution, to invalidate the decision of the Attorney General (made under authority delegated by Congress) to allow a particular deportable alien to remain in the United States.

🏛 RULE OF LAW

Because it constitutes an exercise of legislative power and is thus subject to the bicameralism and presentment requirements of Article I of the Constitution, the federal statute purporting to authorize a one-house veto of the Attorney General's decision to allow a particular deportable alien to remain in the United States is unconstitutional.

FACTS: Three cases consolidated on appeal all presented the question of the constitutionality of a federal statute that authorized either House of Congress, by resolution, to invalidate the decision of the Attorney General (made pursuant to authority delegated by Congress) to allow a particular deportable alien (P) to remain in the United States. After such a one-house veto effectively overturned the Attorney General's decision to let Chadha (P) and certain other individuals remain in the United States, each instituted action challenging the constitutionality of the aforesaid statute. Chadha (P) filed a petition for a review of his deportation order, with the Immigration and Naturalization Service (INS) (D) actually agreeing with his contention that the statute was unconstitutional. The court of appeals held that the statute violated the doctrine of separation of powers.

ISSUE: Is it constitutional for Congress to statutorily authorize a one-house veto of a decision the Attorney General makes, under authority delegated to him by Congress, to allow a particular deportable alien to remain in the United States?

HOLDING AND DECISION: (Burger, C.J.) No. The Constitution does not permit Congress to statutorily authorize a one-house veto of a decision the Attorney General makes, pursuant to authority delegated to him by Congress, to allow a particular deportable alien to remain in the United States. Such an action is clearly an exercise of legislative power, which makes it subject to the bicameralism and presentment requirements of Article I of the Constitution unless one of the express constitutional exceptions authorizing one House to act alone applies here. None of them applies here. Thus, to accomplish what has been attempted by one House of Congress in this case, requires action in conformity with the express procedures of the Constitution's prescription for legislative action; passage by a majority of both Houses and presentment to the President (for his signing or his veto). Such requirements were built into the Constitution to act as enduring checks on each branch and to protect the people from the improvident exercise of power by mandating certain prescribed steps. In attempting to bypass those steps, Congress has acted unconstitutionally. Affirmed.

CONCURRENCE: (Powell, J.) This case should be decided on the narrower ground that Congress assumes a judicial function in violation of the principle of separation of powers when it finds that a particular person does not satisfy the statutory criteria for permanent residence in this country. The Court's broader decision will apparently invalidate every use of the legislative veto, which is a procedure that has been much used by Congress and one it clearly views as essential to controlling the delegation of power to administrative agencies. While one may reasonably disagree with Congress's assessment of the veto's utility, the respect due its judgment as a coordinate branch of government cautions that our holding should be no more extensive than necessary to decide this case.

DISSENT: (White, J.) Today's decision sounds the death knell for nearly two hundred statutory provisions in which Congress has reserved a "legislative veto," which has become a central means by which Congress secures the accountability of executive and independent agencies. Without this particular tool, Congress faces a Hobson's choice: either to refrain from delegating the necessary authority, leaving itself with a hopeless task of writing laws with the requisite specificity to cover endless special circumstances across the entire policy landscape, or in the alternative, to abdicate its lawmaking function to the executive branch and independent agencies. Thus, the apparent sweep of the Court's decision today, which appears to invalidate all legislative vetoes irrespective of form or subject, is regrettable. Furthermore, the Court's decision fails to recognize that the legislative veto is not the type of action subject to the bicameralism and presentment requirements of Article 1. Only bills and their equivalent are subject to such requirements. The initial legislation delegating to the Attorney General the power to make a decision on the deportation of a particular alien complied with the Article I requirements. Congress's power to exercise a legislative veto over that decision cannot be viewed, then, as the power to write new law without bicameral approval or presidential consideration. If Congress can delegate lawmaking power to executive agencies, it is most difficult to understand Article I

Continued on next page.

as forbidding Congress from simply reserving a check on legislative power for itself. Without the veto, agencies to whom power has been delegated may issue regulations having the force of law without bicameral approval and without the President's signature. It is thus not apparent why the reservation of a veto over the exercise of that legislative power must be subject to a more exacting test. In both cases, it is enough that the initial statutory authorizations comply with the Article I requirements.

▶ *ANALYSIS*

It is only within the last 50 years that the legislative veto has come into widespread use. When the federal government began its massive growth in response to the Depression, the legislative veto was "invented" as one means of keeping a check on the sprawling new structure. While many commentators, upon the Court's announcement of this decision, opined that the result was a major shift of power from the Legislative Branch to the executive branch, Congress through more restrictive draftsmanship should actually see minimal diminishment of its control of those areas over which it desires to retain control.

■■■

Quicknotes

BICAMERALISM The necessity of approval by a majority of both houses of Congress in ratifying legislation or approving other legislative action.

■■■

Bowsher v. Synar

Comptroller General (D) v. Union (P)

478 U.S. 714 (1986).

NATURE OF CASE: Appeal from decision that the Gramm-Rudman-Hollings Act violated the doctrine of separation of powers.

FACT SUMMARY: In Synar's (P) action against Bowsher (D), the Comptroller General of the United States, who was assigned by Congress, under the Gramm-Rudman-Hollings Act, the duty of effectuating across-the-board spending reductions in the federal government, Synar (P) contended that the Act was unconstitutional because Bowsher (D) was authorized, under the Act, to exercise executive functions, violating the doctrine of separation of powers.

RULE OF LAW
When Congress elects to exercise its legislative power, it may not authorize a lesser representative of the legislative branch to act on its behalf.

FACTS: Under the Balanced Budget and Emergency Deficit Control Act of 1985, the "Gramm-Rudman-Hollings Act," Bowsher (D), the Comptroller General of the United States, was assigned the duty of effectuating across-the-board spending reductions in the federal government. Synar (P) sued Bowsher (D) on behalf of the National Treasury Employees Union, which claimed that its members were injured because Bowsher's (D) spending reductions suspended certain cost-of-living benefit increases. Synar (P) contended that the Act was unconstitutional because the Comptroller General (D) was authorized, under the Act, to exercise executive functions, violating the doctrine of separation of powers. A three-judge district court held the Act unconstitutional on the grounds alleged by Synar (P), and Bowsher (D) appealed.

ISSUE: When Congress elects to exercise its legislative power, may it authorize a lesser representative of the legislative branch to act on its behalf?

HOLDING AND DECISION: (Burger, C.J.) No. When Congress elects to exercise its legislative power, it may not authorize a lesser representative of the legislative branch to act on its behalf. It is clear that Congress has consistently viewed the Comptroller General as an officer of the legislative branch. To permit an officer controlled by Congress to execute the law that Congress enacts would be, in essence, to permit a congressional veto. Congress could simply remove, or threaten to remove, an officer for executing the laws in any fashion found to be unsatisfactory to Congress. This kind of congressional control over the execution of the laws is unconstitutionally impermissible. Here, Congress has retained removal authority over Bowsher (D), as Comptroller General, so that Bowsher (D) may not be entrusted with executive powers. Under the Gramm-Rudman-Hollings Act, Bowsher (D) would have the ultimate authority to decide budget cuts to be made. Interpreting a law enacted by Congress to implement the legislative mandate is the very essence of "execution" of the law. Bowsher (D) is, therefore, being given the authority to "execute," under the Act, Congress's mandate. This is unconstitutional.

CONCURRENCE: (Stevens, J.) The Comptroller General (D) must be characterized as an agent of Congress because of his long-standing statutory responsibilities. The powers assigned to the Comptroller General (D) under the Gramm-Rudman-Hollings Act require him to make policy that will bind the nation. Therefore, the Act contains a constitutional infirmity so severe that this flawed provision may not stand.

DISSENT: (White, J.) The Act vesting budget-cutting authority in the Comptroller General (D) represents Congress's judgment that the delegation of such authority to counteract ever-mounting deficits is "necessary and proper" to the exercise of the powers granted the federal government by the Constitution. Under such circumstances, the role of this Court is limited to determining whether the Act so alters the balance of authority among the branches of government to pose a threat to the basic division between the lawmaking power and the power to execute the law. No such threat was apparent here.

▶ ANALYSIS

The test for validity of a federal act is whether Congress might reasonably find that the act relates to one of the federal powers. If the act bears some reasonable relationship to a grant of power to the federal government, the law must be upheld. If the act relates to such an end, then it is valid so long as it does not violate a specific check on governmental action such as those contained in the Bill of Rights.

■■■■■

Quicknotes

SEPARATION OF POWERS DOCTRINE Each branch of government is precluded from interfering with the authority of another.

■■■■■

Morrison v. Olson

Federal government (D) v. Attorney (P)

487 U.S. 654 (1988).

NATURE OF CASE: Appeal of challenge to the independent counsel provisions of the Ethics in Government Act.

FACT SUMMARY: Olson (P) challenged the independent counsel law as violating the Appointments Clause and the separation of powers doctrine.

🏛 RULE OF LAW
The independent counsel provisions of the Ethics in Government Act are constitutional.

FACTS: In 1978, Congress enacted the Ethics in Government Act. Part of the Act created an "independent counsel." The Act provided that when the Attorney General had reasonable grounds to believe that certain federal crimes had been committed by federal officials, he was to report to a specially created court. The court would then appoint a special prosecutor, who would be vested with all the investigative and prosecutorial powers of the Justice Department. The counsel would have certain reporting requirements to the special court and to Congress. The counsel's position could be terminated by the Attorney General, special court, or congressional impeachment. Olson (P), an Environmental Protection Agency (EPA) attorney under investigation by a special counsel, challenged the Act as violative of the Appointments Clause and the separation of powers doctrine. The court of appeals struck down the Act, and the Supreme Court granted review.

ISSUE: Are the independent counsel provisions of the Ethics in Government Act constitutional?

HOLDING AND DECISION: (Rehnquist, C.J.) Yes. The independent counsel provisions of the Ethics in Government Act are constitutional. The Constitution mandates that the President shall appoint what amounts to "principal" executive officers, but permits Congress to delegate to courts the appointment of "inferior" officers. This Court concludes that the independent counsel is an inferior officer. His term is limited, as is his jurisdiction. Also, he must answer to both Congress and the special court. Since Congress may empower courts to appoint inferior officers, the Act does not run afoul of the Appointments Clause. It does not violate Article III's "case or controversy" requirement. While the special court may be participating in a matter insufficient in concreteness to be considered a case or controversy, its role is largely ministerial, and federal courts may play a ministerial role in actions not amounting to a case or controversy. Finally, the Act does not violate the separation of powers doctrine. The independent counsel, although appointed by a court, is a member of the executive branch, and may be removed by the Attorney General, subject to judicial review. This is not a

congressional encroachment upon executive powers, and therefore does not violate separation of powers. Reversed.

DISSENT: (Scalia, J.) The Constitution provides that all, not some, of the executive power shall be vested in the President. The Act places some executive power in the hands of the other branches. Any statute depriving the President of exclusive executive power must fall.

▌ ANALYSIS

This was the third major separation of powers decision of the 1980's. The other two were *INS v. Chadha*, 462 U.S. 919 (1983), and *Bowsher v. Synar*, 478 U.S. 714 (1986). In both of these cases, the Court found the doctrine of separation of powers to be violated. The difference in the present case appears to have been the fact that the independent counsel was found to be an inferior officer, part of the executive branch, and answerable to the President.

■══■

Quicknotes

ETHICS IN GOVERNMENT ACT Allows for the appointment of special independent counsel to investigate high ranking government officials.

SEPARATION OF POWERS DOCTRINE Each branch of government is precluded from interfering with the authority of another.

■══■

Equality and the Constitution

Quick Reference Rules of Law

PAGE

1. **Slavery and the Constitution.** Slavery is not inconsistent with a constitutional declaration that all men are by nature free. (State v. Post) — *51*

2. **Slavery and the Constitution.** Individuals of the Negro race are not to be considered "citizens" in the constitutional sense. (Dred Scott v. Sandford) — *52*

3. **Reconstruction and Retreat.** Segregation of the races is reasonable if based upon the established custom, usage, and traditions of the people in the state. (Plessy v. Ferguson) — *53*

4. **The Attack on Jim Crow.** The "separate but equal" doctrine has no application in the field of education and the segregation of children in public schools based solely on their race violates the Equal Protection Clause. (Brown v. Board of Education of Topeka (Brown I)) — *54*

5. **The Attack on Jim Crow.** The cases are remanded to the lower courts to enter orders consistent with equitable principles of flexibility and requiring the defendant to make a prompt and reasonable start toward full racial integration in public schools. (Brown v. Board of Education of Topeka (Brown II)) — *55*

6. **Rational Basic Review.** A public authority may deny employment to methadone users as a class. (New York City Transit Authority v. Beazer) — *56*

7. **Heightened Scrutiny and the Problem of Race.** A state may not prevent one from serving on a jury because of race or color. (Strauder v. West Virginia) — *57*

8. **Heightened Scrutiny and the Problem of Race.** Apprehension by the proper military authorities of the gravest imminent danger to the public safety can justify the curtailment of the civil rights of a single racial group. (Korematsu v. United States) — *58*

9. **Heightened Scrutiny and the Problem of Race.** A state law restricting the freedom to marry solely because of racial classification violates the Equal Protection Clause. (Loving v. Virginia) — *59*

10. **Facially Nonracial Classifications that Disadvantage Racial Minorities: When Does Heightened Scrutiny Apply?** The administration of a race-neutral test on relevant criteria to employment applicants does not violate the equal protection clause where the test results in the elimination of a disproportionate number of racial minorities as opposed to whites. (Washington v. Davis) — *60*

11. **Facially Nonracial Classifications that Disadvantage Racial Minorities: When Does Heightened Scrutiny Apply?** Capital cases require an evaluation of the motivations of individual jurors in sentencing; thus raw abstract statistical data are not dispositive of a lack of equal protection. (McCleskey v. Kemp) — *61*

12. **Race-Specific Classifications Designed to Benefit Racial Minorities.** Federal contracting set-asides for minorities are unconstitutional unless they are narrowly tailored to remedy demonstrable past discrimination. (Adarand Constructors, Inc. v. Pena) — *62*

13. **Race-Specific Classifications Designed to Benefit Racial Minorities.** Student body diversity is a compelling state interest that can justify the use of race in university admissions. (Grutter v. Bollinger) — *63*

CHAPTER 5

14. **The Synthesis of *Brown* and Affirmation Action.**   Racial balance between local   65
high-school districts is not a compelling government interest under the Equal Protection
Clause. (Parents Involved in Community Schools v. Seattle School District No.1)

15. **Intermediate Scrutiny.**   Laws that establish classifications by gender must serve important   67
governmental objectives and must be substantially related to achievement of those
objectives to be constitutionally in line with the Equal Protection Clause. (Craig v. Boren)

16. **Archaic and Overbroad Generalizations versus "Real" Differences.**   Public schools   69
may not exclude women. (United States v. Virginia)

17. **The Problem of Sexual Orientation.**   States may not enact laws prohibiting localities from   70
proscribing discrimination against a class of persons. (Romer v. Evans)

18. **Alienage.**   A state may not refuse all civil service positions on the basis of alienage alone.   71
(Sugarman v. Dougall)

State v. Post

State (D) v. Abolitionists (P)

N.J. Sup. Ct., 20 N.J.L. 368 (1845).

NATURE OF CASE: Appeal of constitutional attack on slavery.

FACT SUMMARY: Slavery was challenged as being contrary to the New Jersey State Constitution.

🏛 RULE OF LAW
Slavery is not inconsistent with a constitutional declaration that all men are by nature free.

FACTS: The New Jersey Constitution proclaimed that all men were free and independent and endowed with certain rights such as liberty and property. The slave system was challenged as being inconsistent with this.

ISSUE: Is slavery inconsistent with a constitutional declaration that all men are by nature free?

HOLDING AND DECISION: (Nevius, J.) No. Slavery is not inconsistent with a constitutional declaration that all men are by nature free. No one is absolutely free. In a civilized state, all residents give up a portion of their freedoms in exchange for the benefits of civilization. Freedom, then, must be looked at in the context of its society. At the time the New Jersey Constitution was adopted, slavery was an accepted part of society and was not considered incompatible with a free society. This court is not inclined to change that view.

▶ ANALYSIS

Numerous attacks on slavery were mounted in the pre-Civil War era. Some were successful, and others turned out as did this action. The most (in)famous pre–Civil War slavery case was, of course, *Scott v. Sanford*, 60 U.S. 393 (1857).

∎▬∎

Dred Scott v. Sandford

Slave (P) v. Owner (D)

60 U.S. (19 How.) 393 (1857).

NATURE OF CASE: Appeal of challenge by slave to slave status.

FACT SUMMARY: Scott (P), a slave, sued for his freedom after having been taken to a free state and returned to a slave state.

🏛 RULE OF LAW
Individuals of the Negro race are not to be considered "citizens" in the constitutional sense.

FACTS: Scott (P) was born a slave. He had been taken to Illinois, a free state, by his master. Scott (P) was taken to several other free states or territories. Scott (P) was then taken to Missouri, a slave state, and sold to Sandford (D). Scott (P) then sued for his freedom, contending that his having been taken into free states made him free. Jurisdiction was predicated on diversity of citizenship.

ISSUE: Are individuals of the Negro race considered to be "citizens" in the constitutional sense?

HOLDING AND DECISION: (Taney, C.J.) No. Individuals of the Negro race are not considered to be "citizens" in the constitutional sense. "Citizens," for constitutional purposes, refers to the sovereign people of the United States as they were understood to be at the time of the Constitution's adoption. At that time, the Negro was considered to be an inferior class, one having no inherent liberty or property rights. A state may confer rights upon individuals living in it as it sees fit. It cannot, however, confer rights as a U.S. citizen by virtue of state law. The fact that in Illinois Scott (P) could not be a slave does not alter the fact that Illinois' ability to make Scott (P) a free man extends no further than its borders and does not confer upon Scott (P) rights and privileges of U.S. citizenship. Therefore, Scott (P) was not a citizen of a state in U.S. constitutional sense and not entitled to sue in U.S. courts. Affirmed.

▶ ANALYSIS

Dred Scott is, without a doubt, the most vilified decision in Supreme Court history. Under analysis, however, the decision was fairly consistent with the ideals of strict constructionism, a judicial philosophy that has been in and out of fashion for much of the twentieth century. The Court basically looked to the intent of the Framers of the Constitution and attempted to be consistent with them.

Quicknotes

CONSTRUCTION The examination and interpretation of statutes.

Plessy v. Ferguson
Negro (D) v. State (P)

163 U.S. 537 (1896).

NATURE OF CASE: Appeal from criminal prosecution for violating a state railway accommodation segregation law.

FACT SUMMARY: Plessy (D) was arrested for trying to sit in a railroad car that was designated "for whites only."

🏛 RULE OF LAW
Segregation of the races is reasonable if based upon the established custom, usage, and traditions of the people in the state.

FACTS: Plessy (D) who was 7/8 Caucasian and whose skin color was white was denied a seat in an all-white railroad car. When he (D) resisted, he was arrested for violating a state law that provided for segregated "separate but equal" railroad accommodations. Plessy (D) appealed the conviction on the basis that separation of the races stigmatized colored people and stamped them with the badge of inferiority. He (D) claimed that segregation violated the Thirteenth and Fourteenth Amendments. The trial court found Plessy (D) guilty on the basis that the law was a reasonable exercise of the state's police powers based upon custom, usage, and tradition in the state.

ISSUE: Is segregation of the races reasonable if based upon the established custom, usage, and traditions of the people of the state?

HOLDING AND DECISION: (Brown, J.) Yes. Segregation of the races is reasonable if based upon the established custom, usage, and traditions of the people in the state. This is a valid exercise of the state's police power. Where this has been the established custom, usage, or tradition in the state, it may continue to require such segregation as is reasonable to preserve order and the public peace. Such decisions have been continuously upheld. This is not a badge of "slavery" under the Thirteenth Amendment and it violates no provision of the Fourteenth Amendment. The enforced separation of the races is not a badge of servitude or inferiority regardless of how Plessy (D) and other colored people deem to treat it. The conviction is sustained.

DISSENT: (Harlan, J.) The statute interferes with the personal freedom of individuals to freely associate with others. The Constitution is color-blind. All citizens should and must be treated alike. Colored people are not subordinate or inferior things. They are citizens and are entitled to all of the privileges that this entails. Enforced separation is an impermissible burden on these privileges and freedoms. The conviction should be overturned.

▌ANALYSIS

Plessy is of importance only for its historical perspective. Later cases borrowed the "separate but equal" phraseology and turned it around 180 degrees. In *Brown v. Board of Education*, 347 U.S. 483 (1954), the Court, 58 years after *Plessy*, held that separate could never be considered equal. It thus expressly overruled *Plessy*.

Quicknotes

SEGREGATION The use of separate institutions and facilities for persons of different races, nationalities, religions, etc.

Brown v. Board of Education of Topeka (Brown I)

Students (P) v. School board (D)

347 U.S. 483 (1954).

NATURE OF CASE: Action seeking order to desegregate public schools.

FACT SUMMARY: Negro children were denied admission to public schools attended by white children.

🏛 RULE OF LAW

The "separate but equal" doctrine has no application in the field of education and the segregation of children in public schools based solely on their race violates the Equal Protection Clause.

FACTS: Negro children had been denied admission to public schools attended by white children under laws requiring or permitting segregation according to race. It was found that the Negro children's schools and the white children's schools had been or were being equalized with respect to buildings, curricula, qualifications, and salaries of teachers.

ISSUE: Does segregation of children in public schools solely on the basis of race, even though the physical facilities are equal, deprive the children of the minority group of equal protection of the law?

HOLDING AND DECISION: (Warren, C.J.) Yes. The "separate but equal" doctrine has no application in the field of education and the segregation of children in public schools based solely on their race violates the Equal Protection Clause. First of all, intangible as well as tangible factors may be considered. Hence, the fact that the facilities and other tangible factors in the schools have been equalized is not controlling. Segregation of white and Negro children in public schools has a detrimental effect on the Negro children because the policy of separating the races is usually interpreted as denoting the inferiority of the Negro children. A sense of inferiority affects children's motivation to learn. Segregation tends to deprive Negro children of some of the benefits they would receive in an integrated school. Any language in *Plessy v. Ferguson*, 163 U.S. 537 (1896), contrary to this is rejected. The "separate but equal" doctrine has no place in the field of education. Separate facilities are inherently unequal. Such facilities deprive Negro children of their right to equal protection of the laws.

▶ ANALYSIS

In *Plessy v. Ferguson*, the Court sustained a Louisiana statute requiring "equal, but separate, accommodations" for black and white railway passengers. The separate but equal doctrine was born and under it a long line of statutes providing separate but equal facilities was upheld. Justice Harlan was the only dissenter in *Plessy*. He stated, "The arbitrary separation of citizens, on the basis of race, while they are on a public highway . . . cannot be justified upon any legal grounds. The thin disguise of equal accommodations for passengers in railway cars will not mislead anyone, nor atone for the wrong done this day." After the 1954 decision in *Brown v. Board of Education*, the Court found segregation unconstitutional in other public facilities as well. Despite the emphasis on the school context in *Brown*, the later cases resulted in per curiam orders simply citing *Brown*. Facilities that were desegregated included beaches, buses, golf courses, and parks.

∎▬∎

Quicknotes

EQUAL PROTECTION CLAUSE A constitutional provision that each person be guaranteed the same protection of the laws enjoyed by other persons in like circumstances.

SEGREGATION The use of separate institutions and facilities for persons of different races, nationalities, religions, etc.

∎▬∎

Brown v. Board of Education of Topeka (Brown II)

(Implementation Decision)

349 U.S. 294 (1955).

NATURE OF CASE: Decision to determine the manner in which relief from segregation in public schools is to be accorded.

FACT SUMMARY: In May 1954, the Court decided that racial discrimination in public education is unconstitutional. It requested further arguments on the question of relief.

🏛 RULE OF LAW
The cases are remanded to the lower courts to enter orders consistent with equitable principles of flexibility and requiring the defendant to make a prompt and reasonable start toward full racial integration in public schools.

FACTS: These cases were decided in May 1954. The opinions declared that racial discrimination in public education is unconstitutional. They are incorporated here. Because the cases arose under various local conditions and their disposition will involve a variety of local problems, the Court requested additional arguments on the question of relief. All provisions of federal, state, and local laws that permit segregation in public schools must be modified.

ISSUE: Shall relief in the public school racial desegregation cases be accorded by remanding the cases to the lower courts to enter orders requiring integration?

HOLDING AND DECISION: (Warren, C.J.) Yes. School authorities have the primary responsibility for assessing and solving the problem of achieving racial integration in the public schools. It will be for courts to consider whether the school authorities' actions are good-faith implementations of the governing constitutional principles. Because of their proximity to local conditions and the possible need for further hearings, the courts that originally heard these cases can best perform this judicial appraisal. In doing so, the courts will be guided by the equitable principles of practical flexibility in shaping remedies and the facility for adjusting and reconciling public and private needs. The courts will require that the defendants make a prompt and reasonable start toward full racial integration in the public schools. Once such a start is made, the courts may determine that additional time is required to carry out the May 1954 ruling. However, the burden rests upon the defendant to determine that such time is necessary and consistent with good-faith compliance with the Constitution. The courts may consider problems related to administration, the facilities, school transportation systems, and revision of school districts and local laws. They will also consider the adequacy of any plans proposed by the defendants and will retain jurisdiction during the transition period. The cases are remanded to the lower courts to enter orders consistent with this opinion as necessary to insure that the parties to these cases are admitted to public schools on a racially nondiscriminatory basis with all deliberate speed.

▶ ANALYSIS

After its promulgation of general guidelines in *Brown II* in 1955, the Court maintained silence about implementation for several years. Enforcement of the desegregation requirement was left largely to lower court litigation. In 1958, the Court broke its silence in *Cooper v. Aaron*, 358 U.S. 1 (1958), where it reaffirmed the *Brown* principles in the face of official resistance in Little Rock, Arkansas. It was not until the early sixties, however, that the Court began to consider the details of desegregation plans. During the late 1960s, Court rulings on implementation came with greater frequency, specificity, and urgency. Finally, in *Alexander v. Holmes County Board of Education*, 369 U.S. 19 (1969), the Court called for an immediate end to dual school systems.

Quicknotes

SEGREGATION The use of separate institutions and facilities for persons of different races, nationalities, religions, etc.

New York Transit Authority v. Beazer

Public authority (D) v. Methadone users (P)

440 U.S. 568 (1979).

NATURE OF CASE: Appeal of court order invalidating certain employment policies.

FACT SUMMARY: A N.Y. Transit Authority (D) policy of not hiring methadone users was challenged as unconstitutional.

🏛 RULE OF LAW
A public authority may deny employment to methadone users as a class.

FACTS: The N.Y. Transit Authority (D) had a rule denying employment to anyone using methadone, a synthetic narcotic used in treating heroin addition. Beazer (P) brought a class action suit alleging that this rule denied equal protection. The evidence showed that at least half of all methadone users were employable. The district court issued an injunction barring enforcement of the rule. The court of appeals affirmed.

ISSUE: May a public authority deny employment to methadone users as a class?

HOLDING AND DECISION: (Stevens, J.) Yes. A public authority may deny employment to methadone users as a class. Methadone users do not have the characteristics of a suspect class, these being distinguishing, immutable characteristics. For this reason all that must be shown is a rational relationship between the end, here safety and efficiency, and the means, here denial of employment. The record does not show that the means do not rationally achieve the ends, so the rule is valid. Reversed.

DISSENT: (White, J.) A rule lumping successful methadone patients with unsuccessful ones is overinclusive. Such an arbitrary rule is unconstitutional.

▶ *ANALYSIS*

For most of the history of civil rights jurisprudence, the "two-tier" system employed here has been the norm. If a classification is suspect, that is, one involving a group that either has immutable distinguishing characteristics or a history of discrimination, strict review of classifications will be made. If, as here, the classification is not suspect, a much more lax standard will be used.

■═■

Quicknotes

RATIONAL BASIS REVIEW A test employed by the court to determine the validity of a statute in "equal protection" actions, whereby the court determines whether the challenged statute is rationally related to the achievement of a legitimate state interest.

SUSPECT CLASSIFICATION A class of persons that have historically been subject to discriminatory treatment; statutes drawing a distinction between persons based on a suspect classification, i.e., race, nationality or alienage, are subject to a strict scrutiny standard of review.

■═■

Strauder v. West Virginia

Criminal defendant (D) v. State (P)

100 U.S. (10 Otto) 303 (1880).

NATURE OF CASE: Appeal from murder conviction.

FACT SUMMARY: [Strauder (D), a black man, was convicted of murder by a jury from which blacks were excluded.]

🏛 RULE OF LAW
A state may not prevent one from serving on a jury because of race or color.

FACTS: [Strauder (D), a black man, was indicted for murder and after a trial was convicted of the charge. On appeal, Strauder (D) argued that at the trial he was denied rights to which he was entitled under the Constitution and laws of the United States because under state law blacks were ineligible to serve on the grand or petit jury.]

ISSUE: May a state prevent one from serving on a jury because of race or color?

HOLDING AND DECISION: (Strong, J.) No. A state may not prevent one from serving on a jury because of race or color. The Fourteenth Amendment was designed to assure to the race recently emancipated the enjoyment of all the civil rights that are under the law enjoyed by white persons, and to give that race the protection of the general government in that enjoyment, whenever it is attempted to be denied by the states. The Fourteenth Amendment not only provided citizenship and its privileges to the colored race, but denies to any state the power to withhold from them the equal protection of the laws, and authorized Congress to enforce its provisions by legislation appropriate to that objective. Although the words of the Amendment are prohibitory, they contain a necessary implication of a positive immunity and valuable right to the colored race: the right to exemption from unfriendly legislation against them because of their color, exemption from legal discrimination, implying inferiority in civil society, and discriminations that constitute steps towards reducing them to the condition of a subject race. Legislation preventing colored people from serving on juries clearly constitutes a prohibited discrimination. It is well known that prejudices often exist against particular classes in the community. These prejudices may sway juror judgment, and, thus, might operate to deny to persons of those classes the full enjoyment of the protections that others enjoy. Reversed.

▶ ANALYSIS

This case, one of the earliest decisions interpreting the Fourteenth Amendment, discusses two themes that later became significant in determining whether a group constituted a suspect classification, and whether the legislation in question violates constitutional prohibitions. The first is whether the class, as in the case of blacks, is one that has historically been the victim of societal discrimination. The second is whether the legislation in question tends to stigmatize that class in the eyes of society.

■══■

Quicknotes

FOURTEENTH AMENDMENT Declares that no state shall make or enforce any law that shall abridge the privileges and immunities of citizens of the United States. No state shall deny to any person within its jurisdiction the equal protection of the laws.

■══■

Korematsu v. United States

Japanese American citizen (D) v. Federal government (P)

323 U.S. 214 (1944).

NATURE OF CASE: Appeal from a conviction for violation of exclusion order No. 34.

FACT SUMMARY: Korematsu (D), an American citizen of Japanese ancestry, was convicted of violating exclusion order No. 34, a World War II decree that ordered all persons of Japanese ancestry to leave the military area of the Western United States.

🏛 RULE OF LAW
Apprehension by the proper military authorities of the gravest imminent danger to the public safety can justify the curtailment of the civil rights of a single racial group.

FACTS: Korematsu (D), an American citizen of Japanese ancestry, was convicted in federal district court for remaining in San Leandro, California, a "military area," contrary to civilian exclusion order No. 34 of the commanding general of the western command. The order directed that after May 9, 1942, all persons of Japanese ancestry should be excluded from the area in order to protect against acts of sabotage and espionage during World War II. Those of Japanese ancestry were to report to and temporarily remain in an assembly center and go under military control to a relocation center for an indeterminate period. Korematsu (P) appealed on grounds that the order denied equal protection.

ISSUE: Can apprehension by the proper military authorities of the gravest imminent danger to the public safety justify the curtailment of the civil rights of a single racial group?

HOLDING AND DECISION: (Black, J.) Yes. Apprehension by the proper military authorities of the gravest imminent danger to the public safety can justify the curtailment of the civil rights of a single racial group. While such a classification is immediately suspect and is subject to the most rigid scrutiny, pressing public necessity may sometimes justify such exclusions. When under conditions of modern warfare the country is threatened, "the power to protect must be commensurate with the threatened danger." Korematsu (D) was excluded because the United States was at war with the Empire of Japan, because the proper military authorities feared invasion of the West Coast and believed security required exclusion, and because Congress, placing its confidence in the military, determined that the military should have that power. Affirmed.

DISSENT: (Murphy, J.) It cannot be reasonably assumed that all persons of Japanese ancestry may have a dangerous tendency to commit enemy acts.

DISSENT: (Jackson, J.) A civil court should not be made to enforce an order that violates constitutional limitations even if it is a reasonable exercise of military authority.

▶ ANALYSIS

This case has received severe and growing criticism over the years. However, Chief Justice Warren has expressed the view that in some circumstances the Court will simply not be in a position to reject descriptions by the executive of the degree of military necessity. Where time is of the essence, the court could only reject the necessity not on grounds of factual unassailability, but for insufficiency. Justice Douglas, 30 years later, wrote, "the decisions were extreme and went to the verge of wartime power . . . It is easy in retrospect to denounce what was done, as there actually was no attempted Japanese invasion of our country . . . but those making plans for the defense of the nation had no such knowledge and were planning for the worst." *De Funis v. Odegaard*, 416 U.S. 312 (1974).

Quicknotes

SUSPECT CLASSIFICATION A class of persons that have historically been subject to discriminatory treatment; statutes drawing a distinction between persons based on a suspect classification, i.e., race, nationality or alienage, are subject to a strict scrutiny standard of review.

Loving v. Virginia

Interracial couple (D) v. State (P)

388 U.S. 1 (1967).

NATURE OF CASE: Appeal after conviction for violation of state law barring interracial marriage.

FACT SUMMARY: Loving (D), a white man, and Jeter (D), a Negro woman, both Virginia residents, were married in the District of Columbia. When they returned to Virginia, they were indicted for violating the state's ban on interracial marriage.

🏛 RULE OF LAW
A state law restricting the freedom to marry solely because of racial classification violates the Equal Protection Clause.

FACTS: In June 1958, Loving (D) a white man, and Jeter (D), a Negro woman, both Virginia residents, were married in the District of Columbia, pursuant to its laws. Shortly after their marriage, the Lovings (D) returned to Virginia and were indicted for violating the state's law barring interracial marriage. They pleaded guilty and were sentenced to one year in jail. The trial judge suspended the sentence for 25 years on the condition that the Lovings (D) leave the state and not return for 25 years. In 1963, they filed a motion to have the judgment vacated and set aside.

ISSUE: Does a state law restricting the freedom to marry solely because of racial classification violate the Equal Protection Clause?

HOLDING AND DECISION: (Warren, C.J.) Yes. A state law restricting the freedom to marry solely because of racial classification violates the Equal Protection Clause. The Clause demands that racial classifications, especially suspect in criminal statutes, be subjected to the most rigid scrutiny. The clear and central purpose of the Fourteenth Amendment was to eliminate all official state sources of invidious discrimination. There can be no question but that Virginia's (P) miscegenation statutes rest solely upon distinctions drawn according to race. The statutes proscribe generally accepted conduct if engaged in by members of different races. Here, there is patently no legitimate overriding purpose of this legislation independent of invidious racial discrimination. The fact that Virginia (P) prohibits only interracial marriages involving white persons demonstrates that the racial classifications could qualify only as a measure designed to maintain White Supremacy. In fact, the very title of the legislation is "An Act to Preserve Racial Integrity." The Court has consistently denied the constitutionality of measures that restrict the rights of citizens on account of race. Reversed.

CONCURRENCE: (Stewart, J.) It is simply not possible for a state law to be valid under the Constitution, which makes the criminality of an act depend upon the race of the actor.

▌ ANALYSIS

In *McLaughlin v. Florida*, 379 U.S. 184 (1964), a state law banning habitual nighttime cohabitation between whites and blacks not married to each other was held to violate the Equal Protection Clause, since other nonmarried couples were not subject to prosecution for the same acts. Ordinances establishing ghettos in which blacks must reside were found to violate the clause (*Buchanan v. Warley*, 245 U.S. 60 (1917)), as was judicial enforcement of covenants restricting ownership of land to whites (*Shelley v. Kramer*, 334 U.S. 1 (1948)). Racial discrimination in the selection of jurors (*Patton v. Mississippi*, 332 U.S. 463 (1947)), hiring blacks for certain occupations, and establishing racial qualifications for public offices (*Anderson v. Martin*, 375 U.S. 399 (1964)) have all been held to violate equal protection.

■=■

Quicknotes

EQUAL PROTECTION CLAUSE A constitutional provision that each person be guaranteed the same protection of the laws enjoyed by other persons in like circumstances.

■=■

Washington v. Davis

Federal district (D) v. Employment applicant (P)

426 U.S. 229 (1976).

NATURE OF CASE: Appeal from reversal of order sustaining validity of employment qualification test.

FACT SUMMARY: Washington (D) administered a written test of verbal skills, vocabulary, and reading comprehension to applicants for jobs in the Police Department, and since four times as many blacks failed the test as whites, Davis (P) brought suit alleging the invalidity of the test due to its discriminatory impact.

🏛 RULE OF LAW
The administration of a race-neutral test on relevant criteria to employment applicants does not violate the Equal Protection Clause where the test results in the elimination of a disproportionate number of racial minorities as opposed to whites.

FACTS: Applicants for jobs as police officers with the District of Columbia Metropolitan Police Department were required by Washington (D) to take a qualifying test that was developed by the Civil Service Commission for use throughout the federal employment system, known as "Test 21." Four times as many black applicants failed this test as white applicants. Davis (P) brought this suit alleging that the disproportionate effect on racial minorities of the test rendered it a denial of equal protection, despite the facts that there was no proof of discriminatory intent, the test was race-neutral, and the test tested verbal skills, vocabulary, and reading comprehension, all of which are relevant to the performance of a police officer's duties. The district court upheld the test due to the absence of proof of intent, but the court of appeals reversed, holding that the discriminatory impact alone was sufficient to show the constitutional violation alleged. The Supreme Court granted certiorari.

ISSUE: Does the administration of a race-neutral test on relevant criteria to employment applicants violate the Equal Protection Clause where the test results in the elimination of a disproportionate number of racial minorities as opposed to whites?

HOLDING AND DECISION: (White, J.) No. The administration of a race-neutral test on relevant criteria to employment applicants does not violate the Equal Protection Clause where the test results in the elimination of a disproportionate number of racial minorities as opposed to whites. The central purpose of the Equal Protection Clause of the Fourteenth Amendment is the prevention of official conduct that discriminates on the basis of race. It has never been held that a law or other official action is unconstitutional solely because it has a racially disproportionate impact. The school desegregation cases have held that a racially discriminatory purpose must be behind law if it is to be found invidiously discriminatory. The Constitution does not prevent the government from seeking to upgrade the communicative skills of its employees by employing a test of those skills that is racially neutral. The administration of a race-neutral test on relevant criteria to employment applicants does not violate the Equal Protection Clause where the tests result in the elimination of a disproportionate number of racial minorities. Some discriminatory intent or purpose must be shown. Reversed.

CONCURRENCE: (Stevens, J.) The line between discriminatory purpose and discriminatory impact is not nearly as bright, and perhaps not quite as critical, as the reader of the Court's opinion might assume. However, "Test 21" survives the challenge of Davis (P) because it serves a neutral and legitimate purpose and is used on all applicants for the job in question, in addition to many others. The evidence of discrimination in this case is therefore insufficient.

▶ ANALYSIS

It is possible to conceive of a test that is race-neutral on its face, but which nonetheless is part of a plan—or purpose—to discriminate. If such a showing is made, the neutrality on the face of the test will not save it, as de jure discrimination will be found if the evidence shows the plan, purpose, or intent. It is only held here that discriminatory effect standing alone is insufficient to invoke the Equal Protection Clause.

Quicknotes

EQUAL PROTECTION CLAUSE A constitutional provision that each person be guaranteed the same protection of the laws enjoyed by other persons in like circumstances.

McCleskey v. Kemp

Inmate (D) v. State (P)

481 U.S. 279 (1987).

NATURE OF CASE: Appeal from denial of writ of habeas corpus.

FACT SUMMARY: McCleskey (D) contended he was denied equal protection when sentenced to death because blacks were statistically more likely to be so sentenced, and such was racially based.

RULE OF LAW

Capital cases require an evaluation of the motivations of individual jurors in sentencing; thus raw abstract statistical data are not dispositive of a lack of equal protection.

FACTS: McCleskey (D), an African American, was sentenced to death for killing a white. He petitioned for a writ of habeas corpus presenting a statistical study indicating blacks were more likely to be sentenced to death, and that such was racially motivated. The district court and the court of appeals rejected the statistical data as irrelevant to the disposition, and the Supreme Court granted certiorari.

ISSUE: May statistical data be used in a capital case to determine an absence of equal protection?

HOLDING AND DECISION: (Powell, J.) No. Capital cases require an evaluation of the motivations of individual jurors in sentencing; thus raw abstract statistical studies are irrelevant and not dispositive of a lack of equal protection. Each jury is unique in its composition, rendering statistical studies useless. Each case must be evaluated on its own merits. Thus, these data were properly excluded. Affirmed.

DISSENT: (Brennan, J.) Georgia's (P) legacy of a race-conscious criminal justice system, as well as the Court's own recognition of the persistent danger that racial attitudes may affect criminal proceedings, indicate that McCleskey's (D) claim is not a fanciful product of mere statistical artifice. The fact that one must always act without the illumination of complete knowledge cannot induce paralysis when confronted with what is literally an issue of life and death.

ANALYSIS

The Court appeared reluctant to rely upon statistical data in overturning a jury verdict. The statistical manipulations and fact-gathering methodology in such studies may give a false conclusion regarding the result. Extrapolation and mathematical interpretation was felt to unreasonably impact upon the ultimate conclusion. Any individual jury, after voir dire, can be as independent as necessary, according to the Court, and thus such statistics merely cloud the issue.

Quicknotes

VOIR DIRE Examination of potential jurors on a case.

Adarand Constructors, Inc. v. Pena

Contractor (P) v. Administrative agency (D)

515 U.S. 200 (1995).

NATURE OF CASE: Challenges to federal program encouraging the awarding of federal contracts to minority-owned businesses.

FACT SUMMARY: A federal program giving preferences in federal contracting to minority-owned businesses was challenged as unconstitutional.

🏛 RULE OF LAW
Federal contracting set-asides for minorities are unconstitutional unless they are narrowly tailored to remedy demonstrable past discrimination.

FACTS: The U.S. Department of Transportation (D) awarded a construction contract. The contractor solicited subcontracts. Adarand Constructors, Inc. (Adarand) (P) submitted the low bid, but because of federal incentives favoring minority contracts, Adarand (P) was rejected in favor of a minority-owned business. Adarand (P) brought an action, contending that the incentive program was a violation of equal protection. The Ninth Circuit rejected the challenge, and the Supreme Court granted review.

ISSUE: Are federal contracting set-asides for minorities unconstitutional if they are not narrowly tailored to remedy demonstrable past discrimination?

HOLDING AND DECISION: (O'Connor, J.) Yes. Federal contracting set-asides for minorities are unconstitutional unless they are narrowly tailored to remedy demonstrable past discrimination. There is no "equal protection" provision in the Fifth Amendment, such as is found in the Fourteenth. However, it is clear that the federal government's due process obligations under the Due Process Clause require it to treat similarly situated individuals in a similar fashion, much as states must do. While there is some prior authority for the proposition that "benign" racial discrimination by Congress is subject to less rigorous scrutiny than traditional discrimination, these decision were in error. Racial classification of any sort is subject to the highest level of judicial review: the classification must be narrowly tailored to serve a compelling state interest. The eradication of racism in contracting is such an interest, but the means to achieve it must be carefully drawn. It is not sufficient that a general history of discrimination be shown. Rather, specific patterns of discrimination must be shown, as well as a remedy that was chosen to be narrowly tailored to address the problem. This was not done in the present case. Reversed and remanded.

CONCURRENCE: (Scalia, J.) Government can never "make up" for past discrimination by present discrimination. In our constitutional system, there can never be a debtor race or a creditor race. The Constitution protects persons, not races.

CONCURRENCE: (Thomas, J.) There is no racial paternalism exception to the principle of equal protection.

DISSENT: (Stevens, J.) Congress has greater leeway in remedying past discrimination than do the states.

DISSENT: (Ginsburg, J.) Large deference is owed by the Judiciary to Congress's institutional competence authority to overcome historic racial subjugation.

▌ ANALYSIS

In 1989, the Court decided *Richmond v. J.A. Croson Co.*, 488 U.S. 469 (1989). In that case, the Court applied strict scrutiny to a municipal preference scheme. The Court left open the question of whether this would also be the case with respect to congressional action. This question was answered by the present opinion.

■■■■■

Quicknotes

DUE PROCESS CLAUSE Clauses found in the Fifth and Fourteenth Amendments to the United States Constitution providing that no person shall be deprived of "life, liberty, or property, without due process of law."

■■■■■

Grutter v. Bollinger

Law school applicant (P) v. Law school (D)

539 U.S. 306 (2003).

NATURE OF CASE: Appeal in racial discrimination case.

FACT SUMMARY: When Grutter (P), a white Michigan resident, was denied admission to the University of Michigan Law School (D), she sued the latter in federal district court, alleging racial discrimination against her in violation of the Equal Protection Clause on the basis of the law school's (D) express consideration of race as a factor in the admissions process.

RULE OF LAW

Student body diversity is a compelling state interest that can justify the use of race in university admissions.

FACTS: To attempt to achieve student body diversity, the University of Michigan Law School (D) admissions committee required admissions officials to evaluate each applicant based on all the information in the file, including a personal statement, letters of recommendation, a student's essay, grades, LSAT score, as well as so-called "soft variables." The admissions policy, furthermore, specifically stressed the law school's (D) long-standing commitment to racial and ethnic diversity. When Grutter (P), a white Michigan resident, applied for admission but was denied, she sued the law school (D) in federal district court, alleging racial discrimination against her in violation of the Equal Protection Clause. [The district court upheld Grutter's (P) claim. The court of appeals reversed, and Grutter (P) appealed.]

ISSUE: Is student body diversity a compelling state interest that can justify the use of race in university admissions?

HOLDING AND DECISION: (O'Connor, J.) Yes. Student body diversity is a compelling state interest that can justify the use of race in university admissions. Here, the law school's (D) admissions program bears the hallmarks of a narrowly tailored plan. Truly individualized consideration demands that race be used in a flexible, nonmechanical way. It follows from this mandate that universities cannot establish quotas for members of certain racial groups or put members of those groups on separate admissions tracks. Nor can universities insulate applicants who belong to certain racial or ethnic groups from the competition for admission. Universities can, however, as was done here, consider race or ethnicity more flexibly as a plus factor in the context of individualized consideration of each and every applicant. The law school's (D) goal of attaining a critical mass of underrepresented minority students does not transform its program into a quota. The evidence indicated

that the law school (D) engaged in a highly individualized, holistic review of each applicant's file, giving serious consideration to all the ways an applicant might contribute to a "diverse educational environment." Furthermore, evidence showed that the law school (D) gives substantial weight to diversity factors besides race by frequently accepting nonminority applicants with grades and test scores lower than underrepresented minority applicants. There was no law school (D) policy, either de facto or de jure, of automatic acceptance or rejection based on any single "soft" variable. Narrow tailoring does not require exhaustion of every conceivable race-neutral alternative. Nor does it require a university to choose between maintaining a reputation for excellence or fulfilling a commitment to provide educational opportunities to members of all racial groups. Affirmed.

CONCURRENCE: (Ginsburg, J.) From today's vantage point, one may hope, but not firmly forecast, that over the next generation's span, progress toward nondiscrimination and genuinely equal opportunity will make it safe to sunset affirmative action.

DISSENT: (Rehnquist, C.J.) Although the law school claims it must take the steps it does to achieve "critical mass" of underrepresented minority students, its actual program bears no relation to this asserted goal. Stripped of its "critical mass" veil, the law school's (D) program is revealed as a naked effort to achieve racial balancing.

DISSENT: (Kennedy, J.) Refusal of the Court to apply strict scrutiny that is meaningful will lead to serious consequences. By deferring to the law school's (D) choice of minority admissions programs, courts will lose the talents and resources of the faculties and administrators in devising new and fairer ways to ensure individual consideration.

CONCURRENCE AND DISSENT: (Scalia, J.) Unlike a clear constitutional holding that racial preferences in state educational institutions are impermissible, or even a clear anticonstitutional holding, today's decision seems perversely designed to prolong the controversy and the litigation. The Constitution proscribes government discrimination on the basis of race, and state-provided education is no exception.

DISSENT: (Thomas, J.) Blacks can achieve in every avenue of American life without the meddling of university administrators. The majority upholds the law school's (D) racial discrimination not by interpreting the people's Constitution, but by responding to a faddish slogan.

Continued on next page.

▶ *ANALYSIS*

As seen in *Grutter* and predecessor Supreme Court decisions, not every decision influenced by race is equally
objectionable, and "strict scrutiny" is designed to provide
a framework for carefully examining the importance and
the sincerity of the reasons advanced by the governmental
decisionmaker for the use of race in any given context.

Quicknotes

EQUAL PROTECTION CLAUSE A constitutional provision
that each person be guaranteed the same protection of
the laws enjoyed by other persons in like circumstances.

Parents Involved in Community Schools v. Seattle School District No. 1

Parents of unadmitted students (P) v. Public school district (D)

551 U.S. 701 (2007).

NATURE OF CASE: Suits challenging school-assignment plans under the Equal Protection Clause.

FACT SUMMARY: Two metropolitan school districts sought to assign students to schools to achieve racial balance.

RULE OF LAW
Racial balance between local high school districts is not a compelling government interest under the Equal Protection Clause.

FACTS: The Seattle School District (Seattle) (D) implemented a student assignment plan designed to achieve numerically defined racial balance between Seattle's (D) ten public high schools. Seattle (D), however, had never been found to run racially segregated schools. The Jefferson County Public Schools in Louisville, Kentucky (Louisville), was under a desegregation order from 1975 to 2000; the order was dissolved in 2001 when a federal court ruled that Louisville (D) had reached unitary status by largely eliminating the district's earlier racial segregation. After the decree was dissolved, Louisville (D) voluntarily adopted a student assignment plan that required specific minimum and maximum enrollment percentages for black students. Parents (P) of students who were denied admission in each school district sued their respective district, alleging, in part, violations of the Equal Protection Clause. After the intermediate appellate courts in both cases upheld the assignment plans, the parents (P) petitioned the U.S. Supreme Court for further review.

ISSUE: Is racial balance between local high school districts a compelling government interest under the Equal Protection Clause?

HOLDING AND DECISION: (Roberts, C.J.) No. Racial balance between local high school districts is not a compelling government interest under the Equal Protection Clause. Because both school districts (D) have apportioned government benefits on the basis of race, the applicable standard of review in these cases is strict scrutiny: Seattle (D) and Louisville (D) must show that their race-based discrimination (1) advances a compelling government interest through (2) means that are narrowly tailored to achieve the intended purpose. The asserted interests in both Seattle (D) and Louisville (D) reduce to nothing more than the goal of numerical racial balance between each district's (D) schools. This Court has consistently found such a purpose illegitimate. *Grutter v. Bollinger*, 539 U.S. 306 (2003), does not control here because *Grutter* involved the specific interests of higher education; it is also instructive, though, that

Grutter upheld the law school admission policy there because racial diversity was only one of a mix of admissions criteria. Here, on the other hand, pure numerical racial balance, by itself, is the government interest, and that interest has never been recognized as valid. The plans at issue here also fail because the school districts (D) have failed to show that they seriously considered other means besides explicit racial classifications. Reversed.

CONCURRENCE: (Thomas, J.) Racial imbalance and racial segregation are not synonymous; it is possible to have racial imbalance through no conscious decision to segregate. Further, forced racial mixing of students may or may not provide educational benefits in general or higher achievement for black students in particular. The color-blind Constitution, then, requires that these student assignment plans be struck down.

CONCURRENCE: (Kennedy, J.) Contrary to the Chief Justice's plurality opinion, race can be considered as one among several factors in examining school enrollments. General, indirect solutions to problems of racial composition of schools are much better than the crude plans in these cases as ways to address those problems. The United States has special obligations to ensure equal opportunity for all children, and government should be permitted to consider race in its attempts to fulfill that mission. As the plurality correctly notes, though, government may not classify students based solely on race without first making a showing that such a step is necessary.

DISSENT: (Stevens, J.) In his demand of strict equality under the Constitution, the Chief Justice forgets that, before *Brown*, only black students were told where they could and could not go to school. Today's plurality decision rewrites the history of our landmark school-desegregation decision.

DISSENT: (Breyer, J.) These voluntary plans bear striking resemblance to plans that this Court has long required, permitted, and encouraged local school districts to formulate and use. Every branch of government has acknowledged that government may voluntarily use race-conscious plans to address race-based problems even when such plans are not constitutionally obligatory. The plurality overlooks the fact that no case has ever decided that all racial classifications should receive precisely the same scrutiny. Actually, our decisions have applied different standards to assess racial classifications depending on whether the government's purpose

Continued on next page.

was to exclude persons from, or to include persons in, government programs. The plurality's interpretation of strict scrutiny, however, would automatically invalidate all race-conscious government action. The school districts' (D) interest here serves remedial, educational, and democratic purposes; such a multiplicity of concerns means that *Grutter*'s rationale controls here and requires upholding these assignment plans. Even under the strictest scrutiny, though, the plans here pass muster under the Equal Protection Clause because they are more narrowly tailored than the plan approved in *Grutter*. Accordingly, these plans are consistent with equal protection of the laws.

▶ *ANALYSIS*

Chief Justice Roberts's plurality opinion in *Parents Involved* focuses on the firm percentages used by Seattle (D) and Louisville (D) in making student-assignment decisions. Despite Justice Breyer's objections in dissent, it is difficult to see how such an overtly numerical approach differs from the quota-based systems that the Court consistently has struck down under the Equal Protection Clause. See, e.g., *Regents of the University of California v. Bakke,* 438 U.S. 265, 307 (1978), "If [the University's] purpose is to assure within its student body some specified percentage of a particular group merely because of its race or ethnic origin, such a preferential purpose must be rejected not as insubstantial but as facially invalid."

■■■■

Quicknotes

EQUAL PROTECTION CLAUSE A constitutional provision that each person be guaranteed the same protection of the laws enjoyed by other persons in like circumstances.

STRICT SCRUTINY The method by which courts determine the constitutionality of a law when a law affects a fundamental right. Under the test, the legislature must have had a compelling interest to enact the law and measures prescribed by the law must be the least restrictive means possible to accomplish its goal.

■■■■

Craig v. Boren

Males 18–20 years of age (P) v. State (D)

429 U.S. 190 (1976).

NATURE OF CASE: Appeal from an action to have an Oklahoma statute declared unconstitutional.

FACT SUMMARY: Craig (P) appealed after a federal district court upheld two sections of an Oklahoma statute prohibiting the sale of "nonintoxicating" 3.2 percent beer to males under the age of 21 and to females under the age of 18 on the ground that such a gender-based differential did not constitute a denial to males 18–20 years of age of equal protection of the laws.

RULE OF LAW

Laws that establish classifications by gender must serve important governmental objectives and must be substantially related to achievement of those objectives to be constitutionally in line with the Equal Protection Clause.

FACTS: Craig (P) brought suit to have two sections of an Oklahoma statute, which prohibited the sale of "nonintoxicating" 3.2 percent beer to males under the age of 21 and to females under the age of 18, declared unconstitutional. Craig (P) contended that such a gender-based differential constituted a denial to males 18–20 years of age of the equal protection of the laws in violation of the Fourteenth Amendment. Boren (D), representing the State of Oklahoma, argued that this law was enacted as a traffic safety measure and that the protection of public health and safety was an important function of state and local governments. Boren (D) introduced statistical data demonstrating that 18–20-year-old male arrests for "driving under the influence" and "drunkenness" substantially exceeded female arrests for the same age range. The district court upheld the ordinance on the ground that it served the important governmental objective of traffic safety. Craig (P) appealed.

ISSUE: Are laws that establish classifications by gender constitutional if they do not serve important governmental objectives and are not substantially related to achievement of those objectives?

HOLDING AND DECISION: (Brennan, J.) No. Laws that establish classifications by gender must serve important governmental objectives and must be substantially related to achievement of those objectives to be constitutionally in line with the Equal Protection Clause. It appears that the objective underlying the statute in controversy is the enhancement of traffic safety. Clearly, the protection of public health and safety represents an important function of state and local governments. However, the statistics presented by Boren (D) in this Court's view cannot support the conclusion that the gender-based distinction closely serves to achieve the objective. The most relevant of the statistical surveys presented as evidence by Boren (D) in support of the statute, arrests of 18–20-year-olds for alcohol-related driving offenses, establish 2 percent more males than females are arrested for that offense. Such a disparity can hardly form the basis for employment of a gender line as a classifying device. Certainly, if maleness is to serve as a proxy for drinking and driving, a correlation of 2 percent must be considered unduly tenuous. Indeed, prior cases have consistently rejected the use of sex as a decision-making factor. Therefore, since the gender-based differential does not serve an important governmental objective, the Oklahoma statute constitutes a denial of the equal protection of the laws to males aged 18–20 and is unconstitutional. The judgment of the district court is reversed.

CONCURRENCE: (Powell, J.) The state legislature, by the classification it has chosen, has not adopted through the enactment of the statute a means that bears a fair and substantial relation to the objective of traffic safety.

CONCURRENCE: (Stevens, J.) It is difficult to believe that the statute in question was actually intended to cope with the problem of traffic safety, since it has only a minimal effect on access to a not-very-intoxicating beverage and does not prohibit its consumption.

DISSENT: (Rehnquist, J.) The Court's disposition of this case is objectionable on two grounds. First, is its conclusion that men challenging a gender-based statute that treats them less favorably than women may invoke a more stringent standard of judicial review than pertains to most other types of classifications. Second, is the court's enunciation of this standard, without citation to any source, as being that "classifications by gender must serve important governmental objectives and must be substantially related to achievement of those objectives." The Equal Protection Clause contains no such language, and none of our previous cases adopts that standard.

ANALYSIS

Cases concerning whether males and females should be considered as reaching a majority age equally has met with some stiff opposition. In *Stanton v. Stanton*, 552 P.2d 112 (1976), Utah Supreme Court Justice Ellett observed: "Regardless of what a judge may think about equality, his thinking cannot change the facts of life. . . . To judicially hold that males and females attain their maturity at the same age is to be blind to the biological facts of life."

Continued on next page.

Quicknotes

EQUAL PROTECTION CLAUSE A constitutional provision that each person be guaranteed the same protection of the laws enjoyed by other persons in like circumstances.

■■■■■

United States v. Virginia

Federal government (P) v. Public institution (D)

518 U.S. 515 (1996).

NATURE OF CASE: Appeal from final judgment upholding a college's male-only admission policy.

FACT SUMMARY: Virginia Military Institute (D), a state sponsored university, had a policy of excluding women from attending.

 RULE OF LAW
Public schools may not exclude women.

FACTS: Since 1839, Virginia Military Institute (VMI) (D), a Virginia (D) public institution, had been a male-only college that sought to train "citizen-soldiers." In 1990, the Attorney General (P) sued VMI (D) and Virginia (D), claiming that the admissions policy violated the Equal Protection Clause. Virginia (D) eventually proposed a remedial plan under which a parallel program would be developed for women. The Virginia Women's Institute for Leadership (VWIL) would be created at Mary Baldwin College. The trial court and an appellate court upheld this remedial plan, but the Attorney General (P) appealed and the Supreme Court granted a writ of certiorari.

ISSUE: May public schools exclude women?

HOLDING AND DECISION: (Ginsburg, J.) No. Public schools may not exclude women. States must show that a sex-based government action serves important governmental objectives and that the discriminatory means employed are substantially related to the achievement of those objectives. There must an exceedingly persuasive justification for the action. This heightened review standard prevents classifications that perpetuate the legal, social, and economic inferiority of women. While single-sex education may provide benefits to some students, Virginia (D) has not shown that it pursued this option as a means to providing a diversity of educational opportunities. On the other hand, the historical record shows that Virginia (D) has systematically prevented women from obtaining higher education until relatively recently. The fact that women have been successfully integrated into the armed forces and service academies demonstrates that VMI's (D) stature will not be downgraded by admitting women. The proposed VWIL does not qualify as VMI's (D) equal in terms of faculty, facilities, course offerings, and its reputation. Accordingly, since Virginia (D) is unable to provide substantial equal opportunities for women who desire to attend VMI (D), the male-only admission policy is unconstitutional. Reversed.

CONCURRENCE: (Rehnquist, J.) The majority decision is correct but there is no basis for stating that states must demonstrate an exceedingly persuasive justification to support sex-based classifications.

DISSENT: (Scalia, J.) The majority sweeps away an institution that has thrived for 150 years and the precedents of this Court to embark on a course of proscribing its own elite opinions on society. Virginia (D) has an important interest in providing education, and single-sex instruction is an approach substantially related to this goal. The proposed VWIL was designed for women and not designed to be exactly equal to VMI (D).

▶ *ANALYSIS*

Justice Scalia's dissent carries a tone of disgust for the majority opinion. As he did in *Romer v. Evans*, 517 U.S. 620 (1996), Scalia states that the majority seeks to satisfy some unidentified group of antimajoritarian elites. This attitude is unusual for a member of the Supreme Court since dissents are usually restricted to attacks on the majority's legal reasoning.

■=■

Quicknotes

EQUAL PROTECTION CLAUSE A constitutional provision that each person be guaranteed the same protection of the laws enjoyed by other persons in like circumstances.

■=■

Romer v. Evans

Municipality (P) v. State (D)

517 U.S. 620 (1996).

NATURE OF CASE: Review of order striking down state constitutional amendment.

FACT SUMMARY: A Colorado law that preempted local ordinances prohibiting discrimination against homosexuals was challenged as unconstitutional.

🏛 RULE OF LAW
States may not enact laws prohibiting localities from proscribing discrimination against a class of persons.

FACTS: In 1992, a statewide initiative was adopted by Colorado voters. The law, known as Amendment 2, preempted local ordinances from prohibiting discrimination on the basis of sexual preference. The Colorado Supreme Court struck down the law as contrary to Equal Protection. The U.S. Supreme Court granted review.

ISSUE: May states enact laws prohibiting localities from proscribing discrimination against a class of persons?

HOLDING AND DECISION: (Kennedy, J.) No. States may not enact laws prohibiting localities from proscribing discrimination against a class of persons. Amendment 2 has the peculiar property of imposing a broad rule on a singled named group, as it places a particular burden in terms of access to the political process. Groups not affected by this law have greater access to this process. This clearly implicates the Equal Protection Clause of the Fourteenth Amendment. Such a law must bear a rational relationship to a legitimate government purpose. Amendment 2 is a status-based law undertaken for its own sake without serving any legitimate interest. Therefore, it is unconstitutional. Affirmed.

DISSENT: (Scalia, J.) Amendment 2 is a modest attempt against assaults on basic morals by a politically powerful interest group. States must be free to disfavor conduct its citizens find reprehensible.

▶ ANALYSIS

Interestingly, the majority opinion here did not mention the last major case involving homosexuality, *Bowers v. Hardwick*, 478 U.S. 18 (1986). That case held it constitutional for a state to criminalize homosexual conduct. Assuming *Bowers* to still be good law, it seems that states can criminalize homosexual conduct, but cannot preempt local laws regarding homosexuals as a class.

Quicknotes

EQUAL PROTECTION A constitutional guarantee that no person shall be denied the same protection of the laws enjoyed by other persons in life circumstances.

RATIONAL BASIS REVIEW A test employed by the court to determine the validity of a statute in equal protection actions, whereby the court determines whether the challenged statute is rationally related to the achievement of a legitimate state interest.

SUSPECT CLASSIFICATION A class of persons that have historically been subject to discriminatory treatment; statutes drawing a distinction between persons based on a suspect classification, i.e., race, nationality or alienage, are subject to a strict scrutiny standard of review.

Sugarman v. Dougall

State (D) v. Alien (P)

413 U.S. 634 (1973).

NATURE OF CASE: Appeal of ruling invalidating state law prohibiting aliens from civil service employment.

FACT SUMMARY: New York (D) had a statutory system prohibiting aliens from civil service positions involving competitive examinations.

🏛 RULE OF LAW
A state may not refuse all civil service positions on the basis of alienage alone.

FACTS: New York (D) prohibited aliens from civil service positions requiring competitive examinations. All civil service positions not involving election or appointment were based on examination scores. Dougall (P), an alien, challenged this as a violation of equal protection. The lower court held the system unconstitutional.

ISSUE: May a state refuse all civil service positions on the basis of alienage alone?

HOLDING AND DECISION: (Blackmun, J.) No. A state may not refuse all civil service positions on the basis of alienage alone. Aliens have a history of being a discrete and insular minority, and therefore classifications based on alienage trigger strict scrutiny, which means the classification must advance a compelling interest and be narrowly drawn. New York (D) argues that it has an interest in allowing into the civil service system only those free of competing loyalties. This is an important interest, but the statute excludes from alien employment positions in which this interest is irrelevant, while not including higher-level positions where the interest is greater. As the statute is both under- and over-inclusive, it must fail. Affirmed.

DISSENT: (Rehnquist, J.) Unlike race, alienage should not trigger heightened scrutiny, so all that New York (D) should have been required to show was a rational basis for the classification, something it could have done.

▶ ANALYSIS

Several factors are taken into account in deciding upon whether a class will be suspect. As the Court said in the opinion, a history of being a discrete minority is a factor. Other factors are a history of discrimination and immutable distinguishing characteristics. Obviously, not all factors must be present at all times, as alienage is not an immutable characteristic.

Quicknotes

EQUAL PROTECTION CLAUSE A constitutional provision that each person be guaranteed the same protection of the laws enjoyed by other persons in like circumstances.

Implied Fundamental Rights

Quick Reference Rules of Law

PAGE

1. **The Privileges or Immunities Clause.** The Privileges and Immunities Clause of the Fourteenth Amendment only guarantees those federal rights protected as of the time of the amendment's adoption. (The Slaughter-House Cases) 75

2. **Substantive Due Process: The Protection of Economic Interests and the Question of Redistribution.** To be a fair, reasonable, and appropriate use of a state's police power, an act must have a direct relation, as a means to an end, to an appropriate and legitimate state objective. (Lochner v. New York) 76

3. **Fundamental Interests and the Equal Protection Clause.** A statute that arbitrarily excludes a class from its purview violates the Equal Protection Clause of the Fourteenth Amendment where fundamental rights are involved. (Skinner v. Oklahoma) 78

4. **Denial of the "Right to Vote."** The right to vote is a fundamental and basic right, and where such rights are asserted under the Equal Protection Clause, classifications that might restrain those rights must be closely scrutinized and carefully confined. Lines drawn on the basis of wealth or property, like those of race, are traditionally disfavored. (Harper v. Virginia State Board of Elections) 79

5. **Denial of the "Right to Vote."** A statute that grants the right to vote to some residents of requisite age and citizenship and denies this right to others must be subjected to strict scrutiny by the court. (Kramer v. Union Free School District) 80

6. **Dilution of the "Right to Vote."** As nearly as practicable, a state apportionment system must reflect a state's population distribution. (Reynolds v. Sims) 81

7. **Dilution of the "Right to Vote."** An at-large voting system, not created specifically to discriminate against a minority's voting power, is not unconstitutional. (City of Mobile v. Bolden) 82

8. **Travel.** Any classification that serves to penalize the exercise of a constitutional right is unconstitutional unless it is shown to be necessary to promote a compelling governmental interest, rather than merely shown to be rationally related to a legitimate purpose. (Shapiro v. Thompson) 83

9. **Education.** A public education financing system that involves substantial disparities in expenditure amounts between the districts is not unconstitutional. (San Antonio Independent School District v. Rodriguez) 85

10. **Education.** Absent a showing that such a policy furthers a substantial state interest, a state may not deny a public education to the children of undocumented aliens. (Plyler v. Doe) 86

11. **The Right of Privacy.** The right to privacy, although not explicitly stated in the Bill of Rights, is a penumbra, formed by certain other explicit guarantees. As such, it is protected against state regulation that sweeps unnecessarily broad. (Griswold v. Connecticut) 87

CHAPTER 6

12. Abortion. The right of privacy found in the Fourteenth Amendment's concept of personal liberty and restrictions upon state action is broad enough to encompass a woman's decision whether or not to terminate her pregnancy. (Roe v. Wade) ... *88*

13. Abortion. A law is unconstitutional as an undue burden on a woman's right to an abortion before fetal viability, if the law places a substantial obstacle in the path of a woman seeking to exercise her right. (Planned Parenthood of Southeastern Pennsylvania v. Casey) ... *90*

14. Abortion. The Partial-Birth Abortion Ban Act does not place a substantial obstacle to late-term, but pre-viability, abortions. (Gonzales v. Carhart) ... *92*

15. Family and Other "Privacy" Interests. Legislation that makes consensual sodomy between adults in their own dwelling criminal violates due process. (Lawrence v. Texas) ... *93*

16. The Right to Die. A state may require clear and convincing evidence of consent by an individual prior to the cessation of life support procedures upon that individual. (Cruzan v. Director, Missouri Department of Health) ... *94*

17. The Right to Die. The "liberty" protections of the Due Process Clause of the Fourteenth Amendment do not include a right to commit suicide with another's assistance. (Washington v. Glucksberg) ... *95*

18. Liberty and Property Interests. A public employee who can be discharged only for cause is entitled to a pretermination hearing. (Cleveland Board of Education v. Loudermill) ... *96*

19. What Process is Due. An evidentiary hearing is not required prior to the termination of disability benefits. (Mathews v. Eldridge) ... *97*

20. The Contracts Clause. Legislation postponing enforcement of mortgages, when tailored to an emergency situation, does not violate the Contracts Clause. (Home Building & Loan Association v. Blaisdell) ... *98*

21. The Eminent Domain Clause. While private property may be regulated to a certain degree, a taking under the Fifth Amendment will be found if the regulation results in a severe diminution of value. At a certain magnitude, there must be an exercise of eminent domain and compensation to sustain the regulatory act. While considerable deference is to be given the legislature's judgment, each case will turn upon its particular facts. (Pennsylvania Coal Co. v. Mahon) ... *99*

22. The Eminent Domain Clause. The state does not exceed its constitutional powers by deciding upon the destruction of one class of private property in order to save another which, in the judgment of the legislature, is of greater value to the public. Where the choice is unavoidable, there is no denial of due process, and compensation need not be given the private owners affected. (Miller v. Schoene) ... *101*

23. The Eminent Domain Clause. A city may, as part of a comprehensive landmark preservation scheme, place restrictions on development affecting the landmark without paying "just compensation." (Penn Central Transportation Co. v. New York City) ... *102*

24. The Eminent Domain Clause. Where regulation prohibits all economically beneficial use of land, and the proscribed use could not have been prohibited under state nuisance law, the regulation is a "taking" that requires "just compensation" to be paid to the landowner. (Lucas v. South Carolina Coastal Council) ... *103*

25. The Eminent Domain Clause. A landowner not deprived of all economic use of property by a state's designation as coastal wetlands, has not had the property taken in violation of the Takings Clause of the Fifth Amendment. (Palazzolo v. Rhode Island) ... *104*

The Slaughter-House Cases

Slaughterhouses (P) v. State (D)

83 U.S. (16 Wall.) 36 (1873).

NATURE OF CASE: Appeal of ruling upholding a state-imposed slaughterhouse monopoly.

FACT SUMMARY: The State of Louisiana granted a monopoly to a certain slaughterhouse, and this was challenged as being contrary to the Fourteenth Amendment.

RULE OF LAW

The Privileges and Immunities Clause of the Fourteenth Amendment only guarantees those federal rights protected as of the time of the amendment's adoption.

FACTS: The State of Louisiana (D) conferred by statute a monopoly in the slaughterhouse business on a certain slaughterhouse. Competing slaughterhouses (P) challenged this as an abridgement of the right to own and use property, which the plaintiffs contended was a right guaranteed by the Privileges and Immunities Clause of the Fourteenth Amendment. The lower courts upheld the statute.

ISSUE: Does the Privileges and Immunities Clause of the Fourteenth Amendment only guarantee those federal rights protected as of the time of the amendment's adoption?

HOLDING AND DECISION: (Miller, J.) Yes. The Privileges and Immunities Clause of the Fourteenth Amendment only guarantees those federal rights protected as of the time of the amendment's adoption. The amendment must be interpreted in light of its purpose. The first section overrules the *Dred Scott* decision, 60 U.S. (19 How.) 393 (1987), by conferring both national and state citizenship on those born in the United States. It would be a major leap to presume, however, that the amendment was intended to change the nature of the privileges granted by the United States vis-à-vis the states. Certain federally guaranteed rights do exist, but, by and large, the extent to which individual freedoms and rights have been granted is a matter of state prerogative, and the Court is not inclined to hold that the amendment alters that. Affirmed.

DISSENT: (Field, J.) The amendment should be construed as guaranteeing basic freedoms for all U.S. citizens. Even holding, as the Court does, that the clause goes no further than the Privileges and Immunities Clause of Article IV, the result should be different. The freedom to engage in one's livelihood is a basic freedom.

DISSENT: (Bradley, J.) The right to follow one's employment of choice is the most basic of rights and should be protected by the clause.

▶ ANALYSIS

The Slaughter-House Cases represents the first major Supreme Court pronouncement on the Fourteenth Amendment. It was argued that the Privileges and Immunities Clause applied the Bill of Rights to the states and this was rejected. The Court has, of course, largely done this by using the Equal Protection and Due Process Clauses. Some have said that the Court would have been more honest in applying the Bill of Rights to the states by overruling the *Slaughter-House Cases*, but it has not seen fit to do this.

Quicknotes

DUE PROCESS CLAUSE Clauses found in the Fifth and Fourteenth Amendments to the United States Constitution providing that no person shall be deprived of "life, liberty, or property, without due process of law."

EQUAL PROTECTION CLAUSE A constitutional provision that each person be guaranteed the same protection of the laws enjoyed by other persons in like circumstances.

FOURTEENTH AMENDMENT Declares that no state shall make or enforce any law that shall abridge the privileges and immunities of citizens of the United States. No state shall deny to any person within its jurisdiction the equal protection of the laws.

Lochner v. New York

Bakery owner (D) v. State (P)

198 U.S. 45 (1905).

NATURE OF CASE: Appeal from conviction for violation of a labor law.

FACT SUMMARY: A state labor law prohibited employment in bakeries for more than 60 hours a week or more than 10 hours a day. Lochner (D) permitted an employee in his bakery to work over 60 hours in one week.

🏛 RULE OF LAW
To be a fair, reasonable, and appropriate use of a state's police power, an act must have a direct relation, as a means to an end, to an appropriate and legitimate state objective.

FACTS: Lochner (D) was fined for violating a state labor law. The law prohibited employment in bakeries for more than 60 hours a week or more than 10 hours a day. Lochner (D) permitted an employee to work in his bakery for more than 60 hours in one week.

ISSUE: To be a fair, reasonable, and appropriate use of a state's police power, must an act have a direct relation, as a means to an end, to an appropriate and legitimate state objective?

HOLDING AND DECISION: (Peckham, J.) Yes. To be a fair, reasonable, and appropriate use of a state's police power, an act must have a direct relation, as a means to an end, to an appropriate and legitimate state objective. The general fight to make a contract in relation to one's business is part of the liberty of the individual protected by the Fourteenth Amendment. The right to purchase or sell labor is part of the liberty protected by this amendment. However, the states do possess certain police powers relating to the safety, health, morals, and general welfare of the public. If the contract is one that the state, in the exercise of its police power, has the right to prohibit, the Fourteenth Amendment will not prevent the state's prohibition. When, as here, the state acts to limit the right to labor or the right to contract, it is necessary to determine whether the rights of the state or the individual shall prevail. The Fourteenth Amendment limits the state's exercise of its police power; otherwise the state would have unbounded power once it stated that legislation was to conserve the health, morals, or safety of its people. It is not sufficient to assert that the act relates to public health. Rather, it must have a more direct relation, as a means to an end, to an appropriate state goal, before an act can interfere with an individual's right to contract in relation to his labor. In this case, there is no reasonable foundation for holding the act to be necessary to the health of the public or of bakery officials. Statutes such as this one are mere meddlesome interferences with the rights of the individual. They are invalid unless there is some fair ground to say that there is material danger to the public health or to the employees' health if the labor hours are not curtailed. It cannot be said that the production of healthy bread depends upon the hours that the employees work. Nor is the trade of a baker an unhealthy one to the degree that would authorize the legislature to interfere with the rights to labor and of free contract. Lochner's (D) conviction is reversed.

DISSENT: (Harlan, J.) Whether or not this would be wise legislation is not a question for this Court. It is impossible to say that there is not substantial or real regulation between the statute and the state's legitimate goals. This decision brings under the court's supervision matters that supposedly belonged exclusively to state legislatures.

DISSENT: (Holmes, J.) The word "liberty" in the Fourteenth Amendment should not invalidate a statute unless it can be said that a reasonable person would say that the statute infringes fundamental principles of our people and our law. A reasonable person might think this statute valid. Citizens' liberty is regulated by many state laws that have been held to be valid, i.e., the Sunday laws, the lottery laws, and laws requiring vaccination.

▶ ANALYSIS

From the *Lochner* decision in 1905 to the 1930's the Court invalidated a considerable number of laws on substantive due process grounds, such as laws fixing minimum wages, maximum hours, prices, and laws regulating business activities. The modern Court claims to have rejected the *Lochner* doctrine. It has withdrawn careful scrutiny in most economic areas but has maintained and increased intervention with respect to a variety of non-economic liberties. However, not only economic regulations were struck down under *Lochner*. That doctrine formed the basis for absorbing rights such as those in the First Amendment into the Fourteenth Amendment concept of liberty. *Lochner* also helped justify on behalf of other non-economic rights such as the right to teach in a foreign language (*Meyers v. Nebraska*, 262 U.S. 390). *Meyers* was to be relied upon in the birth control decision, *Griswold v. Connecticut*.

■■■

Continued on next page.

Quicknotes

DUE PROCESS CLAUSE Clauses found in the Fifth and Fourteenth Amendments to the United States Constitution providing that no person shall be deprived of "life, liberty, or property, without due process of law."

FOURTEENTH AMENDMENT Declares that no state shall make or enforce any law that shall abridge the privileges and immunities of citizens of the United States. No state shall deny to any person within its jurisdiction the equal protection of the laws.

Skinner v. Oklahoma

Criminal (D) v. State (P)

316 U.S. 535 (1942).

NATURE OF CASE: Constitutional challenge to state law.

FACT SUMMARY: Skinner (D) was deemed to be a habitual criminal and was ordered sterilized under a state (P) statute.

🏛 RULE OF LAW
A statute that arbitrarily excludes a class from its purview violates the Equal Protection Clause of the Fourteenth Amendment where fundamental rights are involved.

FACTS: Skinner (D) was convicted of crimes on three separate occasions. Under an Oklahoma (P) statute he could be declared a habitual criminal and could be ordered to be sterilized to prevent the passing on of criminal genetic traits. The statute applied to those convicted of two or more crimes amounting to felonies involving moral turpitude. The Attorney General could maintain a suit to have the convicted party sterilized. A full trial would be held. The issue was confined to whether the party was a habitual criminal and whether he should be sterilized. Offenses arising out of violations of prohibitory laws, revenue acts, embezzlement, or political offenses were not within the purview of the Act. Skinner (D) was adjudged a habitual criminal and was ordered sterilized. Skinner (D) challenged the constitutionality of the statute.

ISSUE: May a state arbitrarily discriminate between like classes where fundamental rights are involved?

HOLDING AND DECISION: (Douglas, J.) No. A statute that arbitrarily excludes a class from its purview violates the Equal Protection Clause of the Fourteenth Amendment where fundamental rights are involved. We do not pass on the constitutionality of sterilization of habitual criminals or the state's procedure. We do find that the State (P) statute is unconstitutional under the Equal Protection Clause of the Fourteenth Amendment. We are dealing herein with a fundamental right, i.e., the right to have children. Statutes dealing with such rights are closely scrutinized. While a state may treat classes unequally based on experience, it may not arbitrarily seek to add or exclude a particular group from treatment. There must be a rational basis for the distinction. The law treats the embezzler in the same manner as other criminals, e.g., those convicted of grand larceny. There is no viable difference between their offenses or gene traits. Failure to treat them equally under the sterilization statute cannot be supported and violates the Equal Protection Clause. The statute is unconstitutional on its face. Reversed.

CONCURRENCE: (Stone, J.) There is no scientific proof that criminal tendencies are inherited. I would find that the statute violates personal liberties secured by the Due Process Clause. The law sets up arbitrary standards that cannot be supported by evidence/fact.

▌ ANALYSIS

A law that condemns, without hearing, all of the individuals of a class to a harsh measure merely because some or many are deserving of such treatment, lacks the basic attributes of due process. *Morrison v. California*, 291 U.S. 82. In *Skinner*, the Court expressly left the constitutional issue as to sterilization open even if the equal protection problem was solved. This is based on the Court's concern to decide all cases on the narrowest possible grounds.

■▬■

Quicknotes

DUE PROCESS CLAUSE Clauses found in the Fifth and Fourteenth Amendments to the United States Constitution providing that no person shall be deprived of "life, liberty, or property, without due process of law."

EQUAL PROTECTION CLAUSE A constitutional provision that each person be guaranteed the same protection of the laws enjoyed by other persons in like circumstances.

FOURTEENTH AMENDMENT Declares that no state shall make or enforce any law that shall abridge the privileges and immunities of citizens of the United States. No state shall deny to any person within its jurisdiction the equal protection of the laws.

■▬■

Harper v. Virginia State Board of Elections

Taxpayers (P) v. Board of elections (D)

383 U.S. 663 (1966).

NATURE OF CASE: Suits challenging the constitutionality of Virginia's poll tax.

FACT SUMMARY: Harper (P) and other Virginia residents brought this suit to have Virginia's (D) poll tax declared unconstitutional.

🏛 RULE OF LAW
The right to vote is a fundamental and basic right, and where such rights are asserted under the Equal Protection Clause, classifications that might restrain those rights must be closely scrutinized and carefully confined. Lines drawn on the basis of wealth or property, like those of race, are traditionally disfavored.

FACTS: Harper (P) and other Virginia residents brought these suits to have Virginia's (D) poll tax declared unconstitutional. The three-judge district court, being bound by the court's decision in *Breedlove v. Suttles*, 302 U.S. 277 (1937), dismissed the complaint. Harper (P) appealed. The law at issue conditions the right to vote in state elections upon the payment of a poll tax.

ISSUE: Is a poll tax, the payment of which is a required prerequisite for voting, constitutional?

HOLDING AND DECISION: (Douglas, J.) No. The right to vote is a fundamental and basic right, and where such rights are asserted under the Equal Protection Clause, classifications that might restrain those rights must be closely scrutinized and carefully confined. Lines drawn on the basis of wealth or property, like those of race, are traditionally disfavored. A state violates the Equal Protection Clause whenever it makes the affluence of the voter or the payment of a fee an electoral standard. The right to vote is a basic and fundamental one, especially since it preserves other rights. Any alleged infringement on the right to vote must be carefully scrutinized. A state's interest, when it comes to voting, is limited to the power to fix qualifications. Wealth, like race or creed or color, is irrelevant to one's ability to participate intelligently in the electoral process. Further lines drawn on the basis of wealth or property, like those of race, are traditionally disfavored. The requirement of the payment of a fee as a condition of obtaining a ballot causes invidious discrimination. *Breedlove* sanctioned this use of the poll tax, and to that extent it is overruled. Reversed.

DISSENT: (Black, J.) So long as a distinction drawn is not irrational, unreasonable, or invidious, it must be upheld. There are certainly rational reasons for Virginia's poll tax, such as the state's desire to collect revenue and its belief that voters who pay a poll tax will be interested in furthering the state's welfare. Hence, the tax must be upheld. If it is to be struck down, it should be done by the legislature, rather than the courts.

DISSENT: (Harlan, J.) The Equal Protection Clause does not impose upon this country an ideology of unrestrained egalitarianism.

⏵ ANALYSIS

If, as the dissenters in *Harper* argue, the poll tax classification is not wholly "irrational," the case represents a greater intervention than the courts undertook under old equal protection. There is some question as to whether this greater scrutiny was because the "fundamental rights" of voting are affected or because "lines drawn on the basis of wealth" are traditionally disfavored. In *McDonald v. Board of Election Commissioners*, 394 U.S. 802 (1969), the Court sees wealth as an independent ground (apart from impact on fundamental rights) for strict scrutiny. There is a series of cases preceding and following *Harper* (among them *Reynolds v. Sims*) that support the invoking of strict scrutiny when voting rights are affected.

Quicknotes

STRICT SCRUTINY The method by which courts determine the constitutionality of a law, when a law affects a fundamental right. Under the test, the legislature must have had a compelling interest to enact the law and measures prescribed by the law must be the least restrictive means possible to accomplish its goal.

Kramer v. Union Free School District

Unmarried taxpayer (P) v. School district (D)

395 U.S. 621 (1969).

NATURE OF CASE: Action challenging the constitutionality of a state law.

FACT SUMMARY: A New York law provided that residents who were otherwise eligible to vote in state and federal elections may vote in the school district election only if they owned or leased taxable property in the district or had custody of children enrolled in local public schools.

RULE OF LAW
A statute that grants the right to vote to some residents of requisite age and citizenship and denies this right to others must be subjected to strict scrutiny by the court.

FACTS: A New York law provided that in certain school districts, residents who were otherwise eligible to vote in state and federal elections may vote in the school district elections only if they owned or leased taxable property within the district or had custody of children enrolled in local public schools. Kramer (P) was a childless bachelor who neither owned nor leased taxable property. He claimed the law violated equal protection.

ISSUE: Must a statute that grants the right to vote to some residents of requisite age and citizenship and denies this right to others be subjected to strict scrutiny by the court?

HOLDING AND DECISION: (Warren, C.J.) Yes. The right to vote in a free and unimpaired manner is preservative of other basic and civil rights. Any unjustified discrimination in determining who may vote undermines the legitimacy of representative government. Hence, a statute that grants the right to vote to some residents of requisite age and citizenship while denying the right to others must be subjected to strict scrutiny by the Court. Such statutes are not granted the presumption of constitutionality given other state laws, and they must be supported by a compelling state interest rather than merely a rational basis. Here, assuming arguendo that, as New York argues, a state can limit the right to vote to those primarily interested, close scrutiny demonstrates that this law does not accomplish this purpose with sufficient precision since it denies the right to many who might be so interested.

DISSENT: (Stewart, J.) This law has a rational basis. A stricter standard is not applicable, since neither a racial classification nor any constitutionally protected right is involved. "The Constitution does not confer the right of suffrage upon anyone."

ANALYSIS

In *Ciariano v. City of Houma*, 395 U.S. 701 (1969), decided the same day as *Kramer*, the Court was unanimous in invalidating a law granting only property taxpayers the right to vote on the approval of the issuance of revenue bonds by a municipal utility. The Court noted that the revenue bonds would be financed from the operation of the utilities, not from property taxes. In a concurring notation, Justices Black and Stewart stated that this case, unlike *Kramer*, involved a voting classification wholly irrelevant to the achievement of the state's objective.

◼◼◼

Quicknotes

STRICT SCRUTINY REVIEW A test employed by the court to determine the constitutionality of a statute, whereby the proponent of the statute must demonstrate that classifications drawn therein serve a compelling interest and are necessary for the furtherance of a state objective.

◼◼◼

Reynolds v. Sims

Parties not identified.

377 U.S. 533 (1964).

NATURE OF CASE: Appeal of ruling invalidating state legislative apportionment schemes.

FACT SUMMARY: The apportionment systems of several states were challenged as not reflecting the states' population distributions.

RULE OF LAW

As nearly as practicable, a state apportionment system must reflect a state's population distribution.

FACTS: The apportionment systems of several states were not based solely on the one-person-one-vote principle but rather took other factors into consideration, with the result being that the various districts had unequal populations. In six companion cases, the constitutionality of this practice was challenged.

ISSUE: As nearly as practicable, must a state apportionment system reflect a state's population distribution?

HOLDING AND DECISION: (Warren, C.J.) Yes. As nearly as practicable, a state apportionment system must reflect a state's population distribution. The right to vote is the most basic right in a democratic society, and all other rights are derivative of this right. To the extent a citizen's right to vote is diluted, his citizenship is diluted. A state may have an interest in protecting certain segments of society, but the giving of unequal voting power is not the way to accomplish it. A state is free, in keeping with the one-person-one-vote principle, to draw districts roughly approximating political subdivisions, so long as that principle is in fact adhered to. The main consideration, however, is not to dilute the voting power of any portion of the electorate. Affirmed and remanded.

DISSENT: (Harlan, J.) The legislative history of the Fourteenth Amendment shows that it was not intended to intrude on the internal workings of a state legislature.

DISSENT: (Stewart, J.) The political process is a way in which to accommodate the competing interests of various groups and regions, and it may well be legitimate to have an apportionment scheme giving greater precedence to this than to the one-person-one-vote principle.

▶ ANALYSIS

An important principle underlying this decision was the protection of majority rule. In some of the states involved in the present action, control was effectively in the hands of political minorities. As the Court made clear, the dilution of the majority's voting power was not the way to protect minority interests.

Quicknotes

FOURTEENTH AMENDMENT Declares that no state shall make or enforce any law that shall abridge the privileges and immunities of citizens of the United States. No state shall deny to any person within its jurisdiction the equal protection of the laws.

City of Mobile v. Bolden

Municipality (D) v. Voters (P)

446 U.S. 55 (1980).

NATURE OF CASE: Appeal of ruling invalidating an at-large voting system.

FACT SUMMARY: The City of Mobile (D) maintained an at-large city commission voting system, rather than one broken into districts.

🏛 RULE OF LAW
An at-large voting system, not created specifically to discriminate against a minority's voting power, is not unconstitutional.

FACTS: The City of Mobile (D) was governed by a three-person board of commissioners. Each commissioner was elected by the city at large, not by a district. No black had ever been elected to the commission. The at-large voting structure was challenged as unconstitutionally submerging the voting power of minorities. The lower court found the system unconstitutional without finding any purposeful discrimination in the system, and ordered the City (D) to change to a mayor-council system.

ISSUE: Is an at-large voting system, not created specifically to discriminate against a minority's voting power, unconstitutional?

HOLDING AND DECISION: (Stewart, J.) No. An at-large voting system not created specifically to discriminate against a minority's voting power is not unconstitutional. Only if there is purposeful discrimination by a governmental entity does an equal protection violation occur. There is no inherent right to proportional representation of any political group. Since the evidence did not prove intentional discrimination, no violation of a constitutional right occurred. Reversed and remanded.

CONCURRENCE: (Blackmun, J.) While the evidence does show purposeful discrimination, the remedy ordered by the district court was too far-reaching.

CONCURRENCE: (Stevens, J.) The proper standard for weighing a voting system should be whether it has a significant adverse impact on a political group, has any neutral justification, and was the product of a routine political decision.

DISSENT: (Brennan, J.) Proof of discriminatory impact is all that is needed for a plaintiff to prevail.

DISSENT: (White, J.) The facts do support purposeful discrimination.

DISSENT: (Marshall, J.) Equal protection is not the issue here, the denial of a fundamental right is. Each political group has a fundamental right to political representation. When fundamental rights are involved, a discriminatory impact is all that is required.

▶ ANALYSIS

The present decision was a plurality one. It is not clear whether or not a precedent has been set that there is no inherent right to group representation. If one looks at the issue presented here as one of equal protection and not of fundamental rights, as the Court did, the Court's holding would appear consistent with the jurisprudence of equal protection.

■━■

Quicknotes

EQUAL PROTECTION CLAUSE A constitutional provision that each person be guaranteed the same protection of the laws enjoyed by other persons in like circumstances.

■━■

Shapiro v. Thompson

Parties not identified

394 U.S. 618 (1969).

NATURE OF CASE: Appeal from decisions holding residency requirements for welfare applicants unconstitutional.

FACT SUMMARY: Statutory provisions deny welfare assistance to residents who have not resided within their jurisdiction for at least one year.

🏛 RULE OF LAW

Any classification that serves to penalize the exercise of a constitutional right is unconstitutional unless it is shown to be necessary to promote a compelling governmental interest, rather than merely shown to be rationally related to a legitimate purpose.

FACTS: A three-judge district court held unconstitutional certain state and District of Columbia statutory provisions. The provisions denied welfare assistance to residents of the state or district who have not resided within their jurisdictions for at least one year immediately preceding their applications for such assistance.

ISSUE: Does a statutory prohibition of welfare benefits to residents of less than a year create a classification denying them equal protection of the laws?

HOLDING AND DECISION: (Brennan, J.) Yes. Any classification that serves to penalize the exercise of a constitutional right is unconstitutional unless it is shown to be necessary to promote a compelling governmental interest, rather than merely shown to be rationally related to a legitimate purpose. The states justify the waiting period requirement as a protective device to preserve the fiscal integrity of their public assistance programs, by discouraging needy families from entering their jurisdictions. However, this act of inhibiting migration by needy persons into the state is constitutionally impermissible, since the right to travel from state to state is protected by the Constitution from laws or regulations that would unreasonably burden such movement. If a law has no other purpose than to chill the assertion of constitutional rights by penalizing those who choose to exercise them, it is patently unconstitutional. Further, the statutes create two classes of persons, different only in that one class has been in the area for one year. A state has a valid interest in preserving the fiscal integrity of its programs. But it cannot accomplish this purpose by invidious discrimination between classes of its citizens. The saving of welfare costs cannot be an independent ground for invidious classification. The states also assert that the waiting period serves certain administrative goals. They contend that a mere showing of a rational relationship and these permissible state goals will justify the classification. This is not true. As stated above, the right to travel is a constitutional right. Any classification that serves to penalize the exercise of a constitutional right is unconstitutional unless it is shown to be necessary to promote a compelling governmental interest. All of the administrative arguments advanced are either unfounded, irrational, or may be accomplished by a less drastic means. The district court's judgment is affirmed.

CONCURRENCE: (Stewart, J.) Contrary to the view of Justice Harlan in his dissent, this decision does not create a new "fundamental right" but merely gives force to a long-recognized constitutional right, the right to travel.

DISSENT: (Warren, C.J.) Since Congress has imposed a residency requirement in the District of Columbia and authorized the states, who receive federal funds for their welfare programs, to do the same, the real issue is whether Congress can create minimal residency requirements. Congress's right to enact a variety of restrictions upon interstate travel pursuant to its commerce power has been upheld in a number of prior cases. They require only that Congress have a rational basis for finding that a chosen regulatory scheme is necessary to the furtherance of interstate commerce. Congress had a rational basis for concluding that the insubstantial restriction imposed by residence requirements would, in the end, foster a climate more conducive to an enhanced flow of commerce and, in the long run, to personal mobility.

DISSENT: (Harlan, J.) The equal protection argument accepted by the majority has, in reality, two branches. Since any departure from equal protection requires a compelling governmental interest as justification under this theory, there are actually two separate types of equal protection violations. The "suspect classification" branch is well-founded in the racial groupings from which the Fourteenth Amendment sprang. But the other branch is far more troubling, since it looks to "fundamental rights." But the traditional equal protection approach required only that the state show a rational justification for its acts. To now require a "compelling interest" in these cases is to create in this Court a super legislature somehow imbued with a special intelligence and expertise in regulating the internal affairs of the states. Using the traditional, and proper, approach to equal protection, there are perfectly adequate rational justifications for the states to impose a welfare residency requirement and this Court has no authority to create new "fundamental rights" as it has done in this case.

Continued on next page.

▶ *ANALYSIS*

Many agreed with Harlan's dissent that the Court was simply resurrecting the judicial intervention of substantive due process under the guise of a new stricter equal protection test. One commentator warned, "Looming down the path is the specter of economic due process, of judges riding to the rescue of Oklahoma's opticians or the Railway Express Agency." Supporters of the new doctrine answered that it was limited to minorities that seem permanently voiceless and invisible and whom the power structure in the political process tends to ignore. Subsequent decisions have shown the Court to be willing to expand the number of suspect classifications to include national origin and sex as well as race.

■▬■

Quicknotes

EQUAL PROTECTION CLAUSE A constitutional provision that each person be guaranteed the same protection of the laws enjoyed by other persons in like circumstances.

■▬■

San Antonio Independent School District v. Rodriguez

School district (D) v. Students (P)

411 U.S. 1 (1973).

NATURE OF CASE: Appeal of ruling invalidating a public school system financing scheme.

FACT SUMMARY: The San Antonio School District (D) had a property tax-based financing system whereby schools in the more affluent neighborhoods received a higher per-pupil expenditure than those in poorer areas.

🏛 RULE OF LAW
A public education financing system that involves substantial disparities in expenditure amounts between the districts is not unconstitutional.

FACTS: The San Antonio School District (D) was largely funded by property taxes, with the taxes of each subdistrict being spent on the school in that district. The result of this was that the per-pupil expenditures in schools in affluent neighborhoods were much higher than those in poorer ones. This disparity was challenged in federal court and the district court, applying strict scrutiny, held the system unconstitutional.

ISSUE: Is a public education financing system that involves substantial disparities in expenditure amounts between the districts unconstitutional?

HOLDING AND DECISION: (Powell, J.) No. A public education financing system that involves substantial disparities in expenditure amounts between the districts is not unconstitutional. Such a system will be subject to strict scrutiny only if it abridges a fundamental right or involves a suspect class. Wealth (or the lack thereof) triggers heightened scrutiny only when that class is completely deprived of some desired benefit. This was not the case here, as it was not contended that the education the plaintiffs received under the system is worthless. Education is, of course, a basic right that might trigger strict scrutiny, but that right was not denied here because, as stated above, it was not contended that the plaintiffs are receiving no education. Since strict scrutiny is not called for, all that must be shown is that the school financing system is rational. Financing public education is a particularly local endeavor, and the Court is reluctant to interfere with it. Reversed.

DISSENT: (White, J.) No showing was made here that the state school financing system was rationally related to any legitimate state interest.

DISSENT: (Marshall, J.) The right to a public education is fundamental. Deprivation of this right need not consist of absolute deprivation. Substandard provision of a right is also deprivation. Also, no legitimate state interest appears to be served by the financing scheme. Finally, strict adherence to the two-tier system of review is proving insufficient as a standard of constitutional review.

▶ ANALYSIS

Despite the protestations of Justice Marshall, the Court declined to declare public education a fundamental right. The Court, which has since been loath to carve out new fundamental rights, has not reversed itself. It does seem odd that something like travel would be considered a fundamental right while education is not, but that is the status of the law.

Quicknotes

HEIGHTENED SCRUTINY A purposefully vague judicial description of all levels of scrutiny more exacting than minimal scrutiny.

STRICT SCRUTINY REVIEW A test employed by the court to determine the constitutionality of a statute, whereby the proponent of the statute must demonstrate that classifications drawn therein serve a compelling interest and are necessary for the furtherance of a state objective.

Plyler v. Doe

State (D) v. Children of undocumented aliens (P)

457 U.S. 202 (1982).

NATURE OF CASE: Constitutional challenge to a state educational restriction statute.

FACT SUMMARY: A class action suit challenged a Texas law that prohibited the use of state funds to educate the children of undocumented aliens.

RULE OF LAW

Absent a showing that such a policy furthers a substantial state interest, a state may not deny a public education to the children of undocumented aliens.

FACTS: In a class action suit, a Texas statute [Tex. Educ. Code Ann. §21.031 (1981)] was sought to be invalidated on the ground that it unconstitutionally denied equal protection to the children of undocumented aliens. The statute prohibited the use of state funds for the education of any children not legally admitted to the United States. Both the district court and the Fifth Circuit Court of Appeals held that §21.031 violated the Equal Protection Clause of the Fourteenth Amendment. Texas (D) appealed, contending that the statute was not unduly discriminatory and was, in fact, justified for three reasons: (1) it was designed to protect the state from an influx of illegal immigrants; (2) it would relieve some of the special burdens that educating undocumented aliens imposes on the educational system; and (3) it would relieve the state of the burden of educating children who are less likely to remain in the state and contribute than other children.

ISSUE: May a state deny a public education to the children of undocumented aliens, absent a showing that such a policy is justified by a substantial state interest?

HOLDING AND DECISION: (Brennan, J.) No. Absent a showing that such a policy furthers a substantial state interest, a state may not deny a public education to the children of undocumented aliens. To begin with, the proper standard of judicial scrutiny must be identified. As the people involved (undocumented aliens) are not members of a suspect class and as the right to an education, although clearly important, has not been held to constitute a fundamental constitutional right, the statute in question will be upheld if it is found to be rationally related to a substantial state interest. Upon examination, however, none of the three state interests advanced by Texas (D)—protection from an influx of illegal immigrants; relief from special burdens on the educational system; or relief from the burdens of educating children who will be more likely to leave the state—justify the statute in question. The legislative scheme found in §21.031 cannot in any way be deemed as advancing the interests asserted by the state (even assuming that these interests are "substantial state interests").

Denying children who are not responsible for their status a public education will stigmatize them with the heavy burden of illiteracy for the rest of their lives. They will be unable to participate in our civic institutions. The cost to the nation over their life spans will be greater than the cost of providing them an education now. As such, the statute must fall, as it is in violation of the equal protection clause. Affirmed.

CONCURRENCE: (Marshall, J.) While joining in the Court's opinion, I do so without in any way retreating from my opinion in *Rodriguez*.

CONCURRENCE: (Blackmun, J.) Today's decision is consistent with *Rodriguez* since the Court there reserved judgment on the constitutionality of a state system that occasioned an absolute denial of educational opportunities to any of its children.

CONCURRENCE: (Powell, J.) The unique nature of this case must be emphasized. Texas (D) has attempted to "visit the sins of the parents" on their innocent children, and has asserted no substantial state interest justifying its doing so. Such a policy cannot be constitutionally upheld.

DISSENT: (Burger, C.J.) The Court oversteps its bounds in striking down the Texas (D) statute. Once it is conceded that neither a suspect class nor a fundamental right is involved only a rational relationship to a legitimate state interest need be found to uphold the law. Despite the fact that it may not be the same course the members of the Court would take if they were legislating, it cannot be said that the Texas (D) law is irrational. As such, it is a valid law.

ANALYSIS

As mentioned in Justice Marshall's concurrence, the Court seems to be taking one step closer to the "sliding scale" approach of equal protection analysis that has long been advocated by certain legal theorists. Under this approach, a court would have greater flexibility than merely identifying the analysis required as being either "strict scrutiny" or "rational basis," and, as such, could better tailor the legal analysis to the facts of the case and the interests involved.

Quicknotes

DUE PROCESS CLAUSE Clauses found in the Fifth and Fourteenth Amendments to the United States Constitution providing that no person shall be deprived of "life, liberty, or property, without due process of law."

Griswold v. Connecticut

Director/Doctor (D) v. State (P)

381 U.S. 479 (1965).

NATURE OF CASE: Appeal from conviction for violating state laws prohibiting the counseling of married persons to take contraceptives.

FACT SUMMARY: Doctor (D) and layman (D) were prosecuted for advising married persons on the means of preventing conception.

🏛 RULE OF LAW
The right to privacy, although not explicitly stated in the Bill of Rights, is a penumbra, formed by certain other explicit guarantees. As such, it is protected against state regulation that sweeps unnecessarily broad.

FACTS: Griswold (D), the Executive Director of the Planned Parenthood League of Connecticut, and Dr. Buxton (D) were convicted under a Connecticut law that made counseling of married persons to take contraceptives a criminal offense.

ISSUE: Is the right to privacy although not explicitly stated in the Bill of Rights, a penumbra, formed by certain other explicit guarantees?

HOLDING AND DECISION: (Douglas, J.) Yes. The right to privacy, although not explicitly stated in the Bill of Rights, is a penumbra, formed by certain other explicit guarantees. As such, it is protected against state regulation that sweeps unnecessarily broad. The various guarantees that create penumbras, or zones, of privacy include the First Amendment's right of association, the Third Amendment's prohibition against the peacetime quartering of soldiers, the Fourth Amendment's prohibition against unreasonable searches and seizures, the Fifth Amendment's self-incrimination clause, and the Ninth Amendment's reservation to the people of unenumerated rights. The Connecticut (P) law by forbidding the use of contraceptives, rather than regulating their manner of sale, seeks to achieve its goals by means having a maximum destructive impact upon that relationship. Reversed.

CONCURRENCE: (Goldberg, J.) The Ninth Amendment, while not constituting an independent source of rights, suggests that the list of rights in the first eight amendments is not exhaustive. This right is a "fundamental" one that cannot be infringed on the state's slender justification in protecting marital fidelity.

CONCURRENCE: (Harlan, J.) To say that the state may not pry into the intimate affairs of a married couple does not, and need not, derive from the Bill of Rights. Rather, the right of marital privacy is implicit in any society concerned with individual liberty. These rights necessary in a free society derive directly from the Due Process Clause and not from the Bill of Rights by way of the clause.

CONCURRENCE: (White, J.) The Due Process Clause should be the test in determining whether such laws are reasonably necessary for the effectuation of a legitimate and substantial state interest and are not arbitrary or capricious in application. Here, the causal connection between married persons engaging in extramarital sex and contraceptives is too tenuous.

DISSENT: (Black, J.) While the law is offensive, neither the Ninth Amendment nor the Due Process Clause invalidates it. Both lead the Court into imposing its own notions as to what are wise or unwise laws. That which constitutes "fundamental" values this Court is incapable of determining. Keeping the Constitution "in tune with the times" is accomplished only through the amendment process. Similarly, the Due Process Clause is too imprecise and lends itself to subjective interpretation.

DISSENT: (Stewart, J.) The Due Process Clause is not the "guide" because there was no claim here that the statute is unconstitutionally vague, or that the defendants were denied any of the elements of procedural due process at their trial. The Ninth Amendment simply restricts the federal government to a government of express and limited powers. Finally, the Constitution is silent on the "right to privacy."

▶ ANALYSIS

Although the theory of "substantive due process" has declined as a means to review state economic regulation—at least since 1937—the Court, as here, has freely applied strict scrutiny of state laws affecting social areas.

■━■

Quicknotes

DUE PROCESS CLAUSE Clauses found in the Fifth and Fourteenth Amendments to the United States Constitution providing that no person shall be deprived of "life, liberty, or property, without due process of law."

NINTH AMENDMENT The Ninth Amendment to the United States Constitution provides that the enumeration of any rights contained therein, are not to be construed as denying or disparaging other rights retained by the people.

■━■

Roe v. Wade

Single woman (P) v. State (D)

410 U.S. 113 (1973).

NATURE OF CASE: Challenge to state laws making it a crime to procure an abortion except by medical advice to save the life of the mother.

FACT SUMMARY: [Roe (P), a single woman, wished to have her pregnancy terminated by an abortion.]

🏛 RULE OF LAW
The right of privacy found in the Fourteenth Amendment's concept of personal liberty and restrictions upon state action is broad enough to encompass a woman's decision whether or not to terminate her pregnancy.

FACTS: [The Texas abortion laws challenged here were typical of those adopted by most states. The challengers were Roe (P), a single pregnant woman, a childless couple with the wife not pregnant (J and M Doe), and a licensed physician with two criminal charges pending (Halford). Only Roe (P) was found to be entitled to maintain the action. Although her 1970 pregnancy had been terminated, her case was not found moot since pregnancy "truly could be capable of repetition, yet evading review."]

ISSUE: Does the constitutional right of privacy include a woman's right to choose to terminate her pregnancy?

HOLDING AND DECISION: (Blackmun, J.) Yes. The right of privacy found in the Fourteenth Amendment's concept of personal liberty and restrictions upon state action is broad enough to encompass a woman's decision whether or not to terminate her pregnancy. While the Constitution does not explicitly mention any right of privacy, such a right has been recognized. This right of privacy, whether founded in the Fourteenth Amendment's concept of personal liberty and restrictions upon state action, as this Court feels it is, or in the Ninth Amendment's reservation of rights to the people, is broad enough to encompass a woman's decision to terminate her pregnancy. A statute regulating a fundamental right, such as the right to privacy, may be justified only by a compelling state interest and such statutes must be narrowly drawn. Here, Texas (D) argued that the fetus is a person within the meaning of the Fourteenth Amendment whose right to life is guaranteed by that amendment. However, there are no decisions indicating such a definition for "fetus." The unborn have never been recognized in the law as persons in the whole sense. Texas (D) may not, by adopting one theory of life, override the rights of the pregnant woman that are at stake. However, neither are the woman's rights to privacy absolute. The state does have a legitimate interest in preserving the health of the pregnant woman and in protecting the potentiality of life. Each of these interests grows in substantiality as the woman approaches term, and, at a point, each becomes compelling. During the first trimester, mortality in abortion is less than mortality in childbirth. After that point, in promoting its interest in the mother's health, the state may regulate the abortion procedure in ways related to maternal health (i.e., licensing of physicians, facilities, etc.). Prior to viability, the physician, in consultation with the pregnant woman, is free to decide that a pregnancy should be terminated without interference by the state. Subsequent to viability, the state, in promoting its interest in the potentiality of life, may regulate, and even proscribe, abortion, except where necessary to save the mother's life. Because the Texas (D) statute makes no distinction between abortions performed in early pregnancy and those performed later, it sweeps too broadly and is, therefore, invalid.

CONCURRENCE: (Stewart, J.) The Texas statute invaded the "liberty" protected by the Fourteenth Amendment Due Process Clause. That clause protects liberties not explicitly named in the Bill of Rights, including a right of personal choice in matters of marriage and family life.

CONCURRENCE: (Douglas, J.) While childbirth endangers the lives of some women, voluntary abortion at any time and place regardless of medical standards would impinge on a rightful concern of society. The woman's health is part of that concern, as is the life of the fetus, after quickening. These concerns justify the state in treating the procedure as a medical one.

DISSENT: (White, J.) This issue, for the most part, should be left with the people. There is nothing in the language or history of the Constitution to support the Court's opinion.

DISSENT: (Rehnquist, J.) The test to be applied is whether the abortion law has a rational relation to a valid state objective. Here, the Court applies the compelling state interest test. The application of this test requires the Court to examine the legislative policies and pass on the wisdom of those policies, tasks better left to the legislature.

▶ ANALYSIS

Doe v. Bolton, 410 U.S. 179 (1973), was the companion case to *Roe v. Wade*. The Georgia laws attacked in *Doe* were more modern than the Texas laws. They allowed a physician to perform an abortion when the mother's life was in danger, or when the fetus would likely be born with birth defects or the pregnancy had resulted from rape. The Court held that a physician could consider all attendant

Continued on next page.

circumstances in deciding whether an abortion should be performed. No longer could only the three situations specified be considered. The Court also struck down the requirements of prior approval for an abortion by the hospital staff committee and of confirmation by two physicians. They concluded that the attending physician's judgment was sufficient. Lastly, the Court struck down the requirement that the woman be a Georgia resident.

■═■

Quicknotes

FOURTEENTH AMENDMENT DUE PROCESS CLAUSE Provides that protections mandated by the U.S. Constitution and observed by the federal government are equally applicable, and therefore must be observed by the states.

■═■

Planned Parenthood of Southeastern Pennsylvania v. Casey

Medical clinics/Doctors (P) v. State (D)

505 U.S. 833 (1992).

NATURE OF CASE: Appeal of order upholding abortion statutes, except a husband-notification provision.

FACT SUMMARY: Planned Parenthood (P) facially challenged the constitutionality of Pennsylvania's (D) abortion law.

> ### RULE OF LAW
> A law is unconstitutional as an undue burden on a woman's right to an abortion before fetal viability, if the law places a substantial obstacle in the path of a woman seeking to exercise her right.

FACTS: The Pennsylvania Abortion Control Act required: (a) a doctor to provide a woman seeking an abortion with information designed to persuade her against abortion and imposed a waiting period of at least 24 hours between provision of the information and the abortion; (b) a minor to obtain consent of one parent or a judge's order before having an abortion; (c) a married woman to sign a statement averring that her husband had been notified, her husband was not the father, her husband forcibly had impregnated her, or that she would be physically harmed if she notified her husband; and (d) a public report on every abortion, detailing information on the facility, physician, patient, and steps taken to comply with the Act. The name of the patient was confidential. It provided the first three provisions would not apply in a "medical emergency," i.e., a condition a doctor determines to require immediate abortion to avert death or serious risk of substantial, irreversible impairment of a major bodily function. Five clinics (P), including Planned Parenthood (P), and five doctors (P) sued Pennsylvania (D), including Governor Casey (D), claiming the Act was unconstitutional on its face. The district court held the entire Act invalid under *Roe v. Wade*, 410 U.S. 113 (1973). The court of appeals reversed, upholding the entire Act except the husband-notification requirement. Planned Parenthood et al. (P) appealed.

ISSUE: Is a law unconstitutional as an undue burden on a woman's right to an abortion before fetal viability, if the law places a substantial obstacle in the path of a woman's exercise of her right?

HOLDING AND DECISION: (O'Connor, J.) Yes. A law is unconstitutional as an undue burden on a woman's right to an abortion before fetal viability when it places a substantial obstacle in the path of a woman seeking to exercise her right. For two decades people have organized lives relying on the availability of abortion. The Court rarely resolves a controversy as intensely divisive as in *Roe*. Such a decision should be overturned only if it proves unworkable or if new information arises that renders the decision unjustified in the present. *Roe* is neither unworkable nor based on outdated assumptions. Medical technology has altered the age of viability, but that does not affect the validity of viability as a dividing line. Viability is the point at which a fetus can be said to be an independent life, so that the state's interest in protecting it then outweighs the mother's decision-making interest. The Court and the nation would be seriously damaged if the Court were to overturn *Roe* simply on the basis of a philosophical disagreement with the 1973 Court, or as surrender to political pressure. The liberty rights of women and the personal, intimate nature of child bearing sharply limit state power to insist a woman carry a child to term or accept the state's vision of her role in society. Thus, the integrity of the Court, stare decisis, and substantive due process require the central principle of *Roe* to be reaffirmed: a state may not prevent a woman from making the ultimate decision to terminate her pregnancy before viability. *Roe* also recognized the state interest in maternal health and in protecting potential life. Application of the rigid trimester framework often ignored state interests, leading to striking down abortion regulations that in no real sense deprived women of the ultimate decision. Therefore, the trimester framework must be rejected and undue burden analysis put in its place. Here, the information requirement is not an undue burden. Truthful, nonmisleading information on the nature of abortion procedure, health risks, and consequences to the fetus is reasonable to ensure informed choice, one which might cause a woman to choose childbirth. The 24-hour waiting period does not create a health risk and reasonably furthers the state interest in protecting the unborn. Requiring a period of reflection to make an informed decision is reasonable. A waiting period may increase cost and risk of delay, but on a facial challenge it cannot be called a substantial obstacle. Prior cases establish that a state may require parental consent before abortions by minors, provided there is a judicial bypass procedure. On its face, the statute's definition of "medical emergency" is not too narrow. The reporting requirement is reasonably directed to the preservation of maternal health, providing a vital element of medical research, and the statute protects patient confidentiality. The husband-notification requirement imposes an undue burden on abortion rights of the abused women who fear for their safety and the safety of their children and are likely to be deterred from procuring an abortion as surely as if the state outlawed abortion. A husband has a strong interest in his wife's pregnancy, but before birth it is a biological fact that regulation of the fetus has a far greater impact on the woman. The husband-notification requirement is unconstitutional, and the rest of the statute is valid. Affirmed.

Continued on next page.

CONCURRENCE AND DISSENT: (Blackmun, J.)

The regulation designed to inform the public about public expenditures does not further the state's interest in maintaining maternal health. Such a regulation, therefore, cannot justify a legally significant burden on a woman's right to obtain an abortion. When the state restricts a woman's right to terminate her pregnancy, it deprives a woman of the right to make her own decision about reproduction and family planning—critical life choices that the Court long has deemed central to the right of privacy.

CONCURRENCE AND DISSENT: (Stevens, J.)

A burden is "undue" if it is too severe or lacks legitimate justification. The information and waiting period requirements are invalid. The state interest in protecting potential life is legitimate, but not grounded in the Constitution. A woman has constitutional liberty rights to bodily integrity and to decide personal and private matters. So, the state may promote a preference for childbirth, but decisional autonomy must limit the state's power to interject into a woman's most personal deliberations its own views of what is best. Pennsylvania's law goes too far by requiring a doctor to provide information designed to persuade a woman to opt against abortion, just as she is weighing her personal choice. In contrast, the requirement of informing a woman of the nature and risks of abortion and childbirth enhances decision-making. The 24-hour waiting period illegitimately rests on assumptions that a decision to terminate pregnancy is wrong, and that a woman is unable to make decisions.

CONCURRENCE AND DISSENT: (Rehnquist, C.J.)

Roe was wrongly decided, has led to a confusing body of law, and should be overturned. The Court's decision, replacing *Roe*'s strict scrutiny standard and trimester framework with a new, unworkable undue burden test, cannot be justified by stare decisis. Authentic principles of stare decisis do not require erroneous decisions to be maintained. The Court's integrity is enhanced when it repudiates wrong decisions. Americans have grown accustomed to *Roe*, but that should not prevent the Court from correcting a wrong decision. The Fourteenth Amendment concept of liberty does not incorporate any all-encompassing right of privacy. Unlike marriage, procreation, and contraception, abortion terminates potential life and must be analyzed differently. Historic traditions of the American people, critical to an understanding of fundamental rights, do not support a right to abortion. A woman's interest in having an abortion is liberty protected by due process, but states may regulate abortion in ways rationally related to a legitimate state interest. All provisions of the Pennsylvania law do so and are constitutional. The husband-notification requirement is reasonably related to promoting state interests in protecting the husband's interests, potential life, and the integrity of marriage.

CONCURRENCE AND DISSENT: (Scalia, J.)

The limits on abortion should be decided democratically. The Constitution is silent on abortion, and American traditions have allowed it to be proscribed. Applying the rational basis test, the Pennsylvania law should be upheld in its entirety. *Roe* was wrongly decided. It begged the question by assuming a fetus is merely potential human life. The whole argument of abortion opponents is that the state seeks to protect human life. *Roe* also failed to produce a settled body of law. *Roe* did not resolve the deeply divisive issue of abortion. It made compromise impossible and elevated the issue to a national level where it has proven infinitely more difficult to resolve. Here, the Court claims to rely on stare decisis but throws out *Roe*'s trimester framework. The new undue burden standard is meaningless in application, giving a district judge freedom to strike down almost any abortion restriction he does not like. The Court's suggestion that public opposition to an erroneous decision mitigates against overturning it is appalling.

▶ ANALYSIS

The Court also affirmed *Roe*'s holding that after viability the state may regulate, or even proscribe, abortion, except where it is necessary to preserve the life or health of the mother. This is only the second time in modern Supreme Court jurisprudence that an opinion has been jointly authored. Justice Kennedy's portion of the opinion addresses the importance of public faith in and acceptance of the Court's work by opening with the statement: "Liberty finds no refuge in a jurisprudence of doubt." Justice O'Connor expounds on the essential nature of a woman's right to an abortion, while Justice Souter performs the stare decisis analysis, concluding that there is no reason to reverse the essential holding of *Roe*. It appears that the instant case marks the first time the Court has downgraded a fundamental right to a protected liberty and by so doing removed from the usual strict scrutiny standard of review.

■■■

Quicknotes

FOURTEENTH AMENDMENT Declares that no state shall make or enforce any law that shall abridge the privileges and immunities of citizens of the United States. No state shall deny to any person within its jurisdiction the equal protection of the laws.

STARE DECISIS Doctrine whereby courts follow legal precedent unless there is good cause for departure.

UNDUE BURDEN A burden that is unlawfully oppressive or troublesome.

■■■

Gonzales v. Carhart

Attorney General (D) v. Abortion doctor (P)

550 U.S. 124 (2007).

NATURE OF CASE: Facial due process challenge to the federal Partial-Birth Abortion Ban Act.

FACT SUMMARY: Congress passed a statute that criminalized doctors' performance of partial-birth abortions.

🏛 RULE OF LAW
The Partial-Birth Abortion Ban Act does not place a substantial obstacle to late-term, but pre-viability, abortions.

FACTS: In 2003, Congress enacted the Partial-Birth Abortion Ban Act, which criminalized doctors' performance of partial-birth abortions. The Act explicitly and precisely defined "partial-birth abortion," in part as an abortion following the "deliver[y] [of] a living fetus." [Carhart (P), a doctor who performed partial-birth abortions, filed suit for injunctive relief to prohibit the Act from being applied against him. The trial court granted the injunction, and the intermediate appellate court affirmed.] The Government (D) sought further review in the U.S. Supreme Court.

ISSUE: Does the Partial-Birth Abortion Ban Act place a substantial obstacle to late-term, but pre-viability, abortions?

HOLDING AND DECISION: (Kennedy, J.) No. The Partial-Birth Abortion Ban Act ("the Act") does not place a substantial obstacle to late-term, but pre-viability, abortions. The Act can be construed as not prohibiting the standard form of partial-birth abortion invalidated in *Stenberg v. Carhart*, 530 U.S. 914 (2000), and the Act therefore is not facially invalid on that basis. Further, instead of placing a substantial obstacle to a partial-birth abortion, the Act simply respects human life—an objective that lies within the legislative power. The Act advances that objective by ensuring that women will be fully informed about the methods of abortion to which they consent. Moreover, Congress can legitimately legislate even in the face of the medical uncertainty on whether such a prohibition on one form of abortion subjects women "to significant health risks." Such uncertainty does not support a facial challenge to the Act. The proper way to attack the Act would be through an as-applied challenge that would permit review of a more precise factual scenario. [Reversed.]

CONCURRENCE: (Thomas, J.) The Court correctly applies existing law, but the Constitution provides no basis at all for the Court's abortion jurisprudence.

DISSENT: (Ginsburg, J.) This decision mocks *Casey*, 505 U.S. 833 (1992), and *Stenberg*, and it flies in the face of medical approval of abortion procedures. The Act does subject women to significant health risks by forcing them to choose less-safe methods of abortion—and, in the process the statute does not save even one fetus because the Act merely criminalizes a method of abortion, not abortion itself. As the Court suggests, the real basis for today's decision is "moral concerns" for what the majority sees as emotionally fragile women. This rationale circumvents the concerns for stare decisis that have supported our prior decisions in this area. Today's decision is actually only a veiled attempt to undermine, in a piecemeal fashion, a woman's established right to an abortion.

▶ ANALYSIS

The right to an abortion announced in *Roe v. Wade*, 410 U.S. 113 (1973), remains intact after *Gonzales v. Carhart*. That right is now more difficult to exercise, though, and, as Justice Ginsburg suggests in dissent, the federal statute's omission of safeguards for women's health is at best problematic under the Court's prior abortion decisions.

Quicknotes

DUE PROCESS The constitutional mandate requiring the courts to protect and enforce individuals' rights and liberties consistent with prevailing principles of fairness and justice and prohibiting the federal and state governments from such activities that deprive its citizens of life, liberty, or property interest.

INJUNCTION A court order requiring a person to do, or prohibiting that person from doing, a specific act.

INJUNCTIVE RELIEF A court order issued as a remedy, requiring a person to do, or prohibiting that person from doing, a specific act.

STARE DECISIS Doctrine whereby courts follow legal precedent unless there is good cause for departure.

Lawrence v. Texas

Sodomy convict (D) v. State (P)

539 U.S. 558 (2003).

NATURE OF CASE: Appeal from a criminal conviction.

FACT SUMMARY: When Lawrence (D) and his male partner, both adults, were prosecuted and convicted for consensual sodomy in their own private dwelling, they argued the unconstitutionality of the statute.

RULE OF LAW

Legislation that makes consensual sodomy between adults in their own dwelling criminal, violates due process.

FACTS: Two Houston, Texas, police officers were dispatched to a private residence in response to a reported weapons disturbance. They entered an apartment where Lawrence (D) resided. The right of the police to enter was not an issue. The officers observed Lawrence (D) and another man engaging in sodomy. Both men were arrested, charged, and convicted before a justice of the peace of the statutory crime of "deviate sexual intercourse, namely anal sex, with a member of the same sex." Both men were adults at the time of the alleged offense. Their conduct was in private and consensual. Lawrence (D) and his partner appealed to the U.S. Supreme Court, arguing the Texas statute to be unconstitutional.

ISSUE: Does legislation that makes consensual sodomy between adults in their own dwelling criminal, violate due process?

HOLDING AND DECISION: (Kennedy, J.) Yes. Legislation that makes consensual sodomy between adults in their own dwelling criminal, violates due process. Liberty protects the person from unwarranted government intrusions into a dwelling or other private places. In our tradition, the state is not omnipresent in the home. Furthermore, freedom extends beyond spatial bounds. Liberty presumes freedom of thought, belief, expression, and certain intimate conduct. The penalties and purposes of the Texas statute in the instant case have far-reaching consequences, touching upon the most private human conduct, sexual behavior, and in the most private of places, the home. The statute seeks to control a personal relationship that, whether or not entitled to formal recognition in the law, is within the liberty of persons to choose without being punished as criminals. This Court acknowledges that adults may choose to enter into private relationships in the confines of their own homes and their own private lives and still retain their dignity as free persons. When sexuality finds expression in intimate conduct with another person, the conduct can be but one element in a personal bond that is more enduring. The liberty protected by the Constitution allows homosexual persons the right to make this choice. Here, two adults who, with full and mutual consent from each other, engaged in sexual practices common to a homosexual lifestyle. They are entitled to respect in their private lives. The state cannot demean their existence or control their destiny by making their private sexual conduct a crime. Reversed.

CONCURRENCE: (O'Connor, J.) Rather than relying on the substantive component of the Fourteenth Amendment's Due Process Clause, as the Court does, I base my conclusion of unconstitutionality on the Fourteenth Amendment's Equal Protection Clause.

DISSENT: (Scalia, J.) Homosexual sodomy is not a right deeply rooted in our nation's history and tradition. Constitutional entitlements do not spring into existence because some states choose to lessen or eliminate sanctions on criminal behavior. Today's opinion is the product of a Court that has largely signed onto the so-called homosexual agenda.

DISSENT: (Thomas, J.) Although finding the instant Texas statute to be "uncommonly silly" and would vote to repeal it if I were a member of the Texas Legislature, I nevertheless find no general constitutional right of privacy violated in this situation.

ANALYSIS

In *Lawrence*, the Supreme Court noted that of the 13 states with laws prohibiting sodomy, only four have enforced their legislation. In those states in which sodomy was still proscribed, whether for same-sex or heterosexual conduct, there was a pattern of nonenforcement with respect to consenting adults acting in private. Even Texas admitted in 1994, that as of that date it had not prosecuted anyone under those circumstances.

Quicknotes

DUE PROCESS CLAUSE Clauses found in the Fifth and Fourteenth Amendments to the United States Constitution providing that no person shall be deprived of "life, liberty, or property, without due process of law."

FOURTEENTH AMENDMENT DUE PROCESS CLAUSE Provides that protections mandated by the U.S. Constitution and observed by the federal government are equally applicable, and therefore must be observed by the states.

Cruzan v. Director, Missouri Department of Health

Individual on life support (P) v. State (D)

497 U.S. 261 (1990).

NATURE OF CASE: Review of challenge to state procedural requirement regarding termination of life support.

FACT SUMMARY: Missouri (D) required clear and convincing evidence of prior consent by an individual prior to the cessation of life support systems operating upon that individual.

RULE OF LAW

A state may require clear and convincing evidence of consent by an individual prior to the cessation of life support procedures upon that individual.

FACTS: Cruzan (P) was rendered comatose by an automobile accident, and remained in that state without any reasonable chance of recovery. When her next of kin requested that life support be terminated, the medical personnel caring for her refused to do so, on the basis of state law, requiring clear and convincing evidence of an individual's prior consent in order for the cessation of life support procedures to be effected. An action was brought on behalf of Cruzan (P), alleging that the law violated her constitutional "right to die." This argument was rejected by the Missouri state courts, and the Supreme Court granted review.

ISSUE: May a state require clear and convincing evidence of consent by an individual prior to the cessation of life support procedures upon that individual?

HOLDING AND DECISION: (Rehnquist, C.J.) Yes. A state may require clear and convincing evidence of consent by an individual prior to the cessation of life support procedures upon that individual. For purposes of argument, this Court will assume that the right to refuse artificial hydration and feeding is a liberty interest protected by the Fourteenth Amendment. However, this liberty interest must be weighed against a state's interest in the challenged regulation. In the context of this case, the state's interest involved is the lives of its citizens, a highly compelling interest. A state is free to adopt procedures designed to ensure that, prior to the cessation of artificial life support, the individual undergoing such support had, when competent, desired that such support be withheld. Due to the highly compelling nature of the state's interest in this type of situation, a clear and convincing evidentiary standard does not run afoul of any right to terminate such treatment that may exist. Affirmed.

CONCURRENCE: (O'Connor, J.) A right to deny artificial life support should be clearly recognized. Also, this decision should not be read to apply to a situation involving a surrogate decisionmaker.

CONCURRENCE: (Scalia, J.) As with abortion, the federal courts do not belong in this field, and matters of this type should be left to the states for decision.

DISSENT: (Brennan, J.) An individual has a fundamental interest in avoiding unwanted medical treatment. A state may only effect procedures to determine the wishes of an incompetent individual with the aim of reflecting as accurately as possible those wishes. A clear and convincing evidentiary standard improperly amounts to a presumption against the cessation of treatment.

DISSENT: (Stevens, J.) Missouri (D) insists, without regard to Cruzan's (P) own interests, upon equating her life with the biological persistence of her bodily functions. Cruzan is not now simply incompetent, she is in a persistent vegetative state, and has been so for seven years. The trial court found, and no party contested, that there is no possibility of recovery and no consciousness. Reasonable grounds for believing she has any personal interest in the perpetuation of what the State (D) has decided is her life does not exist. Secular government may not circumscribe the liberties of the people by regulations designed to establish a sectarian definition of life.

ANALYSIS

This case is as important for what it does not say as for what it does say. The Court did not declare, as many expected, that a right to die does or does not exist. Consequently, the invitation for other cases presenting this issue appears to be open.

■━■

Quicknotes

FOURTEENTH AMENDMENT DUE PROCESS CLAUSE Provides that protections mandated by the U.S. Constitution and observed by the federal government are equally applicable, and therefore must be observed by the states.

■━■

Washington v. Glucksberg

State (D) v. Doctor (P)

521 U.S. 707 (1997).

NATURE OF CASE: Appeal in case challenging the constitutionality of prohibition against assisted suicide.

FACT SUMMARY: Glucksberg (P), a Washington state physician, wished to assist his terminally ill patients to commit suicide.

🏛 RULE OF LAW
The "liberty" protections of the Due Process Clause of the Fourteenth Amendment do not include a right to commit suicide with another's assistance.

FACTS: Washington state law makes it a felony to knowingly cause or aid another person to attempt suicide. Glucksberg (P), a Washington state doctor, along with others, wanted to assist his terminally ill, mentally competent patients in ending their lives. In January of 1994, Glucksberg (P) filed a declaratory judgment action, asserting that Washington's (D) ban on assisted suicide violated the Fourteenth Amendment's protection of liberty interests. The district court ruled for Glucksberg (P) and the Ninth Circuit affirmed. Washington (D) appealed.

ISSUE: Do the "liberty" protections of the Due Process Clause include a right to commit suicide with another's assistance?

HOLDING AND DECISION: (Rehnquist, C.J.) No. The "liberty" protections of the Due Process Clause of the Fourteenth Amendment do not include a right to commit suicide with another's assistance. Therefore, Washington's (D) prohibition against assisting a suicide does not violate the Fourteenth Amendment. Here, unlike seeking an abortion or terminating lifesaving medical assistance, Washington's (D) state interests outweigh any personal issues of autonomy that Glucksberg (P) may assert. First, assisted suicide is not a deeply rooted tradition in American culture and the Supreme Court has required a careful description of liberty interests that are protected by the Fourteenth Amendment. No such historical guideposts exist for assisted suicide. Furthermore, an individual's interest in personal autonomy is outweighed by Washington's (D) interest in preventing coercion of patients and discrimination against the terminally ill. This Court has been very cautious in expanding rights under the Fourteenth Amendment, requiring asserted rights to meet a threshold so that those same rights do not ultimately get manipulated in the political process. The asserted right of assisted suicide does not meet any threshold. Reversed.

CONCURRENCE: (O'Connor, J.) While I agree that there is no general right to commit suicide, the narrower question of whether a mentally competent, terminally ill patient has the right to determine his own imminent death does not need to be answered today with the facial challenge to the Washington (D) law.

CONCURRENCE: (Stevens, J.) While there is no general right to commit suicide, the "unqualified interest in the preservation of human life" is not itself sufficient to outweigh the interest in liberty that may justify the only possible means of preserving a dying patient's dignity and alleviating her intolerable suffering. Some allowable circumstances may arise in the future.

CONCURRENCE: (Souter, J.) While assisted suicide may be an accepted right in the future, legislators are in a better position than the courts to determine if such a right is within the confines of the due process protections of the Constitution.

CONCURRENCE: (Ginsburg, J.) J. O'Connor's reasoning is correct.

CONCURRENCE: (Breyer, J.) Our legal tradition may provide greater support for a plaintiff's right to "die with dignity," rather than a "right to commit suicide with another's assistance," but this Court does not need to decide now whether such a right is "fundamental."

▶ ANALYSIS

This unanimous ruling by the Supreme Court decided the most closely watched case of its 1997 term. Note that the Court implied that states could choose to permit doctor-assisted suicide if they so desired. Oregon has in fact voted by referendum to do so. The Court will rule on a challenge to that law in 1998.

━━▪

Quicknotes

FOURTEENTH AMENDMENT DUE PROCESS CLAUSE Provides that protections mandated by the U.S. Constitution and observed by the federal government are equally applicable, and therefore must be observed by the states.

━━▪

Cleveland Board of Education v. Loudermill

Board of Education (D) v. Employee (P)

470 U.S. 532 (1985).

NATURE OF CASE: Appeal of order invalidating termination of public employee without hearing.

FACT SUMMARY: Loudermill (P), a public employee who could only be terminated for cause, was denied a pretermination hearing.

🏛 RULE OF LAW
A public employee who can be discharged only for cause is entitled to a pretermination hearing.

FACTS: It was discovered that Loudermill (P), an Ohio public servant, had falsified data on his employment application. He was discharged without a pretermination hearing. Under Ohio law, he could be discharged only for cause. Loudermill (P) challenged this as a deprivation of due process. Ohio law provided for termination without a hearing. The district court found that this did not violate due process, but the court of appeals reversed.

ISSUE: Is a public employee who can be discharged only for cause entitled to a pretermination hearing?

HOLDING AND DECISION: (White, J.) Yes. A public employee who can be discharged only for cause is entitled to a pretermination hearing. The Constitution does not create property rights; this is the province of the states. However, once a property right is created, the Constitution mandates that such property can be deprived only with due process. Due process requires that the concerned individual be given a predeprivation hearing. Here, Ohio by statute gave Loudermill (P) the right to continue employment, with good behavior, which is a property right. As Loudermill (P) was deprived of it without a hearing, due process was violated. Affirmed.

DISSENT: (Rehnquist, J.) When, as here, the statute conferring the property right provides its own procedures, those procedures are acceptable.

▶ ANALYSIS

The rule announced by the Court will only apply when an employee has a vested interest in continued employment. The Court has held that an employee who can be terminated without cause has no right to a hearing. *Roth v. Board of Regents of State Colleges*, 408 U.S. 564. It should be noted, however, that state laws have recently been expanding in terms of recognizing rights to employment, so the scope of the present case would appear to be ever-expanding.

Quicknotes

DUE PROCESS CLAUSE Clauses found in the Fifth and Fourteenth Amendments to the United States Constitution providing that no person shall be deprived of "life, liberty, or property, without due process of law."

Mathews v. Eldridge

Government agency (D) v. Benefits recipient (P)

424 U.S. 319 (1976).

NATURE OF CASE: Appeal from order of evidentiary hearing.

FACT SUMMARY: [Eldridge's (P) benefits under the federal disability insurance benefits program were terminated after a state agency found that his disability had ceased to exist.]

🏛 RULE OF LAW
An evidentiary hearing is not required prior to the termination of disability benefits.

FACTS: [Eldridge (P), who had been receiving disability insurance benefits under the Social Security Act since 1968, received a questionnaire from the state agency charged with monitoring his medical condition in 1972. After considering Eldridge's (P) reply that he was still disabled as well as the reports of physicians and a psychiatric consultant, the agency informed Eldridge (P) by letter that it had made a tentative decision to terminate his disability payments and gave Eldridge (P) a reasonable time to reply. After Eldridge (P) replied, disputing the agency's findings, the state agency made a final determination against Eldridge (P), which was accepted by the Social Security Agency. Although Eldridge (P) had the right to seek reconsideration of the decision within six months, he instead filed suit challenging the constitutional validity of the administrative procedures used to assess the presence of a continued disability. The court of appeals held that Eldridge (P) had to be afforded an evidentiary hearing prior to termination of disability payments, and Mathews (D), on behalf of the Social Security Agency, appealed.]

ISSUE: Is an evidentiary hearing required prior to the termination of disability benefits?

HOLDING AND DECISION: (Powell, J.) No. An evidentiary hearing is not required prior to the termination of disability benefits. The determination of what due process requires in the way of specific procedures requires consideration of three distinct factors: (1) the private interest that will be affected by the official action; (2) the risk of an erroneous deprivation of such interest through the procedures used and the probable value, if any, of additional or substitute procedural safeguards; and (3) the government's interest, including the function involved and the fiscal and administrative burdens that the additional or substitute procedural requirement would entail. Here, while the deprivation from termination of disability benefits may be significant, the recipient may have access to other forms of private or government assistance. Second, because the decision whether to discontinue disability benefits will usually turn upon routine and unbiased medical reports, there is

little risk of an erroneous deprivation. Third, the government's and the public's interest in conserving scarce fiscal and administrative resources is a significant factor. Thus, the present administrative procedures fully comport with due process. Reversed.

DISSENT: (Brennan, J.) The very legislative determination to provide disability benefits, without any prerequisite determination of need in fact, presumes a need by the recipient that should not be denigrated.

▶ ANALYSIS

In *Sniadich v. Family Finance Corp.*, 395 U.S. 337 (1969), the Court invalidated a Wisconsin statutory garnishment procedure that gave no notice or opportunity to be heard before the in rem seizure of Sniadich's wages. The Court noted that because prejudgment garnishment may impose tremendous hardship on the wage earner and give the creditor enormous leverage, the general rule is that there must be notice and a prior hearing before garnishment.

Quicknotes

NOTICE Communication of information to a person by an authorized person or an otherwise proper source.

PROCEDURAL DUE PROCESS The constitutional mandate that if the state or federal government acts so as to deny a citizen of a life, liberty or property interest the individual is first entitled to notice and the right to be heard.

Home Building & Loan Association v. Blaisdell
Lender (P) v. State (D)

290 U.S. 398 (1934).

NATURE OF CASE: Appeal from ruling upholding state mortgage moratorium law.

FACT SUMMARY: In the midst of the Depression, Minnesota (D) passed a mortgage moratorium law.

🏛 RULE OF LAW
Legislation postponing enforcement of mortgages, when tailored to an emergency situation, does not violate the Contracts Clause.

FACTS: In 1933, during the Depression, Minnesota (D) passed a mortgage moratorium law to provide emergency relief for homeowners threatened with foreclosure. The law allowed courts to postpone mortgage sales and periods of redemption through May 1, 1935, thus modifying lenders' (P) contractual rights of foreclosure. The Minnesota Supreme Court upheld the statute, and lenders (P) appealed.

ISSUE: Does legislation postponing enforcement of mortgages, when tailored to an emergency situation, violate the Contracts Clause?

HOLDING AND DECISION: (Hughes, C.J.) No. When tailored to an emergency situation, legislation postponing enforcement of mortgages does not violate the Contracts Clause. While the Contracts Clause prohibits impairment of contractual obligations, it does not follow that conditions may not arise in which a temporary restraint of enforcement may be constitutional. A court will not use the Contracts Clause to throttle the ability of states to protect their fundamental interests, and the reservation of a state's power to exercise its protection is read into all contracts. In this case, an emergency justified the state's (D) protection of the community's vital interest. The state's (D) legislation aimed to protect the entire society's basic interest, and the conditions are reasonable and temporary. Affirmed.

DISSENT: (Sutherland, J.) The Contracts Clause was adopted following the Revolution, when Americans found themselves impoverished and debtors began to rest their hopes on legislative interference. It cannot be urged that conditions that produced the rule may now be invoked to destroy it. If the provisions of the Constitution are not upheld when they pinch as well as when they comfort, they may as well be abandoned.

▶ ANALYSIS

A state law runs afoul of the Contracts Clause if it: (1) substantially impairs a contractual relationship; (2) serves no significant and legitimate public purpose; and (3) contains conditions that are not reasonable or appropriate to the public purpose.

Pennsylvania Coal Co. v. Mahon

Coal mining company (D) v. Landowner (P)

260 U.S. 393 (1922).

NATURE OF CASE: Action by property owner to enjoin certain operations on adjacent property.

FACT SUMMARY: A Pennsylvania statute forbade the mining of coal in such fashion as to cause the subsidence of any structure used as a human habitation.

🏛 RULE OF LAW
While private property may be regulated to a certain degree, a taking under the Fifth Amendment will be found if the regulation results in a severe diminution of value. At a certain magnitude, there must be an exercise of eminent domain and compensation to sustain the regulatory act. While considerable deference is to be given the legislature's judgment, each case will turn upon its particular facts.

FACTS: In 1878, the Pennsylvania Coal Co. (D) conveyed some land but reserved in the deed the right to remove all coal under the land. The grantee agreed to assume any resulting damage. Mahon (P), who later acquired the land, was bound by the deed. Mahon (P), wanting to prevent further mining under the land, claimed that a 1922 state law changed the coal company's (D) rights. The act forbade the mining of coal in such manner as to cause the subsistence of any structure used as a human habitation with certain exceptions. Mahon's (P) injunction was denied, the trial court maintaining that the Act would be unconstitutional if applied to the present case. On appeal, the state Supreme Court reversed, holding that the statute was a legitimate exercise of the police power.

ISSUE: Must a state which, through legislation, destroys previously existing contractual and property rights between private parties to the extent of severe diminution of property value give compensation to the affected party?

HOLDING AND DECISION: (Holmes, J.) Yes. While private property may be regulated to a certain degree, a taking under the Fifth Amendment will be found if the regulation results in a severe diminution of value. At a certain magnitude, there must be an exercise of eminent domain and compensation to sustain the regulatory act. While considerable deference is to be given the legislature's judgment, each case will turn upon its particular facts. Where damage is inflicted on a single private house, even if similar damage is inflicted on others in different places, there is no public interest. On the other hand, the damage to the coal company's (D) contractual and property rights is considerable. The Act cannot be sustained where, as an exercise of the police power, it affects reserved rights. To make coal mining commercially unprofitable is, in effect, to destroy it. The rights of the public in a street purchased by eminent domain are those it has paid for. A strong public desire to improve the public condition is not enough to justify achieving it by a shorter cut than the constitutional way of paying for the charge. This is a question of degree and cannot be disposed of by general propositions. So long as private individuals or communities take the risk of contracting for or purchasing only surface rights, they must bear the loss. Reversed.

DISSENT: (Brandeis, J.) Every restriction on the use of property is an abridgment by the state of rights in property without making compensation. Here, the restriction was only against a noxious use of property that remains in the Coal Company's (D) possession. The Company (D), once it discontinues its noxious use, is free to enjoy its property as before. A restriction does not cease to be public simply because some individuals may be benefited. The means chosen here may be the only way to prevent the subsistence of land. Because values are relative, the value of the coal kept in place by the restriction should be compared with the value of other parts of the land. The state should not have to follow a theory of reciprocal advantage to justify exercising its police power for the public good. The reciprocal advantage given by the Act to the Coal Company (D) is that of doing business in a civilized community.

▌ ANALYSIS

Eventually, the same analysis of the "taking" issue was used in *United States v. Causby*, 328 U.S. 265 (1946). There, a group of chicken farmers who owned land adjacent to a military airport claimed that, as a result of the noise of planes flying over their property, their chickens were literally frightened to death and egg production fell off. Rejecting the government's argument that any damage was merely consequential of the public's right of freedom of transit, Justice Douglas, writing for the majority, stated, "It is the owner's loss, not the taker's gain, which is the measure of the value of the property taken. . . . The owner's right to possess and exploit the land—that is to say, his beneficial ownership of it—would be destroyed. . . . It would not be a case of incidental damages arising from a legalized nuisance." In dissent, Justice Black warned "the effect of the court's decision is to limit, by the imposition of relatively absolute constitutional barriers, possible future adjustments through legislation and regulation which might become necessary with the growth of air transportation, and [because] the Constitution does not contain such barriers."

■■■

Continued on next page.

Quicknotes

EMINENT DOMAIN The governmental power to take private property for public use so long as just compensation is paid therefor.

TAKING A governmental action that substantially deprives an owner of the use and enjoyment of his property, requiring compensation.

■≡■

Miller v. Schoene

Private property owner (P) v. State entomologist (D)

276 U.S. 272 (1928).

NATURE OF CASE: Appeal from order to cut cedar trees.

FACT SUMMARY: A Virginia statute authorized state official (D) to order, after study, the cutting down of cedar trees growing on private property so as to prevent the spread of rust disease to private apple orchards; no compensation was allowed the owner of the cedar trees.

🏛 RULE OF LAW
The state does not exceed its constitutional powers by deciding upon the destruction of one class of private property in order to save another which, in the judgment of the legislature, is of greater value to the public. Where the choice is unavoidable, there is no denial of due process, and compensation need not be given the private owners affected.

FACTS: A Virginia statute authorized the state entomologist (D) (an official charged with studying and regulating insects) to determine if any cedar trees constituted a menace to the health of any apple orchard. Upon an affirmative finding, the state entomologist (D) could order private owners of property to cut down their cedar trees. No compensation is given by the state for the value of the cedars or any decrease in market value of the realty that results. The statute was designed to curb the spread of cedar rust, a disease fatal to apple orchards, but without effect on the value of the cedar. The disease is carried by spores up to two miles. Compared with the value of apple orchards, red cedar is not valued commercially, but for the most part, only as ornamental. On the other hand, apple growing is a principal crop of Virginia, involving multi-million-dollar investments, jobs, and attendant development. Miller (P) was ordered to cut down his red cedar trees and challenged the constitutionality of the statute as denying him due process of law as applied to the states through the Fourteenth Amendment. The trial court had affirmed the order after a hearing to consider whether his trees were, in fact, infected with rust disease.

ISSUE: May a state, acting through the police power, order the destruction of one class of private property so as to protect another class which, in its estimation, is of greater value to the public interest?

HOLDING AND DECISION: (Stone, J.) Yes. Virginia had to choose between two classes of private property, in close proximity to one another, which were incompatible. If the state had chosen not to pass a statute, this would have been a poor choice, since the apple orchards would almost certainly have been destroyed. There may be a preponderant public interest favoring one property class over another: more is involved than a conflict of private interests and a shifting of loss between them. The police power may place the public interest over the property interest of an individual even to the extent of destroying private property. The Virginia statute is constitutional. Reversed.

▶ ANALYSIS

Although the Fifth Amendment provides that no private property shall "be taken for private use, without just compensation," the U.S. Supreme Court has consistently held that a state, acting through its police powers, may restrict the use of private property; such impositions, even if producing a substantial loss in market value of the property, is not tantamount to a "taking," and so the state is not required to compensate the owner for incidental losses that are the consequence of legitimate regulations infused with the public interest.

Quicknotes

FIFTH AMENDMENT Provides that no person shall be compelled to serve as a witness against himself, or be subject to trial for the same offense twice, or be deprived of life, liberty, or property without due process of law.

TAKING A governmental action that substantially deprives an owner of the use and enjoyment of his property, requiring compensation.

Penn Central Transportation Co. v. New York City

Transportation company (P) v. Municipality (D)

438 U.S. 104 (1978).

NATURE OF CASE: Appeal of action challenging application of municipal landmark preservation law.

FACT SUMMARY: Penn Central (P) was denied a permit to erect a skyscraper over Grand Central Station, a designated landmark.

🏛 RULE OF LAW
A city may, as part of a comprehensive landmark preservation scheme, place restrictions on development affecting the landmark without paying "just compensation."

FACTS: New York (D) enacted a comprehensive landmark preservation ordinance requiring Commission approval prior to development affecting a designated landmark. In exchange for losing development rights, the owners of designated property were permitted to transfer development rights to other property. Grand Central Station, belonging to Penn Central (P), was designated a landmark. The Landmark Commission denied an application for the erection of a skyscraper over the station. Penn Central (P) filed suit, claiming that the ordinance constituted a "taking" in the Fifth Amendment sense. Penn Central (P) did not argue that Grand Central Station was profitable. The New York Court of Appeals held for New York City (D), and Penn Central (P) appealed.

ISSUE: May a city, as part of a comprehensive landmark preservation scheme, place restrictions on development affecting the landmark without paying "just compensation?"

HOLDING AND DECISION: (Brennan, J.) Yes. A city may, as part of a comprehensive landmark preservation scheme, place restrictions on development affecting the landmark without paying "just compensation." No precise rule exists for determining when regulation of private property becomes a taking in the constitutional sense. Some factors include whether a physical invasion occurred, whether the interference is arbitrary or part of a common plan, and whether any reasonable return is left on the property. An analysis of these factors leads to the conclusion that no taking occurred. There was no invasion. The regulation was part of a comprehensive plan. Analysis also reveals that a reasonable return on the property still remains. This is especially true in light of the fact that Penn Central (P) is the beneficiary of transferred development rights. It is settled that a government may deny an owner the most profitable use of his property without a taking occurring, and this rule applies here. Affirmed.

DISSENT: (Rehnquist, J.) The type of legislation involved here was not zoning in the true sense, so rules formulated regarding zoning should not apply. The law imposes an affirmative duty on the part of Penn Central (P) to maintain the property, and this is more than the usual type of zoning regulation. The burden of landmark preservation should not so disproportionately fall on the owner.

▶ ANALYSIS

The Court has been highly deferential to state authority in this area of the law. While examples of holdings in favor of owners do exist (e.g., *Pennsylvania Coal Co. v. Mahon*, 260 U.S. 393 (1922)), it is difficult for an owner to prevail. Generally speaking, in the absence of an invasion or outright destruction, the regulation will not be held to constitute a taking.

■=■

Quicknotes

TAKING A governmental action that substantially deprives an owner of the use and enjoyment of his property, requiring compensation.

■=■

Lucas v. South Carolina Coastal Council

Developer (P) v. State agency (D)

505 U.S. 1003 (1992).

NATURE OF CASE: Appeal of reversal of compensation award for government "taking."

FACT SUMMARY: The Coastal Council (D) prevented Lucas (P) from building homes on his beachfront property.

🏛 RULE OF LAW
Where regulation prohibits all economically beneficial use of land, and the proscribed use could not have been prohibited under state nuisance law, the regulation is a "taking" that requires "just compensation" to be paid to the landowner.

FACTS: In 1986, Lucas (P) purchased two vacant beachfront lots in a residential area. In 1988, South Carolina passed a law creating a coastal zone in which no occupiable improvements could be built. The law's stated purpose was to protect property from storms, tides, and beach erosion, and as an environmental protection. The law prevented Lucas (P) from constructing two homes he had planned. In suing the Coastal Council (D), Lucas (P) did not challenge the state's right to pass the law or its justifications for doing so. He simply claimed the law rendered his property valueless, which amounted to a "taking" under the Fifth Amendment, and, thus, entitled him to just compensation. The trial court agreed, the South Carolina Supreme Court reversed, and Lucas (P) appealed.

ISSUE: Where regulation prohibits all economically beneficial use of land, and the proscribed use could not have been prohibited under state nuisance law, is the regulation a "taking" that requires "just compensation" to be paid to the landowner?

HOLDING AND DECISION: (Scalia, J.) Yes. Where regulation prohibits all economically beneficial use of land, and the proscribed use could not have been prohibited under state nuisance law, the regulation is a "taking" that requires that "just compensation" be paid to the landowner. Mandated preservation of private land looks like a conversion of private property to public, a classic "taking." Government cannot be permitted to regulate in this manner without compensation simply by reciting some police power or "prevention of harmful use" rationale. Such regulations must account for owners' traditional understandings as to the state's power over their property rights. The source of these understandings is state public and private nuisance law. Thus, the owner of a lake bed always is aware he may be stopped by law from flooding adjacent property to create a landfill. If the state restricts this use, even to deprive him of all economic benefit, he is not entitled to compensation. Here, however,

South Carolina common law principles probably would not prevent Lucas (P) from building homes on his land. If the state court determines they would not, Lucas (P) is entitled to just compensation. Reversed and remanded.

CONCURRENCE: (Kennedy, J.) Where all economic value is deprived, the issue of compensation turns on the owner's reasonable, investment-backed expectations. However, reasonable expectations must be based on our whole legal tradition, not just nuisance law. Coastal property may present unique concerns not addressed by nuisance law.

DISSENT: (Blackmun, J.) The Court should not create a category that precludes a case-specific inquiry when all economic value is lost. It is well recognized that government may regulate property without compensation no matter how adverse the financial effect on the owner. The Court's injection of nuisance considerations into takings doctrine is misguided and goes beyond what is necessary to secure Lucas's (P) benefit.

DISSENT: (Stevens, J.) Under the Court's new rule, a landowner who loses 95 percent of his property value gets nothing, while one who loses 100 percent recovers the land's full value. The Court's holding today denies the Legislature its traditional power to revise property laws. Even assuming Lucas's (P) land was rendered valueless, the risks inherent in Lucas's (P) type of investment, the generality of the statute, and the compelling purpose motivating the legislature demonstrate that no taking was effected.

▶ ANALYSIS

Traditionally, "takings" were limited to direct appropriation of property by the government. Since this view was rejected in *Pennsylvania Coal Co. v. Mahon*, 260 U.S. 393 (1922), the Court has engaged in a case-by-case, ad hoc determination of when regulation becomes "taking." The *Lucas* majority identified two categories of regulations that constitute takings regardless of the public interest in the regulation. One category is defined in the holding. The other is where the government physically invades the owner's property (e.g., where a city law requires landlords to place cable television facilities in their buildings).

Quicknotes

TAKING A governmental action that substantially deprives an owner of the use and enjoyment of his property, requiring compensation.

Palazzolo v. Rhode Island

Property owner (P) v. State (D)

533 U.S. 606 (2001).

NATURE OF CASE: Appeal from a decision denying compensation in adverse condemnation suit.

FACT SUMMARY: When Anthony Palazzolo's (P) development proposals were rejected by Rhode Island (D) after Rhode Island (D) designated the land on which he owned property as protected coastal wetlands, Palazzolo (P) brought an inverse condemnation suit.

🏛 RULE OF LAW
A landowner not deprived of all economic use of property by a state's designation as coastal wetlands, has not had the property taken in violation of the Takings Clause of the Fifth Amendment.

FACTS: Anthony Palazzolo (P) owned a waterfront parcel of land in Rhode Island (D), most of which was designated as protected coastal wetlands. Palazzolo (P) made several proposals to the Rhode Island Coastal Resources Management Council to develop his property. His proposals were rejected, with the exception that he could build a substantial residence on an 18-acre parcel. The Council stated that his application was "vague and inadequate for a project of this size and nature" and that it would adversely impact the waters and wetlands on and around the prospective development area. Palazzolo (P) brought an inverse condemnation suit against Rhode Island (D), arguing that denial of his application without just compensation constituted a violation of the Takings Clause of the Fifth Amendment. The trial court found against Palazzolo (P), and the Rhode Island Supreme Court affirmed. Palazzolo (P) appealed to the U.S. Supreme Court.

ISSUE: Has a landowner who has not been deprived of all economic use of his or her property by the state's designation as coastal wetlands, had the property taken in violation of the Takings Clause of the Fifth Amendment?

HOLDING AND DECISION: (Kennedy, J.) No. A landowner not deprived of all economic use of his or her property by the state's designation as coastal wetlands, has not had the property taken in violation of the Takings Clause of the Fifth Amendment. Just as a prospective enactment, such as a new zoning ordinance, can limit the value of land without effecting a taking because it may be reasonable to all concerned, other enactments are unreasonable and do not become less so because of the passage of time. While the right to improve property, however, is indeed subject to the reasonable exercise of state authority, including the enforcement of valid zoning and land-use restrictions, the Takings Clause in certain circumstances allows the landowner to assert that a particular exercise of the state's regulatory

power is so unreasonable or onerous as to compel compensation. Here, Rhode Island (D), by designation of the property as coastal wetlands, prevented Palazzolo (P) from using any fill, effectively precluding commercial development of his property in his desired manner. With no fill, there can be no structures and no development on the wetlands. A regulation that denies all economically beneficial or productive use of land will require compensation under the Takings Clause. Even where a regulation places limitations on land that fall short of eliminating all economically beneficial use, a taking may nonetheless have occurred, depending on a complex of factors, including the regulation's economic effect on the landowner, the extent to which the regulation interferes with reasonable investment-backed expectations, and the character of the government action. Here, however, the regulation permitted Palazzolo (P) to build a substantial residence on an 18-acre parcel, which does not leave the property "economically idle." This constitutes far more than simply leaving Palazzolo (P) with "a few crumbs of value" or a token interest. While the Rhode Island Supreme Court did not err in finding that Palazzolo (P) failed to establish a deprivation of all economic value since it is undisputed the parcel retains significant worth for construction of a residence, the latter court did err in finding the claims were unripe because Palazzolo (P) failed to apply for further building permits subsequent to the coastal wetlands designation. Affirmed in part, and reversed in part and remanded.

CONCURRENCE: (O'Connor, J.) Courts properly consider the effect of existing zoning and land-use regulations under the rubric of investment-backed expectations in determining whether a compensable taking has occurred. The salience of these facts cannot be reduced to any set formula. The temptation to adopt what amounts to per se rules in either direction must be resisted.

CONCURRENCE: (Scalia, J.) The fact that a restriction existed at the time the purchaser of property took title should have no bearing upon the determination of whether the restriction is so substantial as to constitute a taking.

CONCURRENCE AND DISSENT: (Stevens, J.) While future generations have a right to challenge unreasonable limitations on the use and value of land, it does not follow that, as the Court assumes, a succeeding property owner may obtain compensation for a taking of property from his or her predecessor in interest. A taking is a discrete event, a governmental acquisition of private property for which the state is required to provide just

Continued on next page.

compensation. Like other transfers of property, it occurs at a particular time, the time being the moment when the relevant property interest is alienated from its owner.

▶ *ANALYSIS*

In *Palazzolo*, the Supreme Court makes clear that the determination whether an existing, general law can limit all economic use of property must turn on objective factors, such as the nature of the land use proscribed.

■■■

Quicknotes

FIFTH AMENDMENT Provides that no person shall be compelled to serve as a witness against himself, or be subject to trial for the same offense twice, or be deprived of life, liberty, or property without due process of law.

TAKINGS CLAUSE Provision of the Fifth Amendment to the United States Constitution prohibiting the government from taking private property for public use without providing just compensation therefor.

■■■

Freedom of Expression

Quick Reference Rules of Law

PAGE

1. **Speech That "Causes" Unlawful Conduct.** An opinion critical of a draft statute, no matter how seditious in nature, cannot be deemed to be advocacy of the violation of that statute unless there is a direct urging of such violation. (Masses Publishing Co. v. Patten) ... *110*

2. **Speech That "Causes" Unlawful Conduct.** The test to determine the constitutionality of a statute restricting free speech is whether, under the circumstances, the speech is of such a nature as to create a clear and present danger that it will bring about the substantive evils that Congress has a right to prevent. (Schenck v. United States) ... *111*

3. **Speech That "Causes" Unlawful Conduct.** [Rule of law not stated in casebook excerpt.] (Abrams v. United States) ... *112*

4. **Speech That "Causes" Unlawful Conduct.** Under its police powers, a state may validly forbid any speech or publication that has a tendency to produce action dangerous to public security, even where such speech or publication presents no "clear and present danger" to the security of the public. (Gitlow v. New York) ... *113*

5. **Speech That "Causes" Unlawful Conduct.** A state may, in the exercise of its police power, punish abuses of freedom of speech where such utterances are inimical to the public welfare as tending to incite crime, disturb the peace, or endanger organized government through threats of violent overthrow. (Whitney v. California) ... *114*

6. **Speech That "Causes" Unlawful Conduct.** In reviewing legislation that restricts freedom of speech, the court, in determining whether a "clear and present danger" exists, must ask whether the gravity of the evil, discounted by its improbability, justifies such invasion of free speech as is necessary to avoid the evil. (Dennis v. United States) ... *116*

7. **Speech That "Causes" Unlawful Conduct.** The constitutional guarantees of freedom of speech and freedom of press do not permit a state to forbid or proscribe advocacy of the use of force or of law violation, except where such advocacy is directed to inciting or producing imminent lawless action and is likely to produce or incite such action. (Brandenburg v. Ohio) ... *118*

8. **Speech That Provokes a Hostile Audience Reaction.** Speech not amounting to a clear and present danger to public health or security may not be abridged under the guise of preserving public peace. (Cantwell v. Connecticut) ... *119*

9. **Speech That Provokes a Hostile Audience Reaction.** When clear and present danger of riot, disorder, interference with traffic on the streets, or other immediate threat to public safety, peace, or order, appears, the state has the power to punish or prevent such disorder. (Feiner v. New York) ... *120*

10. **Speech That Provokes a Hostile Audience Reaction.**   A government may proscribe language tending to incite violence. (Chaplinsky v. New Hampshire)   *121*

11. **Speech That Discloses Confidential Information.**   There is a special presumption that the First Amendment does not permit the use of prior restraints. (New York Times Co. v. United States; United States v. Washington Post Co.)   *122*

12. **Overbreadth and Vagueness.**   Statutes abridging freedom of speech must be narrowly drawn to abridge only unprotected expression. (Gooding v. Wilson)   *124*

13. **Prior Restraint.**   An ordinance that prohibits the distribution of literature of any kind at any time, at any place, and in any manner without a prior permit is unconstitutional in that it subjects the right of freedom of the press to license and censorship. (Lovell v. Griffin)   *125*

14. **Prior Restraint.**   A state statute that authorizes previous restraints on publication violates the liberty of the press guaranteed by the Fourteenth Amendment if such publication relates to the malfeasance of public officials. (Near v. Minnesota)   *126*

15. **False Statements of Fact.**   The First Amendment requires that a public official may not recover damages for defamatory falsehoods relating to his official conduct unless he proves that the statement involved was made with "actual malice—this is, with knowledge that it was false or with reckless disregard of whether it was false or not." (New York Times v. Sullivan)   *127*

16. **"Nonnewsworthy" Disclosures of "Private" Information.**   The First and Fourteenth Amendments prevent state sanctions for publication of truthful information contained in official court records that are open to public inspection. (Cox Broadcasting Corp. v. Cohn)   *129*

17. **Commercial Advertising.**   "The consumer's interest in the free flow of commercial information" makes such information the type of expression that the First Amendment is designed to protect—even if it does "no more than propose a commercial transaction." (Virginia State Board of Pharmacy v. Virginia Citizens Consumer Council)   *130*

18. **Obscenity.**   Material is obscene and not protected by the First Amendment if: (1) the average person, applying contemporary community standards, would find that the work, taken as a whole, appeals to the prurient interest; (2) the work depicts in a patently offensive way sexual conduct specifically defined by the applicable state law; and (3) the work, taken as a whole, lacks serious literary, artistic, political, or scientific value. (Miller v. California)   *131*

19. **Obscenity.**   A state can forbid the dissemination of obscene material to consenting adults in order to preserve the quality of the community and to prevent the possibility of resulting antisocial behavior. (Paris Adult Theatre I v. Slaton)   *132*

20. **The Lewd, the Profane, and the Indecent.**   A state cannot bar the use of offensive words either because such words are inherently likely to cause a violent reaction or because the state wishes to eliminate such words to protect the public morality. (Cohen v. California)   *133*

21. **Hate Speech and Pornography.**   A statute that makes it a crime to libel the members of any class or group is not repugnant to the Constitution. (Beauharnais v. Illinois)   *134*

22. **Hate Speech and Pornography.**   The government may not proscribe some fighting words and permit others, where the distinction is based on content or viewpoint. (R.A.V. v. City of St. Paul)   *135*

23. **Hate Speech and Pornography.**   A provision in a state's cross-burning statute treating   *137*
any cross burning as prima facie evidence of intent to intimidate is unconstitutional. (Virginia
v. Black)

24. **The Public Forum: Other Publicly Owned Property.**   Demonstrators do not have a   *138*
constitutional right to expound their views whenever, wherever, and however they choose.
(Adderley v. Florida)

25. **The Public Forum: Unequal Access and the Problem of Content-Neutrality.**   A state   *139*
may not permit or prohibit peaceful picketing based on the content of the sign. (Police
Department of Chicago v. Mosley)

26. **The Public Forum: Unequal Access and the Problem of Content-Neutrality.**   A city   *140*
that operates a public rapid transit system and sells advertising space on its vehicles is not
required by the First and Fourteenth Amendments to accept paid political advertising on
behalf of a candidate for public office. (Lehman v. City of Shaker Heights)

27. **Symbolic Conduct.**   When speech and nonspeech elements are combined in the same   *141*
course of conduct, a sufficiently important governmental interest in regulating the nonspeech
element can justify incidental limitations on First Amendment freedoms. (United States v.
O'Brien)

28. **Regulation of Political Solicitation, Contribution, Expenditure, and Activity.**   Although   *142*
"the [F]irst [A]mendment protects political association as well as political expression . . .
a limitation upon the amount that any one person or group may contribute to (and
associate with) a candidate or political committee entails only a marginal restriction on the
contributor's ability to engage in free communication (and association)"; but "a restriction
on the amount of money a person or group can spend on political communication (as a
whole) during a campaign (excessively) reduces the quantity of expression by restricting the
number of issues discussed, the depth of their exploration, and the size of the audience
reached." (Buckley v. Valeo)

29. **A Right to "Gather" News?**   The First Amendment's freedom of press does not exempt a   *144*
news reporter from disclosing to a grand jury information that he has received in
confidence. (Branzburg v. Hayes)

30. **Regulating the Press to "Improve" the Marketplace of Ideas.**   Reasonable   *145*
governmental regulations designed to ensure equal access to the airwaves do not violate the
first amendment. (Red Lion Broadcasting Co. v. FCC)

Masses Publishing Co. v. Patten

Publishing company (P) v. Postmaster General (D)

244 F. 535 (S.D.N.Y. 1917).

NATURE OF CASE: Action for preliminary injunction.

FACT SUMMARY: Patten (D) refused Masses Publishing Company's (P) magazine access to the mails for violating the 1917 Espionage Act.

🏛 RULE OF LAW
An opinion critical of a draft statute, no matter how seditious in nature, cannot be deemed to be advocacy of the violation of that statute unless there is a direct urging of such violation.

FACTS: Masses Publishing Company (Masses) (P) published a monthly magazine called "The Masses," which contained cartoons and text of a politically revolutionary nature. During the First World War, Masses (P) ran political material in the magazine violently attacking the draft and the war and expressing sympathy for conscientious objectors. In July of 1917, under directions from the Postmaster General, Patten (D), Postmaster of New York, told Masses (P) that their August issue would be denied use of the mails. Patten (D) stated that the magazine violated the Espionage Act of 1917 by: (1) making false statements with the intent to interfere with the operation of the military forces of the United State; (2) arousing discontent among potential draftees and thereby promoting insubordination among troops already in the war; and (3) counseling resistance and disobedience to the law. Masses (P) brought this suit for a preliminary injunction against Patten's (D) refusal to accept the magazine in the mails.

ISSUE: Where a person's publications or utterances stop short of directly advocating resistance to a law, is that person nonetheless to be held responsible for attempting to cause its violation?

HOLDING AND DECISION: (Hand, J.) No. An opinion critical of a draft statute, no matter how seditious in nature, cannot be deemed to be advocacy of the violation of that statute unless there is a direct urging of such violation. Unless there is some direct advocacy by a person for others to resist a particular law, then that person may not be held responsible for attempting to cause a violation of the law. Here, the publications of Masses (P) may have created national dissension and thereby assisted, indirectly, the cause of the enemy. But the statute in question provided that such publications be willfully false and made with the intent to interfere with military operations. The publications were mere opinions and not publications of facts. Thus, they fell within the scope of the right to criticize, normally the privilege of individuals in countries dependent on free expression of opinions as an ultimate source of authority. The

statute was intended to prevent the spreading of false rumors embarrassing to the military, not the dissemination of inflammatory public opinion. It is also contended by Patten (D) that to allow Masses (P) to arouse discontent among the public as to the conduct of the war and draft caused insubordination among wartime troops. But to interpret the word "causes" too broadly would be to suppress all hostile criticism of the war except those officially sanctioned opinions. There are recognized limits to criticisms of existing laws or policies of war. One may not counsel or advise others to violate the law as it stands. The present statute is limited to punishing direct advocacy of resistance to recruiting and enlistment. Neither the cartoons nor the text of Masses' (P) publications fell with this test. Injunction granted.

▶ ANALYSIS

The present test, later supplanted with the "clear and present danger" test as to what type of conduct constitutes advocacy of resistance to law, focuses on the speaker and the value of the speech. This decision weighs the value of content of freely spoken opinions against its impact on the orderly conduct of governmental policy. The burden is on the government as accuser to show that such speech or publication is so detrimental to the orderly process of government that freedom of speech should bow to governmental will. The *Masses* case takes a liberal view of First Amendment rights, and allows the free expression of opinion that falls short of direct advocacy of resistance to governmental authority. Judge Hand's decision in this case was overturned by the court of appeals on the ground that a person would be held accountable for the natural consequences of his words. If his words strongly imply that a particular law should be violated, that person will not be immune from prosecution merely because he omitted a direct appeal for violations. Judge Hand later wrote to a friend that his opinion in this case had apparently received little or no professional approval.

■━■

Quicknotes

FIRST AMENDMENT Prohibits Congress from enacting any law respecting an establishment of religion, prohibiting the free exercise of religion, abridging freedom of speech or the press, the right of peaceful assembly and the right to petition for a redress of grievances.

■━■

Schenck v. United States

Publisher (D) v. Federal government (P)

249 U.S. 47 (1919).

NATURE OF CASE: Appeal from conviction for conspiracy to violate the Espionage Act, conspiracy to use the mails for transmissions of nonmailable material, and unlawful use of the mails.

FACT SUMMARY: During a time of war, Schenck (D) mailed circulars to draftees that were calculated to cause insubordination in the armed services and to obstruct the U.S. recruiting and enlistment program in violation of military laws.

🏛 RULE OF LAW
The test to determine the constitutionality of a statute restricting free speech is whether, under the circumstances, the speech is of such a nature as to create a clear and present danger that it will bring about the substantive evils that Congress has a right to prevent.

FACTS: During a time of war, Schenck (D) mailed circulars to draftees. The circulars stated that the Conscription Act was unconstitutional and likened conscription to conviction. They intimated that conscription was a monstrous wrong against humanity in the interest of Wall Street's chosen few, and described nonconscription arguments as coming from cunning politicians and a mercenary capitalist press. They urged: "Do not submit to intimidation," but advised only peaceful actions such as a petition to repeal the Conscription Act. Schenck (D) did not deny that the jury could find that the circulars could have no purpose except to influence draftees to obstruct the carrying out of the draft.

ISSUE: Does the right to freedom of speech depend upon the circumstances in which the speech is spoken?

HOLDING AND DECISION: (Holmes, J.) Yes. The test to determine the constitutionality of a statute restricting free speech is whether, under the circumstances, the speech is of such a nature as to create a clear and present danger that it will bring about the substantive evils that Congress has a right to prevent. The character of every act depends on the circumstance in which it is done. The most stringent protection of free speech would not protect a person's falsely shouting "fire" in a theatre and causing a panic. "The question in every case is whether the words are used in such circumstances and are of such a nature as to create a clear and present danger that they will bring about the substantive evils that Congress has a right to prevent. It is a question of proximity and degrees." During a war, things that could be said during peaceful times may be such a hindrance to the war effort that they will not be permitted. Affirmed.

▶ ANALYSIS

The Court's first significant encounter with the problem of articulating the scope of constitutionally protected speech came in a series of cases involving agitation against the draft and war during World War I (*Schenck, Frohwerk* (249 U.S. 204 (1919)), and *Debs* (249 U.S. 211 (1919)). *Schenck* announces the "clear and present danger" test, the test for determining the validity of legislation regulating speech. In *Schenck,* Holmes rejected perfect immunity for speech. But he also rejected a far more restrictive, far more widely supported, alternative test: that "any tendency in speech to produce bad acts, no matter how remote, would suffice to validate a repressive statute."

Quicknotes

FIRST AMENDMENT Prohibits Congress from enacting any law respecting an establishment of religion, prohibiting the free exercise of religion, abridging freedom of speech or the press, the right of peaceful assembly and the right to petition for a redress of grievances.

Abrams v. United States

Publisher (D) v. Federal government (P)

250 U.S. 616 (1919).

NATURE OF CASE: Appeal of conviction for publishing materials with intent to hinder American war efforts.

FACT SUMMARY: In response to American military intervention in post-czarist Russia, Abrams (D) circulated a leaflet calling for a strike.

 RULE OF LAW
[Rule of law not stated in casebook excerpt.]

FACTS: Following the Marxist takeover of Russia, the United States sent a military expedition to that country. Abrams (D) circulated a leaflet decrying U.S. efforts to undercut the Russian revolution and calling for a general strike by U.S. workers. Abrams (D) was convicted of "publishing materials with the intent to hinder American war efforts." Abrams (D) appealed.

ISSUE: [Issue not stated in casebook excerpt.]

HOLDING AND DECISION: (Clarke, J.) [The Court summarily rejected Abrams's (D) First Amendment claims.]

DISSENT: (Holmes, J.) The First Amendment is meant to encourage the free exchange of ideas in the marketplace, and this applies to all ideas, no matter how unpopular. Only when expression presents an immediate danger may it be curtailed, and this was not the case here.

▶ *ANALYSIS*

J. Holmes's dissent was, at the time, probably the most libertarian treatise on the First Amendment that a Court member had made. The concept of "clear and present danger" as being the only basis for curtailment of expression first saw its pronouncement here. This concept would later be expanded upon by the Court itself.

■■■

Quicknotes

FIRST AMENDMENT Prohibits Congress from enacting any law respecting an establishment of religion, prohibiting the free exercise of religion, abridging freedom of speech or the press, the right of peaceful assembly and the right to petition for a redress of grievances.

■■■

Gitlow v. New York
Publisher (D) v. State (P)
268 U.S. 652 (1925).

NATURE OF CASE: Appeal from a conviction for criminal anarchy.

FACT SUMMARY: Gitlow (D) printed and circulated literature advocating a Communist revolt against the U.S. government.

🏛 RULE OF LAW
Under its police powers, a state may validly forbid any speech or publication that has a tendency to produce action dangerous to public security, even where such speech or publication presents no "clear and present danger" to the security of the public.

FACTS: Gitlow (D) was a member of the Left Wing Section of the Socialist Party in New York, and he was responsible for printing the official organ of the Left Wing called the Revolutionary Age. In this paper, Gitlow (D) printed articles advocating the accomplishment of the Communist revolution through militant revolutionary socialism. Gitlow (D) further advocated a class struggle, mobilization of the proletariat through mass industrial revolts and political strikes to conquer and destroy the U.S. government and replace it with a dictatorship of the proletariat. Although there was no evidence that these writings resulted in any such action, Gitlow (D) was arrested, tried, and convicted for advocating the overthrow of the government by force under a New York (P) criminal anarchy act. At trial, Gitlow's (D) counsel urged that since there was no resulting action flowing from the publication of the Gitlow (D) "Manifesto," the statute penalized the mere utterance of doctrine having no propensity toward incitement of concrete action.

ISSUE: Is a state statute punishing the mere advocacy of overthrowing the government by force an unconstitutional denial of the freedom of speech and press as protected under the First Amendment and applied to the states by the Fourteenth Amendment?

HOLDING AND DECISION: (Sanford, J.) No. Under its police powers, a state may validly forbid both speech and publication if they have a tendency to result in action that is dangerous to public security, even though such utterances present no "clear and present danger" to the security of the public. The New York (P) criminal anarchy act did not punish the utterance of abstract doctrine, having no quality of incitement to action. It prohibits advocacy to overthrow organized government by unlawful means. These words imply advocacy of action. Clearly, Gitlow's (D) "Manifesto," which spoke in terms of "mass action" of the proletariat for the "Communist reconstruction of society" is language of direct incitement. The means suggested imply force and violence and are inherently unlawful in a consti-

tutional form of government based on law and order. Although freedom of speech and press are protected by the First and Fourteenth Amendments, it is fundamental that this freedom is not absolute. The police power extends to a state the right to punish those who abuse this freedom by advocating action inimical to the public welfare, tending to corrupt public morals, to incite crime, or to threaten the public security. The state need not wait for such dangers to arise. It may punish utterances likely to bring about such substantive evils. The "clear and present danger" test announced in the *Schenck* case, 249 U.S. 47 (1919), does not apply here since the legislature has previously determined the danger of the substantive evils that may arise from specified utterances. So long as the statute is constitutional and the use of the language sought to be penalized comes within the prohibition, the statute will be upheld. And it is not necessary that the defendant advocate some definite or immediate act of force or violence. It is sufficient if they were expressed in general terms. Affirmed.

DISSENT: (Holmes, J.) The "clear and present danger" test applies, and there was no clear and present danger here. The followers of Gitlow (D) were too few to present one. Every idea is an incitement. The only meaning of free speech is to allow everyone to have their say.

▶ ANALYSIS
The *Gitlow* case is an example of what has been termed the "bad tendency" test. This test punishes utterances whose meaning lies somewhere between "clear and present danger" and mere advocacy of abstract ideas. The key question here is whether the language "tends" to produce action resulting in a danger to public security. The holding of the Court in this case, while recognizing Gitlow's (D) constitutional rights of free speech and press, bypassed these rights by saying that the New York (P) statute did not unduly restrict such freedom. However, in light of the modern test of "clear and present danger," it seems that the "bad tendency" test is all but dead. The "clear and present danger" test requires language that results in imminent lawless action. Tendency is not enough. It is important to note that the "bad tendency" test has not been used by the Court since *Gitlow*.

Quicknotes
POLICE POWERS The power of a state or local government to regulate private conduct for the health, safety and welfare of the general public.

Whitney v. California

Communist Party member (D) v. State (P)

274 U.S. 357 (1927).

NATURE OF CASE: Appeal from conviction for violation of criminal syndicalism act.

FACT SUMMARY: Whitney (D), organizer and member of the Communist Labor Party of California, was convicted of aiding in that organization's violation of the Criminal Syndicalism Act.

🏛 RULE OF LAW
A state may, in the exercise of its police power, punish abuses of freedom of speech where such utterances are inimical to the public welfare as tending to incite crime, disturb the peace, or endanger organized government through threats of violent overthrow.

FACTS: In 1919, Whitney (D) attended a convention of the Socialist Party. When the convention split into factions, Whitney (D) went with the radicals and helped form the Communist Labor Party. Later that year, Whitney (D) attended another convention to organize a new California unit of CLP. There Whitney (D) supported a resolution that endorsed political action and urged workers to vote for CLP member-candidates at all elections. This resolution was defeated and a more extreme program of action was adopted, over Whitney's (D) protests. At trial, upon indictment for violation of the California Criminal Syndicalism Act, which held it unlawful to organize a group that advocated unlawful acts of violence as a means of effecting change in industrial ownership and in political change, Whitney (D) contended that she never intended the CLP to become a terrorist organization. Whitney (D) further contended that since she had no intent to aid the CLP in a policy of violent political reform, her mere presence at the convention was not a crime. Whitney (D) contended that the Act thus deprived her of her liberty without due process, and freedom of speech, assembly and association.

ISSUE: Is a state statute that punishes a person for becoming a knowing member of an organization that advocates the use of unlawful means to effect its aims, a violation of due process and a restraint of freedom of speech, assembly and association secured by the Constitution?

HOLDING AND DECISION: (Sanford, J.) No. A state may, in the exercise of its police power, punish abuses of freedom of speech where such utterances are inimical to the public welfare as tending to incite crime, disturb the peace, or endanger organized government through threats of violent overthrow. At her trial, Whitney (D) testified that it was not her intention that the Communist Labor Party of California should be an instrument of terrorism or violence. Nevertheless, by its enactment of the Criminal Syndicalism Act, California (P) has declared that for an individual to knowingly be or become a member of an organization that advocates criminal syndicalism, involves such danger to the public peace and security of the state that these acts should be penalized in the exercise of California's (P) police power. That determination must be given great weight. Here, the essence of the offense denounced by the legislation is of the nature of a criminal conspiracy. It is clear that such united and joint action involves even greater danger to the public peace and security than the mere isolated utterances and acts of individual persons. Accordingly, the Court cannot hold that, as here applied, the Criminal Syndicalism Act constitutes an unreasonable or arbitrary exercise of California's (P) police power. Affirmed.

CONCURRENCE: (Brandeis, J.) Whitney (D) is here punished for a step in the preparation of incitement that only threatens the public remotely. The Syndicalism Act of California aims at punishing those who propose to preach not put into action, criminal syndicalism. The right of freedom of speech, assembly and association, protected by the Due Process Clause of the Fourteenth Amendment and binding on the states, are restricted if they threaten political, moral or economic injury to the state. However, such restriction does not exist unless speech would produce a clear and imminent danger of some substantive evil to the state. The Court has not yet fixed standards in determining when a danger shall be clear. But no danger flowing from speech can be deemed clear and present unless the threatened evil is so imminent that it may strike before an opportunity for discussion on it. There must be, however, a probability of serious injury to the state. As to review by this court of an allegation of unconstitutionality of a criminal syndicalism act, whenever fundamental rights of free speech and assembly are alleged to have been invaded, the defendant must be allowed to present the issue of whether a clear and present danger was imminent by his actions. Here, mere advocacy of revolution by mass action at some future date was within the Fourteenth Amendment protection. But our power of review was lacking since there was evidence of a criminal conspiracy and such precludes review by this court of errors at a criminal trial absent a showing that constitutional rights were deprived.

▌ ANALYSIS

The *Whitney* case is important for having added to the *Schenck* test of "clear and present danger" the further requirement that the danger must be "imminent." *Schenk v. United States*, 249 U.S. 47 (1919). The opinion by Justice

Continued on next page.

Brandeis in the *Whitney* case should be viewed as a dissenting opinion. His addition of "imminent" flies directly in the face of the majority opinion that punished "mere advocacy" of threatened action against the state. The "mere advocacy" test has not survived. Modernly, through the Smith Act that continues to punish criminal syndicalism, "mere advocacy" is not punishable. The urging of action for forcible overthrow is necessary before punishment will be imposed. Thus, the "urging of action" is the modern test of "clear and present imminent danger" espoused by Justice Brandeis in *Whitney*.

■▬■

Quicknotes

DUE PROCESS CLAUSE Clauses found in the Fifth and Fourteenth Amendments to the United States Constitution providing that no person shall be deprived of "life, liberty, or property, without due process of law."

FOURTEENTH AMENDMENT Declares that no state shall make or enforce any law that shall abridge the privileges and immunities of citizens of the United States. No state shall deny to any person within its jurisdiction the equal protection of the laws.

■▬■

Dennis v. United States

Communist Party members (D) v. Federal government (P)

341 U.S. 494 (1951).

NATURE OF CASE: Appeal from conviction of violating the Smith Act.

FACT SUMMARY: Ringleaders (D) of the American Communist Party were convicted, under the Smith Act, of knowingly advocating the overthrow of government by violent means, and conspiracy.

🏛 RULE OF LAW

In reviewing legislation that restricts freedom of speech, the court, in determining whether a "clear and present danger" exists, must ask whether the gravity of the evil, discounted by its improbability, justifies such invasion of free speech as is necessary to avoid the evil.

FACTS: The Smith Act, passed by Congress in 1940, made it a crime for anyone to knowingly advocate the overthrow of government by force or violence, or by the assassination of any officer. The Act also prohibited an attempt or conspiracy to accomplish the same. Dennis (D) and other ringleaders (D) of the American Communist Party had been conducting seminars, making speeches, and writing articles advocating the overthrow of the U.S. government (P). They were charged with conspiracy in violation of the Smith Act. At their trial, the judge instructed the jury that their only duty was to determine whether a violation of the Act had occurred, and if so, as a matter of law, he had determined that there is sufficient danger of a substantive evil that Congress had a right to prevent that justified the Act's application under the first amendment. Dennis (D) and the other leaders (D) were convicted, and they appealed.

ISSUE: Is the Smith Act, as applied against the leaders of the American Communist Party, constitutional?

HOLDING AND DECISION: (Vinson, C.J.) Yes. In reviewing legislation that restricts freedom of speech, the court, in determining whether a "clear and present danger" exists, must ask whether the gravity of the evil, discounted by its improbability, justifies such invasion of free speech as is necessary to avoid the evil. [The Court initially held that Congress has the power to pass the Smith Act since government has a right to protect itself against armed rebellion.] Congress, by passing the Act, intended not to prohibit the free discussion of political theories, but only advocacy of a dangerous nature. The words of the standard test, "clear and present danger," cannot mean that before the government may act, it must wait until the rebellion is about to be executed, the plans have been laid, and the signal is awaited. The fact that those plotting the rebellion are small and weak, while the government is strong, is irrelevant; success or

probability of success is not the criterion. In determining whether a "clear and present danger exists," the court must determine the gravity of the evil as discounted by the improbability of its occurrence. In the present case, the trial court concluded that the Communist Party, composed of rigidly disciplined members subject to call at the will of the leaders, posed a sufficient danger to justify an intrusion on First Amendment rights. Furthermore, the doctrine that there must be a clear and present danger of a substantive evil that Congress has a right to prevent is a judicial rule to be applied as a matter of law by the courts. The convictions are affirmed.

CONCURRENCE: (Frankfurter, J.) The independence of the judiciary would be jeopardized were courts to become embroiled in the passions of the day and assume primary responsibility in choosing between competing political, economic, and social pressures. How best to reconcile competing interests is the business of legislatures and should not be second-guessed by the judiciary if there is any reasonable basis to sustain it.

CONCURRENCE: (Jackson, J.) The "clear and present danger" test should be applied only in those cases where the issue is criminality of a hot-headed speech on a street corner or circulation of a few pamphlets, etc. It should not be applied in cases like the instant one where the Court must appraise imponderables, including international and national phenomena that baffle the best informed foreign offices and our most experienced politicians.

DISSENT: (Black, J.) The First Amendment as construed in the light of "reasonableness" is not likely to protect any but those safe or orthodox views that rarely need its protection.

DISSENT: (Douglas, J.) Defendants here were indicted for organizing people to teach, and themselves teach, certain books. These books, by Marx and Lenin, may lawfully remain on library shelves. Thus, the Smith Act punishes not what is said, but on the intent with which it is said. Furthermore, pure speech, without seditious conduct, is prohibited. The "clear and present danger" test requires that before speech can be curtailed, conditions must be so critical that there will be no time to avoid the evil that is threatened. That is not the situation here; while the force of Communism may be prevalent in the world, its strength in this country is minimal.

▌ ANALYSIS

After *Dennis,* the Court retreated from its apparent carte blanche approval of congressional attempts to fight domestic

Continued on next page.

Communism. In *Yates v. United States*, 354 U.S. 298 (1957), the Court held that in order for a defendant to be convicted under the Smith Act, the trial judge must instruct the jury to acquit, unless it found that there had been some advocacy of action and not merely an argument for the desirability of the action.

■━■

Quicknotes

SMITH ACT Federal law prohibiting the violent overthrow of government.

■━■

Brandenburg v. Ohio

Ku Klux Klan member (D) v. State (P)

395 U.S. 444 (1969).

NATURE OF CASE: Appeal from conviction for violation of the Ohio Criminal Syndicalism statute.

FACT SUMMARY: Brandenburg (D) was convicted under a state statute that proscribes advocacy of the duty, necessity, or propriety of crime, sabotage, violence, or unlawful methods of terrorism as a means of accomplishing reform.

🏛 RULE OF LAW
The constitutional guarantees of freedom of speech and freedom of press do not permit a state to forbid or proscribe advocacy of the use of force or of law violation, except where such advocacy is directed to inciting or producing imminent lawless action and is likely to produce or incite such action.

FACTS: Brandenburg (D), a Klu Klux Klan leader, was convicted under Ohio's Criminal Syndicalism statute. The statute prohibits advocacy of the duty, necessity, or propriety of crime, sabotage, violence, or unlawful methods of terrorism as a means of accomplishing reform, and the assembling with any group formed to teach or advocate the doctrine of criminal syndicalism. The case against Brandenburg (D) rested on some films. One film showed 12 hooded figures, some carrying firearms, gathered around a wooden cross that they burned. Scattered words could be heard that were derogatory to Jews and Negros. Brandenburg (D) made a speech and stated, "We are not a revengent group, but if our President, our Congress, and our Supreme Court, continues to suppress the white, Caucasian race, it's possible that there might have to be some revengence taken."

ISSUE: Does a statute that proscribes advocacy of the use of force without more violate the rights guaranteed by the First and Fourteenth amendments?

HOLDING AND DECISION: (Per curiam) Yes. The constitutional guarantees of freedom of speech and freedom of press do not permit a state to forbid or proscribe advocacy of the use of force or of law violation, except where such advocacy is directed to inciting or producing imminent lawless action and is likely to incite or produce such action. The mere abstract teaching of the moral propriety or even moral necessity for a resort to force and violence, is not the same as preparing a group for violent action steering it to such action. A statute that fails to draw this distinction impermissibly intrudes upon the freedoms guaranteed by the First and Fourteenth Amendments. It sweeps within its condemnation speech that the Constitution has immunized from governmental control. The Ohio statute purports to punish mere advocacy and to forbid assembly with others merely to advocate the described type of action. Hence, it cannot be sustained. Brandenburg's (D) conviction is reversed.

CONCURRENCE: (Black, J.) The doctrine of "clear and present danger" should have no place in the interpretation of the First Amendment.

CONCURRENCE: (Douglas, J.) It is doubtful that the "clear and present danger" is congenial with the First Amendment. "The line between what is permissible and not subject to control and what may be made impermissible and subject to regulation is the line between ideas and overt acts." Apart from where "speech is brigaded with action," speech should be immune from prosecution.

▶ ANALYSIS

This case demonstrates that the imminence of danger is an essential requirement to the validity of any statute curbing freedom of speech. This requirement was reiterated in *Bond v. Floyd*, 385 U.S. 116 (1966), in which the Court reversed a state legislature's resolution excluding Bond from membership. The exclusion was based on the ground that Bond could not take the oath to support the state and U.S. Constitutions after his endorsement of a SNCC statement and his remarks criticizing the draft and the Vietnam War. The Court found no incitement to violation of law in Bond's remarks.

Quicknotes

FIRST AMENDMENT Prohibits Congress from enacting any law respecting an establishment of religion, prohibiting the free exercise of religion, abridging freedom of speech or the press, the right of peaceful assembly and the right to petition for a redress of grievances.

FOURTEENTH AMENDMENT Declares that no state shall make or enforce any law that shall abridge the privileges and immunities of citizens of the United States. No state shall deny to any person within its jurisdiction the equal protection of the laws.

Cantwell v. Connecticut

Jehovah's Witness (D) v. State (P)

310 U.S. 296 (1940).

NATURE OF CASE: Appeal of conviction for breach of the peace.

FACT SUMMARY: Cantwell (D), on a public street, played a recording of virulent anti-Catholic nature, for which he was convicted of breach of the peace.

RULE OF LAW

Speech not amounting to a clear and present danger to public health or security may not be abridged under the guise of preserving public peace.

FACTS: Cantwell (D), a Jehovah's Witness, positioned himself on a sidewalk and then played to passersby a recording denouncing all other religions in general and Catholicism in particular. Cantwell (D) did not attempt to intimidate anyone into listening against their will. The recording, while insulting, did not call for violence. Cantwell (D) was convicted of breaching the peace, and he appealed.

ISSUE: May speech not amounting to a clear and present danger to public health or security, be abridged under the guise of preserving public peace?

HOLDING AND DECISION: (Roberts, J.) No. Speech not amounting to a clear and present danger to public health or security may not be abridged under the guise of preserving public peace. The Constitution holds that the free communication of ideas is an important value, and something more than a desire to conserve desirable conditions is required to suppress it. An immediate threat to the public is required. Here, the recording in question may have been offensive to some, but it was not a call to violence or other threat to the public. Reversed.

▶ ANALYSIS

A portion of the Court's opinion is interesting to note. Justice Roberts pointed out that Cantwell (D) was not convicted because of the noise his phonograph made, but rather the ideas therein. The inference could be that regulation of the noise would have been permissible. This can be seen as an intimation of the doctrine that content-neutral abridgements of speech will be given greater latitude than content-regulatory ones.

Quicknotes

FIRST AMENDMENT Prohibits Congress from enacting any law respecting an establishment of religion, prohibiting the free exercise of religion, abridging freedom of speech or the press, the right of peaceful assembly and the right to petition for a redress of grievances.

Feiner v. New York

Public speaker (D) v. State (P)

340 U.S. 315 (1951).

NATURE OF CASE: Appeal from conviction for disorderly conduct.

FACT SUMMARY: Feiner (D) gave an open-air speech before a racially mixed audience. The crowd that gathered forced pedestrians into the street. Feiner (D) urged black people to rise up in arms against whites and fight for equal rights. He refused to stop when asked to do so by a police officer and was arrested.

🏛 RULE OF LAW
When clear and present danger of riot, disorder, interference with traffic on the streets, or other immediate threat to public safety, peace, or order, appears, the state has the power to punish or prevent such disorder.

FACTS: Feiner (D) addressed an open-air meeting. A racially mixed crowd of about eighty people gathered. The crowd forced pedestrians walking by into the street. In response to a complaint about the meeting, two police officers arrived. They heard Feiner (D) urge black people to take up arms and fight against whites for equal rights. The remarks stirred up the crowd a little, and one person commented on the police's inability to control the crowd. Another threatened violence if the police did not act. The officers finally "stepped in to prevent it all resulting in a fight." They asked Feiner (D) twice to stop speaking. He ignored them, and they arrested him.

ISSUE: When clear and present danger of riot, disorder, interference with traffic on the streets, or other immediate threat to public safety, peace, or order, appears, does the state has the power to punish or prevent such disorder?

HOLDING AND DECISION: (Vinson, C.J.) Yes. When clear and present danger of riot, disorder, interference with traffic on the streets, or other immediate threat to public safety, peace, or order, appears, the state's has the power to prevent or punish such disorder. Here, the crowd's behavior and Feiner's (D) refusal to obey the police requests presented a sufficient danger to warrant his arrest and to persuade the court that Feiner's (D) conviction for violation of public peace, order and authority does not exceed the bounds of proper state police action. Feiner (D) was neither arrested nor convicted for the making or the content of his speech. Rather, it was the reaction it engendered. The community's interest in maintaining peace and order on its streets must be protected. Hence, Feiner's (D) conviction is affirmed.

DISSENT: (Black, J.) "... will have no part or parcel in this holding which ... view as a long step toward totalitarian authority. Disagreement, mutterings, and objections from a crowd do not indicate imminent threat of a riot; nor does one threat to assault the speaker. Even assuming that a critical situation existed, it was the duty of the police to protect Feiner's (D) right to speak, which they made no effort to do. Finally, a person making a lawful address is not required to be silent merely because an officer so directs. Here, Feiner (D) received no explanation as to why he was being directed to stop speaking. This decision means that the police have the discretion to silence minority views in any city as soon as the customary hostility to such views develops."

▶ *ANALYSIS*

As *Feiner* demonstrates, free speech is not an absolute right. The conflicting interest of community order must also be considered. *Feiner* points out the question of whether the boundaries of protected speech depend on the content of the speech and the speaker's words or on the environment, the crowd reaction or potential crowd reaction. This question arose again in *Gregory v. Chicago*, 394 U.S. 111 (1969), which reversed convictions of disorderly conduct. There, participants in a "peaceful and orderly procession" to press their claims for desegregation were arrested when, after the number of bystanders increased, and some became unruly, they were asked to disperse and did not. The majority asserted that this was a simple case as the marchers' peaceful conduct was a protected activity within the First Amendment. The concurring opinion saw *Gregory* as involving some complexities, since, as the judge noted, both the demonstrators and the officers had tried to restrain the hecklers but were unable to do so. He concluded that "this record is a crying example of a need for some narrowly drawn law," rather than the sweeping disorderly conduct law.

Quicknotes

FIRST AMENDMENT Prohibits Congress from enacting any law respecting an establishment of religion, prohibiting the free exercise of religion, abridging freedom of speech or the press, the right of peaceful assembly and the right to petition for a redress of grievances.

Chaplinsky v. New Hampshire

Jehovah's Witness (D) v. State (P)

315 U.S. 568 (1942).

NATURE OF CASE: Appeal of a conviction for violation of statute forbidding utterance of words derisive or annoying to another.

FACT SUMMARY: Chaplinsky (D), a Jehovah's Witness, first denounced all other religions as "rackets" and then called a Marshall a "fascist" and "racketeer."

🏛 RULE OF LAW
A government may proscribe language tending to incite violence.

FACTS: Chaplinsky (D), a Jehovah's Witness, had been calling other religions "rackets." An unfriendly crowd began to assemble. A Marshall warned Chaplinsky (D) that the crowd was getting ugly, whereupon Chaplinsky (D) called the Marshall a "racketeer" and a "fascist." Chaplinsky (D) was convicted under an ordinance prohibiting the utterance of words tending to harass, annoy, or deride another. Chaplinsky (D) appealed.

ISSUE: May a government proscribe language tending to incite violence?

HOLDING AND DECISION: (Murphy, J.) Yes. A government may proscribe language tending to incite violence. It is established that words constituting a clear and present danger to the public health may be banned. So-called "fighting words" do constitute such a danger. The ordinance in question basically is a prohibition of fighting words, and therefore the ordinance is valid. Affirmed.

▶ ANALYSIS

This case presents one of the first enunciations of the concept of "protected" and "unprotected" speech, among them libel, obscenity, and "fighting words." The scope of the former two categories has been the subject of much subsequent analysis.

■=■

Quicknotes

FIGHTING WORDS Unprotected speech under the First Amendment that is likely to instigate a violent reaction.

■=■

New York Times Co. v. United States; United States v. Washington Post Co.

Federal government (P) v. Press (D)

403 U.S. 713 (1971).

NATURE OF CASE: Review of denial of injunctions against newspapers.

FACT SUMMARY: The United States (P) sought to enjoin the further publication of a top secret Defense Department study of the Vietnam War, known as the Pentagon Papers.

RULE OF LAW
There is a special presumption that the First Amendment does not permit the use of prior restraints.

FACTS: When the Washington Post (D) and the New York Times (D) began publishing the Pentagon Papers, the Government (P) sought to enjoin further publication, claiming that further publication of the top secret study would endanger national security and prolong the Vietnam War. The district court and the Court of Appeals for the District of Columbia Circuit held that the Government (P) had not met the heavy burden of showing justification for the imposition of a prior restraint. The New York district court had also ruled that the Government (P) had not met its burden, but the Second Circuit Court of Appeals reversed. Restraining orders were issued while the two cases were appealed. The Supreme Court granted certiorari.

ISSUE: Is there a special presumption that the First Amendment does not permit the use of prior restraints?

HOLDING AND DECISION: (Per curiam) Yes. There is a special presumption that the First Amendment does not permit the use of prior restraints. The Government (P) has not met its heavy burden of showing justification for the imposition of a prior restraint on speech. The Second Circuit's decision is reversed and the other judgments are affirmed.

CONCURRENCE: (Black, J.) The First Amendment abolished the government's power to censor the press. The judiciary cannot make laws enjoining publication of current news and abridging freedom of the press in the name of 'national security.'

CONCURRENCE: (Douglas, J.) That these disclosures may have a serious impact is no basis for sanctioning a previous restraint on the press. Open debate and discussion of public issues are vital to the national health.

CONCURRENCE: (Brennan, J.) It was error to grant any injunctive relief whatever, interim or otherwise. The First Amendment does not tolerate any prior judicial restraints of the press predicated upon surmise or conjecture that untoward consequences may result. Unless and until the government has clearly made its case, the First Amendment commands that no injunction may issue.

CONCURRENCE: (Stewart, J.) The executive branch may promulgate and enforce executive regulations to protect the confidentiality necessary to carry out its responsibilities in international relations and national defense. In the absence of specific regulations or laws, it cannot be said that disclosure of the documents at issue will surely result in direct, immediate, and irreparable damage to the nation. That being so there is only one judicial resolution under the First Amendment.

CONCURRENCE: (White, J.) The Government's (P) failure to justify prior restraints does not measure its constitutional entitlement to a conviction for criminal publication. That the Government (P) mistakenly chose to proceed by injunction does not mean that it could not have successfully proceeded in another way.

CONCURRENCE: (Marshall, J.) Congress has specifically rejected passing legislation that would have clearly given the President the power he seeks here to prevent publication of sensitive material damaging to "national security." It is not for this Court to overrule Congress.

DISSENT: (Burger, C.J.) These are not easy cases because no one knows all the facts. We are in this posture because these cases have been conducted in unseemly haste. When judges are pressured as in these cases the result is a parody of the judicial function.

DISSENT: (Harlan, J.) The Court has been almost irresponsibly feverish in dealing with these cases. The doctrine of separation of powers permits the judiciary to review the initial executive determination that disclosure of these documents would irreparably impair the national security, but it does not permit the judiciary to redetermine for itself the probable impact of disclosure on the national security.

DISSENT: (Blackmun, J.) I would remand to allow the orderly presentation of evidence from both sides. The publication of some of these documents could clearly result in great harm to the nation because it could lead to the death of soldiers, the destruction of alliances, the increased difficulty of negotiations with our enemies, the prolongation of the war, and the further delay in the freeing of U.S. prisoners.

ANALYSIS

These cases illustrate the fact that injunctions are considered to be prior restraints. A prior restraint may be invalid

Continued on next page.

even if the speech at issue would result in a criminal prosecution. The doctrine of prior restraint reflects the historical right of the press to be free from licensing or censorship.

■≡■

Quicknotes

FIRST AMENDMENT Prohibits Congress from enacting any law respecting an establishment of religion, prohibiting the free exercise of religion, abridging freedom of speech or the press, the right of peaceful assembly and the right to petition for a redress of grievances.

PRIOR RESTRAINT A restriction imposed on speech imposed prior to its communication.

■≡■

Gooding v. Wilson

State (P) v. Antiwar demonstrator (D)

405 U.S. 518 (1972).

NATURE OF CASE: Appeal of grant of federal habeas corpus.

FACT SUMMARY: Wilson (D), arrested during an antiwar demonstration, was convicted under a statute proscribing words tending to cause a breach of the peace.

🏛 RULE OF LAW
Statutes abridging freedom of speech must be narrowly drawn to abridge only unprotected expression.

FACTS: Wilson (D) was arrested during an antiwar demonstration. Wilson (D) used threatening and highly derisive language to the officers. He was convicted under a statute proscribing words tending to cause a breach of the peace. Wilson (D) sought and obtained habeas corpus, which was appealed.

ISSUE: Must statutes abridging freedom of speech be narrowly drawn to abridge only unprotected expression?

HOLDING AND DECISION: (Brennan, J.) Yes. Statutes abridging freedom of speech must be narrowly drawn to abridge only unprotected expression. A state may regulate, for instance, "fighting words," which are unprotected. However, this statute, while admittedly pertaining to such language, impermissibly covers other types of language, as the expression of ideas can breach the peace. While it may be true that the speech here would be properly abridged under a more narrowly drawn statute, the statute itself must fall here. Affirmed.

DISSENT: (Burger, C.J.) No danger for sweeping application of the statute in question exists, so it should be upheld.

DISSENT: (Blackmun, J.) It is anomalous on the one hand to admit that a state could proscribe certain conduct and at the same time strike down a statute proscribing such conduct.

▶ ANALYSIS

The present case presents an example of the "overbreadth" doctrine. As the name implies, a court in a First Amendment case will look to the language of a statute. If the statute can be applied to cover protected speech, it will be struck down, even if the speech in question could have been properly circumscribed.

the free exercise of religion, abridging freedom of speech or the press, the right of peaceful assembly and the right to petition for a redress of grievances.

Quicknotes

FIRST AMENDMENT Prohibits Congress from enacting any law respecting an establishment of religion, prohibiting

Lovell v. Griffin

Literature distributor (D) v. Municipality (P)

303 U.S. 444 (1938).

NATURE OF CASE: Appeal from conviction of violation of city ordinance prohibiting the distribution of circulars, handbooks, advertising, or literature of any kind without first obtaining written permission from the City Manager.

FACT SUMMARY: Lovell (D) distributed religious tracts and magazines in the City of Griffin (P), without first obtaining a permit from the City Manager.

🏛 RULE OF LAW
An ordinance that prohibits the distribution of literature of any kind at any time, at any place, and in any manner without a prior permit is unconstitutional in that it subjects the right of freedom of the press to license and censorship.

FACTS: A City of Griffin (P) ordinance provided that no circulars, handbooks, advertising, or literature of any kind will be distributed within the city limits without first obtaining written permission from the City Manager. Lovell (D) distributed a pamphlet and a magazine in the nature of religious tracts, without obtaining written permission from the City Manager. She contended first that the ordinance abridged freedom of the press and the free exercise of her religion.

ISSUE: Does an ordinance that prohibits the distribution of literature of any kind without first obtaining a written permit violate the constitutional right of freedom of the press?

HOLDING AND DECISION: (Hughes, C.J.) Yes. An ordinance that prohibits the distribution of literature of any kind at any time, at any place, and in any manner without a prior permit is unconstitutional in that it subjects the right of freedom of the press to license and censorship. The City of Griffin (P) ordinance was in no way limited to literature that is obscene or offensive to public morals or that advocates unlawful conduct. It embraced literature in the widest sense without any restriction in its application with respect to time or place. It prohibited the distribution of literature of any kind, at any time, at any place, and in any manner without a permit from the City Manager. The ordinance was invalid on its face in that it subjected the freedom of the press to license and censorship. Reversed.

▶ ANALYSIS

What a state may not do by direct regulation, it may not do indirectly through licensing, permit, or registration statutes. As *Lovell* demonstrates, just as a state may not constitutionally ban all speech in public places, it may not require, as a condition precedent to the exercise of free speech in public, that a citizen first obtain a permit, the granting or denial of which is discretionary with local authorities. The Court also invalidated an ordinance that banned the unlicensed communication of any views from door to door. It made canvassing in public subject to a police officer's determination of what could be distributed and who could distribute it. Likewise, it has been held that a requirement that one must register before making a speech in public to enlist support for a lawful movement is quite incompatible with the First Amendment.

■=■

Quicknotes

FIRST AMENDMENT Prohibits Congress from enacting any law respecting an establishment of religion, prohibiting the free exercise of religion, abridging freedom of speech or the press, the right of peaceful assembly and the right to petition for a redress of grievances.

■=■

Near v. Minnesota

News publisher (D) v. State (P)

283 U.S. 697 (1931).

NATURE OF CASE: Action to abate publication of a newspaper as a public nuisance.

FACT SUMMARY: Minnesota (P) sought to have an injunction issued against the Saturday Press (D), which was publishing articles charging public officials with dereliction and complicity in dealing with gangsters.

> **RULE OF LAW**
> A state statute that authorizes previous restraints on publication violates the liberty of the press guaranteed by the Fourteenth Amendment if such publication relates to the malfeasance of public officials.

FACTS: A Minnesota (P) statute authorized abatement as a public nuisance of a "malicious, scandalous and defamatory" newspaper. The law permitted the defense of good motives and justifiable ends. The Saturday Press (D) had published a series of articles charging that gangsters were in control of gambling, bootlegging, and racketeering in Minneapolis, and that public officials were either derelict in their duties, or had illicit relations with the gangsters. Minnesota (P) sought to abate further publication of the Saturday Press (D), which was "malicious, scandalous, or defamatory." The trial court issued a permanent injunction, and the Press (D) appealed.

ISSUE: Is a state statute that authorizes abatement of a newspaper publication dealing with the corruption of public officials unconstitutional?

HOLDING AND DECISION: (Hughes, C.J.) Yes. A state statute that authorizes previous restraints on publication violates the liberty of the press guaranteed by the Fourteenth Amendment if such publication relates to the malfeasance of public officials. It is the chief purpose of the constitutional guaranty of freedom of press to prevent previous restraint on publication. Placing previous restraints on the press endangers the very nature of a free state. Only in exceptional circumstances may previous restraints be imposed. These would include where a government seeks to prevent actual obstruction to its recruiting service or the publication of the sailing dates of transports or the number and location of troops. Similarly, obscene publications and incitements to acts of violence or the overthrow by force of orderly government may be enjoined. However, previous restraint on a publication that seeks to expose the malfeasance of public officials is prohibited by the Fourteenth Amendment. Public officials have recourse against false accusations under the libel law. Finally, requiring newspapers to present proof of their good intentions is merely an additional step to a complete system of censorship. So far as the Minnesota (P)

statute authorized the abatement proceedings against the Saturday Press (D), it was unconstitutional. Reversed.

DISSENT: (Butler, J.) The Minnesota (P) statute does not operate as a "previous restraint on publication" within the proper meaning of that phrase. It does not authorize administrative control in advance such as was formerly exercised by the licensors and censors, but prescribes a remedy to be enforced by a suit in equity. Existing libel laws are ineffective to suppress the evils occasioned by false and malicious publications.

▍ *ANALYSIS*

"The issue is not whether the government may impose a particular restriction of substance in an area of public expression, such as forbidding obscenity in newspapers, but whether it may do so by a particular method, such as advance screening of newspaper copy. In other words, restrictions that could be validly imposed when enforced by subsequent punishment are, nevertheless, forbidden if attempted by prior restraint." Emerson, The Doctrine of Prior Restraint, 20 L. & Contemp. Prob. 648 (1956). Traditionally, the judicial concern in prior restraint cases is on the broad discretion over free expression vested in administrative officers.

■==■

Quicknotes

FOURTEENTH AMENDMENT Declares that no state shall make or enforce any law that shall abridge the privileges and immunities of citizens of the United States. No state shall deny to any person within its jurisdiction the equal protection of the laws.

■==■

New York Times v. Sullivan

News publisher (D) v. Public official (P)

376 U.S. 254 (1964).

NATURE OF CASE: Appeal of defamation judgment.

FACT SUMMARY: The New York Times (D) published an editorial advertisement in which false statements were made that concerned Sullivan (P).

🏛 RULE OF LAW
The First Amendment requires that a public official may not recover damages for defamatory falsehoods relating to his official conduct unless he proves that the statement involved was made with "actual malice—that is, with knowledge that it was false or with reckless disregard of whether it was false or not."

FACTS: Sullivan (P) was a commissioner in the city of Montgomery, Alabama, charged with supervision of the Police Department. During a series of civil rights demonstrations in that city in 1960, the New York Times (D) published an editorial advertisement entitled "Heed Their Rising Voices," in which several charges of terrorism were leveled at the Police Department. The falsity of some of these statements is uncontroverted. The advertisement charged that nine students at a local college had been expelled for leading a march on the state capitol when, in fact, the reason had been an illegal lunch counter sit-in. The advertisement charged that the police had padlocked the dining hall of the college to starve the demonstrators into submission when, in fact, no padlocking had occurred. Other false statements also were made. Sullivan (P) brought a defamation action against the New York Times (D) for these statements and recovered $500,000. Under Alabama law, a publication is libel per se (no special damages need be proved—general damages are presumed), whenever a defamatory falsehood is shown to have injured its subject in his public office or impute misconduct to him in his office. The New York Times (D) appealed the Alabama judgment, challenging this rule.

ISSUE: Are defamatory falsehoods regarding public officials protected by constitutional guarantees of freedom of speech and press?

HOLDING AND DECISION: (Brennan, J.) Yes. The First Amendment requires that a public official may not recover damages for defamatory falsehoods relating to his official conduct unless he proves that the statement involved was made with "actual malice—that is, with knowledge that it was false or with reckless disregard of whether it was false or not." First Amendment protections do not turn upon the truth, popularity, or social utility of ideas and beliefs that are involved. Rather, they are based upon the theory that erroneous statements are inevitable in free debate and must be protected if such freedom is to survive. Only where malice is involved do such protections cease. Here, the Alabama rule

falls short of this standard and the evidence at trial was insufficient to determine its existence. The decision must, therefore, be reversed and remanded.

CONCURRENCE: (Black, J.) The federal Constitution has dealt with this deadly danger to the press in the only way possible without leaving the free press open to destruction—by granting to the press an absolute immunity for criticism of the way public officials do their public duty. "Malice," even as defined by the Court, is an elusive, abstract concept, hard to prove and hard to disprove. The requirement that malice be proved provides at best an evanescent protection for the right critically to discuss public affairs and certainly does not measure up to the sturdy safeguard embodied in the First Amendment.

▶ ANALYSIS

New York Times v. Sullivan is the landmark case in constitutional defamation law. Subsequent cases have expanded this concept even further. In *Rosenblatt v. Baer*, 383 U.S. 75 (1966), the Court defined "public official" as anyone having substantial responsibility for conduct of government affairs. In *Curtis Publishing Co. v. Butts* (decided together with) *Associated Press v. Walker*, 388 U.S. 130 (1967), *New York Times v. Sullivan* was extended to "public figures" as well as officials. In *Gertz v. Robert Welch, Inc.*, 418 U.S. 323 (1974), however, the Court retreated a bit by stating that, "As long as they do not impose liability without fault, the states may define for themselves the appropriate standard of liability for (a) publisher . . . of defamatory falsehood injurious to a private individual." Note that the Court also has taken steps to toughen the *New York Times v. Sullivan*'s recklessness standard. In *St. Amont v. Thompson*, 390 U.S. 727 (1968), the Court ruled that recklessness was not to be measured by the reasonable person standard, but rather by the subjective standard of whether or not the defendant in the case subjectively entertained serious doubts about the truth of his statements.

Quicknotes

DEFAMATION PER SE An intentional false publication of words which, standing alone without proof, communicated publicly in either oral or written form, subject a person to scorn, hatred or ridicule.

FIRST AMENDMENT Prohibits Congress from enacting any law respecting an establishment of religion, prohibiting the free exercise of religion, abridging freedom of speech

Continued on next page.

or the press, the right of peaceful assembly and the right to petition for a redress of grievances.

MALICE The intention to commit an unlawful act with the intent to inflict injury without justification or excuse.

Cox Broadcasting Corp. v. Cohn

Broadcasting company (D) v. Father of rape victim (P)

420 U.S. 469 (1975).

NATURE OF CASE: Appeal from conviction for invasion of privacy.

FACT SUMMARY: Cohn (P) sued the Cox Broadcasting Corp. (D) for invading his privacy by identifying his daughter as a rape victim.

🏛 RULE OF LAW
The First and Fourteenth Amendments prevent state sanctions for publication of truthful information contained in official court records that are open to public inspection.

FACTS: Cohn's (P) daughter was a murder and rape victim. The Georgia code prohibited the publication of the name or identity of a rape victim. At the trial a reporter for the Cox Broadcasting Corp. (D) obtained the Cohn's (P) daughter's name by examining public records. The girl's name was broadcast during a news report concerning the crime and the trial. Cohn (P) sued the Cox Broadcasting Corp. (D) for violating the Georgia code that protects the privacy of rape victims. The trial court granted a judgment for Cohn (P). The Georgia Supreme Court affirmed for Cohn (P). The Cox Broadcasting Corp. (D) appealed.

ISSUE: May a state impose sanctions upon the publication of truthful information contained in official court records open to public inspection?

HOLDING AND DECISION: (White, J.) No. The First and Fourteenth Amendments prevent state sanctions for publication of truthful information contained in official court records open to public inspection. The right to privacy is not invaded by any publication made in a court of justice, and reports of any such proceedings that are open to public inspection may be published without invading a person's right to privacy. If there are privacy interests to be protected in judicial proceedings, the states must respond by means that avoid public documentation or other exposure of private information. Here, the defendant simply published truthful information contained in official court records that were open to public inspection; it did not invade the plaintiff's privacy. Judgment is entered for Cox Broadcasting Corp. (D). Reversed.

▌ ANALYSIS

By declaring that persons have no reasonable expectation of privacy in information contained in public records, the Court in *Cox* materially constricted the constitutional right to privacy. Note that this rule runs contrary to the well established defamation rule that the scope of publication of any statement may increase liability. Note also that this rule runs

the risk of motivating and justifying (especially on the facts of *Cox*) government secrecy "gag orders," etc., under the subterfuge of protecting citizens from press embarrassment. Note also that *Cox* appears, at least theoretically, to threaten the privacy cause of action based on unauthorized disclosure of privileged information—since disclosure here, though not subject to privilege, was illegal.

■══■

Quicknotes

FIRST AMENDMENT Prohibits Congress from enacting any law respecting an establishment of religion, prohibiting the free exercise of religion, abridging freedom of speech or the press, the right of peaceful assembly and the right to petition for a redress of grievances.

FOURTEENTH AMENDMENT Declares that no state shall make or enforce any law that shall abridge the privileges and immunities of citizens of the United States. No state shall deny to any person within its jurisdiction the equal protection of the laws.

GAG ORDER Court order mandating that the parties or reporters not discuss or publicize the case so that the defendant may receive a fair trial.

■══■

Virginia State Board of Pharmacy v. Virginia Citizens Consumer Council

State agency (D) v. Public interest group (P)

425 U.S. 748 (1976).

NATURE OF CASE: Action for declaratory relief.

FACT SUMMARY: A Virginia statute made it illegal for pharmacists to advertise the prices of prescription drugs.

🏛 RULE OF LAW
"The consumer's interest in the free flow of commercial information" makes such information the type of expression the First Amendment is designed to protect—even if it does "no more than propose a commercial transaction."

FACTS: By Virginia law, the advertising of prescription drug prices by pharmacists was deemed "unprofessional conduct" subjecting offending pharmacists to various penalties. The Consumer Council (P), a private public interest organization, filed this action in federal district court, to have the Virginia law declared an unconstitutional violation of the First Amendment rights of both pharmacists and consumers. The Council (P) offered evidence that the advertising ban had resulted in wide price variations from outlet to outlet. From a declaration of unconstitutionality, this appeal followed.

ISSUE: Does the First Amendment protect such purely commercial speech activity as price advertising?

HOLDING AND DECISION: (Blackmun, J.) Yes. The consumer's interest in the free flow of commercial information makes such information the type of expression the First Amendment is designed to protect, even if it does no more than propose a commercial transaction. If there is a kind of speech that lacks all First Amendment protection, it must be distinguished by its content. Yet the speech whose content deprives it of protection cannot simply be speech on a commercial subject. No one would contend that a pharmacist may be prevented from being heard on the subject of whether, in general, pharmaceutical prices should be regulated, or their advertisement forbidden. Nor can it be dispositive that a commercial advertisement is noneditorial, and merely reports a fact. Purely factual matter of public interest may claim protection. Even though an advertiser's interest is a purely economic one, such fact does not disqualify the advertiser from First Amendment protection. A particular consumer's interest in the free flow of commercial information may be as keen, if not keener by far, than his interest in the day's most urgent political debate. As applied to the instant case, when drug prices vary as strikingly as they do, information as to who is charging what becomes more than a convenience. It could mean the alleviation of pain or the enjoyment of basic necessities. Affirmed.

DISSENT: (Rehnquist, J.) The Court's extraordinary decision today not only usurps the power of the state legislature to make policy decisions about professionals, it also opens the door to possible irresponsible advertising and interference in the doctor-patient relationship.

▶ ANALYSIS

This case finally did away with the often criticized rule that the First Amendment does not protect pure commercial speech. In *Bigelow v. Virginia*, 421 U.S. 809 (1975), the Court had invalidated a Virginia statute that made the advertising of abortions illegal. The Court there indicated that abortion was of "public interest" and therefore information about it was constitutionally protected. *Consumer Council* expands that to cover all commercial advertising. Note that this case has stimulated speculation that advertising bans on attorneys are also unconstitutional. Indeed, several state bar associations have recently begun drafting new regulations in this regard.

■■■

Quicknotes

FIRST AMENDMENT Prohibits Congress from enacting any law respecting an establishment of religion, prohibiting the free exercise of religion, abridging freedom of speech or the press, the right of peaceful assembly and the right to petition for a redress of grievances.

■■■

Miller v. California

Advertisment distributor (D) v. State (P)

413 U.S. 15 (1973).

NATURE OF CASE: Criminal prosecution for knowingly distributing obscene matter.

FACT SUMMARY: Miller (D) sent out advertising brochures for adult books to unwilling recipients.

🏛 RULE OF LAW
Material is obscene and not protected by the First Amendment if: (1) the average person, applying contemporary community standards, would find that the work, taken as a whole, appeals to the prurient interest; (2) the work depicts in a patently offensive way sexual conduct specifically defined by the applicable state law; and (3) the work, taken as a whole, lacks serious literary, artistic, political, or scientific value.

FACTS: Miller (D) conducted a mass mailing campaign to advertise the sale of adult books. The advertising brochures were themselves found obscene. These brochures were sent to unwilling recipients who had not requested the material. Miller (D) was convicted of violating a statute that forbade knowingly distributing obscene matter.

ISSUE: Is material that is obscene protected by the First Amendment?

HOLDING AND DECISION: (Burger, C.J.) No. Material is obscene and not protected by the First Amendment if: (1) the average person, applying contemporary community standards, would find that the work, taken as a whole, appeals to the prurient interest; (2) the work depicts in a patently offensive way sexual conduct specifically defined by the applicable state law; and (3) the work, taken as a whole, lacks serious literary, artistic, political, or scientific value. If material meets this definition of obscenity, then the state can prohibit its distribution if the mode of distribution entails the risk of offending unwilling recipients or exposing the material to juveniles. The burden of proof of the *Memoirs* test, (*Memoirs v. Massachusetts,* 383 U.S. 113 (1966), that the material be utterly without redeeming value, is virtually impossible for the prosecution to meet and must be abandoned. There is no fixed national standard of "prurient interest" or "patently offensive" and these first two parts of the test are questions of fact to be resolved by the jury by applying contemporary community standards. Vacated and remanded.

DISSENT: (Douglas, J.) Courts were never given the constitutional power to make definitions of obscenity. The idea that the First Amendment permits punishment for ideas that are "offensive" is astounding. No greater leveler of speech or literature has ever been designed.

DISSENT: (Brennan, J.) The statute in question is unconstitutionally overbroad and therefore invalid on its face.

▶ ANALYSIS

The *Miller* test of obscenity is the most current test. If the three requirements are met, then the material in question is considered obscene and outside the protection of the First Amendment. *Miller* is a turnaround from *Memoirs* for many reasons: the *Memoirs* standard was too difficult to prove; the lower courts had no clear-cut guidelines because *Memoirs* was a plurality opinion; the court decided to use local community standards to allow greater jury power; and the court was beginning to feel institutional pressures, since every obscenity question was a constitutional question. Therefore, *Miller* was an attempt by the Court to decentralize decision-making.

Quicknotes

FIRST AMENDMENT Prohibits Congress from enacting any law respecting an establishment of religion, prohibiting the free exercise of religion, abridging freedom of speech or the press, the right of peaceful assembly and the right to petition for a redress of grievances.

Paris Adult Theatre I v. Slaton

Movie theatres (D) v. State (P)

413 U.S. 49 (1973).

NATURE OF CASE: Civil proceeding to enjoin continued showing of two adult films.

FACT SUMMARY: Two adult films were shown at theaters that advertised the nature of the films and required proof that all patrons were over 21.

🏛 RULE OF LAW
A state can forbid the dissemination of obscene material to consenting adults in order to preserve the quality of the community and to prevent the possibility of resulting antisocial behavior.

FACTS: Two movie theatres in Atlanta showed "adult" films exclusively. The state of Georgia sought to enjoin the showing of sexually explicit movies in these theatres under an obscenity statute. It was determined that the exterior advertising was not obscene or offensive, but that there were signs at the entrance stating that patrons must be 21 years of age and able to prove it. There was a further warning that those who would be offended by nudity should not enter. However, the films in question included, in addition to nudity, various simulated sex acts.

ISSUE: Can a state prohibit the dissemination of obscene material if the material is distributed only to consenting adults?

HOLDING AND DECISION: (Burger, C.J.) Yes. A state can forbid the dissemination of obscene material to consenting adults in order to preserve the quality of the community and to prevent the possibility of resulting antisocial behavior. A state has a valid interest in preventing exposure of obscene material to consenting adults. Even if exposure to juveniles and unwilling observers is prevented, the state has a further interest in preserving the quality of life, the community environment, and possible threats to public safety, which will allow the regulation of obscenity. Even if there is no conclusive scientific proof that exposure to obscenity adversely affects either an individual or society, it is for the legislature, not the courts, to resolve these empirical uncertainties. A legislature can determine that a connection between obscenity and antisocial behavior exists, even in the absence of conclusive proof. Here, even though only consenting adults are involved, the state can make a judgment that public exhibition of obscenity has a tendency to injure the community and can, therefore, enjoin the distribution of obscenity. Vacated and remanded.

DISSENT: (Brennan, J.) Prior obscenity standards have proved unworkable because they fail to give adequate notice of the definition of obscenity, producing a chilling effect on constitutionally protected speech. Because of the vague nature of these standards, every case is marginal, producing a vast number of constitutional questions, which creates institutional stress in the judicial system. States do have a valid interest in protecting children and unconsenting adults from exposure to allegedly obscene material, but other possible state interests, as discussed in the majority opinion, are vague, speculative, and cannot be proven. Therefore, in the absence of threat of exposure to juveniles or unconsenting adults, material cannot be suppressed, but the state can regulate the manner of distribution.

▶ ANALYSIS

The Court, in three companion cases to the principal case, also upheld obscenity convictions on seizures involving the importation of films from a foreign country, the interstate transportation of obscene materials for private use, and the sale of an obscene book that contained no pictures. In 1974, however, the Court overturned an obscenity conviction for the showing of "Carnal Knowledge," a film with an MPAA rating of "R." While asserting that the finding of obscenity was essentially a question of fact for the jury, the Court warned that the jury did not have unbridled discretion in this area. In another case, the Court also stated that the community standard to be applied was local, not national. Justice Brennan dissented, arguing that requiring a national distributor to comply with numerous local standards was totally unreasonable.

◼︎▭◼︎

Quicknotes

FIRST AMENDMENT Prohibits Congress from enacting any law respecting an establishment of religion, prohibiting the free exercise of religion, abridging freedom of speech or the press, the right of peaceful assembly and the right to petition for a redress of grievances.

OBSCENITY Indecency, lewdness or offensive behavior in appearance or expression.

◼︎▭◼︎

Cohen v. California

Wearer of jacket with text (D) v. State (P)

403 U.S. 15 (1971).

NATURE OF CASE: Criminal prosecution for violation of disturbing the peace statute.

FACT SUMMARY: Cohen (D) wore a jacket with the words "Fuck the Draft" on it in a courthouse corridor and was arrested and convicted under a disturbing the peace statute.

🏛 RULE OF LAW
A state cannot bar the use of offensive words either because such words are inherently likely to cause a violent reaction or because the state wishes to eliminate such words to protect the public morality.

FACTS: Cohen (D) was arrested in a courthouse because he was wearing a jacket bearing the words "Fuck the Draft." Cohen (D) did not engage in any act of violence or any other unlawful act. There was also no evidence that anyone who saw the jacket became violently aroused or even protested the jacket. Cohen (D) testified that he wore the jacket to inform people of his feelings against the Vietnam War and the draft. He was convicted under a statute prohibiting "maliciously and willfully disturbing the peace or quiet . . . by offensive conduct." The state court held that "offensive conduct" meant conduct that had a tendency to provoke others to disturb the peace.

ISSUE: Can a state constitutionally prevent the use of certain words on the ground that the use of such words is offensive conduct?

HOLDING AND DECISION: (Harlan, J.) No. A state cannot constitutionally prohibit the use of offensive words. Here, Cohen (D) could not be punished for criticizing the draft, so the statute could be upheld, if at all, only as a regulation of the manner, not the substantive content, of his speech. Cohen's (D) speech does not come within any of the exceptions to the general rule that the form and content of speech cannot be regulated: (1) this is not a prohibition designed to protect courthouse decorum because the statute is not so limited; (2) this is not an obscenity case because Cohen's (D) words were not erotic; (3) this is not a case of fighting words that are punishable as inherently likely to provoke a violent reaction because here the words were not directed as a personal insult to any person; and (4) this is not a captive audience problem since a viewer could merely avert his eyes, there is no evidence of objection by those who saw the jacket, and the statute is not so limited. The state tries to justify the conviction because the words are inherently likely to cause a violent reaction, but this argument cannot be upheld because these are not fighting words and there is no evidence that words that are merely offensive would cause such a response. Next the state justifies the conviction on the ground that the state is guardian of the public morality. This argument is unacceptable because "offensive" is an unlimited concept and forbidding the use of such words would also cause the risk of suppressing the accompanying ideas. Therefore, there are no valid state interests that support the regulation of offensive words in public. Reversed.

DISSENT: (Blackmun, J.) Cohen's (D) conviction can be upheld both because his speech was fighting words and also because his act was conduct and not speech. Additionally, the state court subsequently restricted the statute in question to the fighting words context, so the case should be remanded and reconsidered under this construction.

▶ ANALYSIS

This case reasserts the *Chaplinsky v. New Hampshire*, 315 U.S. 568 (1942), holding that fighting words are not protected by the First Amendment. Fighting words, then, are only those words that are likely to cause an immediate breach of the peace by another person, and are not just offensive words. More importantly, this case holds that a state has no valid interest in preventing the use of offensive words when there is no competing privacy interest. Here, the public in general has no right to protection from hearing either offensive words or offensive ideas.

Quicknotes

FIGHTING WORDS Unprotected speech that inflicts injury by its very utterance and provokes violence from the audience.

Beauharnais v. Illinois

Publisher (D) v. State (P)

343 U.S. 250 (1952).

NATURE OF CASE: Appeal from a criminal conviction.

FACT SUMMARY: Beauharnais (D) was convicted under an Illinois (P) statute making it a crime to publish any material criticizing members of a group in a way that subjects them to ridicule or invited civil unrest.

🏛 RULE OF LAW
A statute that makes it a crime to libel the members of any class or group is not repugnant to the Constitution.

FACTS: An Illinois (P) law made it a crime to publish or exhibit any lithograph, movie, play or sketch that attributed depravity, criminality, or other conduct lacking in virtue to a racial or religious group in such a way as to expose the members of that group to derision or to cause a breach of the peace. Beauharnais (D), president of the White Circle League, arranged for the distribution of lithographs that urged whites to prevent further encroachment by Negroes and that described the alleged criminality, violence, and drug use rampant among Negroes. Beauharnais (D) was charged with violating the State (P) statute, but argued that the enactment deprived him of freedom of speech and press and was unconstitutionally vague. Beauharnais (D) was found guilty and his conviction was affirmed by the Illinois Supreme Court, which identified the challenged statute as "a form of criminal libel law." The United States Supreme Court then agreed to review the conviction.

ISSUE: Is a statute that makes it a crime to libel the members of any class or group repugnant to the Constitution?

HOLDING AND DECISION: (Frankfurter, J.) No. A statute that makes it a crime to libel the members of any class or group is not repugnant to the Constitution. Originally, libel was a common law crime to which even truth was not a defense. In Illinois (P), as in most states, truth is now a defense to a criminal libel charge only if publication was made "with good motives and for justifiable ends." Since Beauharnais's (D) offers of proof made no effort to establish motive or justification, the trial court properly concluded that the lithographs were libelous as a matter of law, and permitted the jury to decide only the issue of publication. Profane or cruelly pejorative expressions may be punished by a state without interfering with anyone's constitutionally guaranteed privileges. Historically, violence and bloodshed have accompanied racial disputes in Illinois (P). Whether or not the contested statute is the best way of dealing with the problem, it is a reasonable exercise of the legislature's power to preserve the peace and protect the public. The statute is drawn with sufficient narrowness and clarity, and punishes only utterances which are indisputably libelous. Therefore, the law is constitutional and Beauharnais's (D) conviction must be affirmed.

DISSENT: (Black, J.) This "group libel law" exemplifies an invidious form of censorship. Traditional criminal libel laws apply only to attacks upon individuals, not groups. In racial controversies, angry accusations are so prevalent that virtually anyone could end up violating a statute such as that enacted by Illinois (P). This law precludes free public discussion, and thus stifles cherished First Amendment rights. It is argued that judicial discretion could prevent Illinois (P) from abusing the statute, but the rights secured to all citizens by the Constitution should not be dispensed at the whim of an arbitrary and sometimes capricious tribunal.

DISSENT: (Douglas, J.) If the First Amendment is to be overridden, the peril of the speech must be so clear and present that failure to curb it will result in disaster.

▌ ANALYSIS

Common law criminal libel statutes were apparently designed to discourage feuding individuals from launching personal attacks upon one another in public. Such laws were not applied to punish allegedly libelous assaults upon groups. Nevertheless, some contemporary commentators argue that group libel laws would be an effective and desirable method of preventing scurrilous public campaigns of hatred against particular races or religious groups. Although such laws would tend to stifle protected First Amendment rights, it may be possible to imagine situations similar to that cited by the *Beauharnais* majority in which such restraint would be justified by a need to protect against threats to the public peace and tranquility.

Quicknotes

FIRST AMENDMENT Prohibits Congress from enacting any law respecting an establishment of religion, prohibiting the free exercise of religion, abridging freedom of speech or the press, the right of peaceful assembly and the right to petition for a redress of grievances.

LIBEL A false or malicious publication subjecting a person to scorn, hatred or ridicule, or injuring him or her in relation to his or her occupation or business.

R.A.V. v. City of St. Paul

Vandal (D) v. Municipality (P)

505 U.S. 377 (1992).

NATURE OF CASE: Appeal of reversal of dismissal of disorderly conduct charge.

FACT SUMMARY: R.A.V. (D) burned a cross and was charged with violating St. Paul's (P) hate crime law.

🏛 RULE OF LAW
The government may not proscribe some fighting words and permit others, where the distinction is based on content or viewpoint.

FACTS: R.A.V. (D) allegedly burned a cross in the yard of a black family and was charged under the "fighting words" ordinance. R.A.V. (D) facially challenged the ordinance on grounds that it was overbroad and impermissibly content-based. The state trial court dismissed the charges. The Minnesota Supreme Court reversed, finding the ordinance not overbroad because prior Minnesota cases had limited the phrase "anger, alarm or resentment in others" to "fighting words" (under the doctrine of *Chaplinsky v. New Hampshire*, 315 U.S. 568 (1942)), i.e., "conduct that itself inflicts injury or tends to incite immediate violence." R.A.V. (D) appealed.

ISSUE: May the government proscribe some fighting words and permit others, where the distinction is based on content or viewpoint?

HOLDING AND DECISION: (Scalia, J.) No. The government may not proscribe some fighting words and permit others where the distinction is based on content or viewpoint. The government may proscribe fighting words, but proscribable categories of speech are not beyond the First Amendment. Speech may be proscribable for one reason, but not for another. For example, a city may ban obscenity, but not just obscenity that criticizes city government. Here, St. Paul (P) may prohibit the conduct that is fighting words, but may not, as it has, ban fighting words only if they go to the topics of "race, color, creed, religion or gender." This ordinance goes beyond content to viewpoint discrimination, prohibiting, for example, fighting words aimed at religion, while permitting fighting words aimed at religious opponents. Content discrimination may permissibly single out speech presenting a heightened version of the harm that is the basis for the category of proscribable speech (e.g., an obscenity law prohibiting only the most lascivious displays of sexual activity). Or it may single out speech with secondary effects (e.g., a law only prohibiting live obscene performances by minors, the secondary effect being harm to minors). These bases for distinction ensure the restriction is not based on opposition to the speaker's message. Here, however, St. Paul (P) certainly attempted to suppress particular ideas. Reversed.

CONCURRENCE: (White, J.) The majority strikes down the ordinance for the wrong reason. This Court has long held fighting words and other categories of unprotected speech outside the First Amendment. Fighting words are worthless to society. It is inconsistent to hold that fighting words may be completely proscribed, but that the government may not treat some fighting words differently than others. The irrationally discriminatory laws the majority is concerned about would be prohibited by the Equal Protection Clause. The majority's exceptions are designed to cover obvious flaws. The St. Paul (P) ordinance singles out certain fighting words that present a special threat of violence. The ordinance should be struck down as overbroad. This approach, unlike the majority's, avoids chilling protected speech. *Chaplinsky* identifies words "which by their very utterance inflict injury." The only injury identified in the ordinance is "anger, alarm or resentment." The mere fact that expression causes hurt feelings, offense, or resentment does not render it unprotected.

CONCURRENCE: (Blackmun, J.) No First Amendment values are compromised by prohibiting attempts to drive minorities from their homes by cross burning, but there is great harm in preventing St. Paul (D) from specifically punishing race-based fighting words that prejudice the community. Nevertheless, the ordinance is overbroad and invalid.

CONCURRENCE: (Stevens, J.) St. Paul's (P) ordinance does not regulate speech based on content or viewpoint. The ordinance regulates a subcategory of speech that causes harm based on race, color, creed, religion or gender. The Court narrowly construes St. Paul's (P) ordinance as not banning all hate speech. R.A.V. (D) is therefore free to burn a cross to announce a rally or express race supremacy views, so long as the burning is not so directed at an individual as to inflict injury. Such proscription scarcely offends the First Amendment.

▶ ANALYSIS

The majority also held that the ordinance did not survive strict scrutiny review. St. Paul (P) had a compelling interest in protecting the rights of certain group members to live where they wish in peace, but the ordinance was held not necessary to achieve this interest. The majority ruled a content-neutral ordinance could have achieved the same results. Justice White disagreed, stating that the Court, as recently as *Burson v. Freeman*, 504 U.S. 191 (1992), has always rejected the view that a narrowly drawn, content-based ordinance is unconstitutional if the object of

Continued on next page.

legislation could be achieved by banning a wider category of speech.

■■■

Quicknotes

CONTENT-BASED   Refers to statutes that regulate speech based on its content.

CONTENT-NEUTRAL   Refers to statutes that regulate speech regardless of their content.

FIGHTING WORDS   Unprotected speech under the First Amendment that is likely to instigate a violent reaction.

OVERBREADTH   Refers to a statute that proscribes lawful as well as unlawful conduct.

■■■

Virginia v. Black

State (P) v. Person convicted under cross-burning statute (D)

538 U.S. 343 (2003).

NATURE OF CASE: Appeal from a criminal conviction.

FACT SUMMARY: When Black (D) was prosecuted and convicted under Virginia's (P) cross-burning statute, he argued its unconstitutionality because of a provision treating any cross burning as prima facie evidence of intent to intimidate.

RULE OF LAW
A provision in a state's cross-burning statute treating any cross burning as prima facie evidence of intent to intimidate is unconstitutional.

FACTS: Black (D) was prosecuted and convicted by a jury under Virginia's (P) cross-burning statute, which bans cross burning with intent to intimidate a person or group of persons. The statute contains a provision that any burning of a cross constitutes prima facie evidence of intent to intimidate a person or group of persons. The Supreme Court of Virginia upheld the conviction, and Black (D) appealed to the U.S. Supreme Court on the grounds that the prima facie evidence provision was unconstitutional.

ISSUE: Is a provision in a state's cross-burning statute treating any cross burning as prima facie evidence of intent to intimidate unconstitutional?

HOLDING AND DECISION: (O'Connor, J.) Yes. A provision in a state's cross burning statute treating any cross burning as prima facie evidence of intent to intimidate is unconstitutional. To this day, regardless of whether the message is a political one or whether the message is also meant to intimidate, the burning of a cross is a symbol of hate. While cross burning sometimes carries no intimidating message, at other times the intimidating message is the only message conveyed. The Court has long held that the government may regulate certain categories of expression consistent with the Constitution and that indeed intimidation in the constitutionally proscribable sense of the word is a type of true threat. The First Amendment, accordingly, permits Virginia (P) to outlaw cross burnings done with the intent to intimidate because burning a cross is a particularly virulent form of intimidation. Furthermore, instead of prohibiting all intimidating messages, Virginia (P) may choose to regulate this subset of intimidating messages in light of cross burnings long and pernicious history as a signal of impending violence. However, this particular cross-burning statute is unconstitutionally overbroad due to its provision stating that any burning of a cross is prima facie evidence of intent to intimidate a person or group of persons. The prima facie provision strips away the very reason why a state may ban cross burning with the intent to intimidate because this provision permits a jury to convict in every cross-burning case in which defendants

exercise their constitutional right not to put on a defense. It is apparent that the provision as so interpreted "would create an unacceptable risk of the suppression of ideas." Anger or hatred is not sufficient to ban all cross burnings in the absence of actual intimidation or threat. The First Amendment does not permit shortcuts.

CONCURRENCE: (Stevens, J.) Cross burning with "an intent to intimidate" unquestionably qualifies as the kind of threat that is unprotected by the First Amendment.

DISSENT: (Thomas, J.) The majority errs in imputing an expressive component to the activity in question. In our culture, cross burning has almost invariably meant lawlessness and understandably instills in its victims well-grounded fear of physical violence. Those who hate cannot terrorize and intimidate to make their point.

CONCURRENCE AND DISSENT: (Souter, J.) While agreeing that the statute makes a content-based distinction within the category of punishable intimidating or threatening expression, I disagree that any exception should save the statute from unconstitutionality. No content-based statute should survive without a high probability that no official suppression of ideas is being encouraged.

ANALYSIS

As articulated by the plurality in the *Black* decision, the prima facie evidence provision in the Virginia cross-burning statute ignored all of the contextual factors that would be necessary in order for a court or jury to decide whether a particular cross burning was in fact intended to intimidate. On the other hand, some legal commentators express the viewpoint such as that conveyed in Justice Thomas's dissent, that a cross burning always and necessarily represents intimidation.

Quicknotes

FIFTH AMENDMENT Provides that no person shall be compelled to serve as a witness against himself, or be subject to trial for the same offense twice, or be deprived of life, liberty, or property without due process of law.

OVERBREADTH That quality or characteristic of a statute, regulation, or order that reaches beyond the problem it was meant to solve causing it to sweep within it activity it cannot legitimately reach.

Adderley v. Florida

Students (D) v. State (P)

385 U.S. 39 (1966).

NATURE OF CASE: Grant of certiorari after conviction on a charge of trespass with a malicious and mischievous intent upon the premises of another.

FACT SUMMARY: Adderley (D) and other students marched to the jail to protest segregation policies. They were told to leave. When they refused, they were arrested.

🏛 RULE OF LAW
Demonstrators do not have a constitutional right to expound their views whenever, wherever, and however they choose.

FACTS: Adderley (D) and 200 other students went to a jail to protest the arrest of other demonstrators the day before and segregation policies. They stood or sat singing, clapping, and dancing on a jail driveway that was normally used to transport prisoners and was not used by the public. They were blocking the driveway and, when the sheriff arrived, he told them they were trespassing on jail property and that they would be arrested if they did not leave within ten minutes. Ten minutes later, he warned them again, and arrested the 107 persons who remained.

ISSUE: Do demonstrators have a constitutional right to expound their views whenever, wherever, and however they choose?

HOLDING AND DECISION: (Black, J.) No. Demonstrators do not have a constitutional right to expound their views whenever, wherever, and however they choose. In this case Adderley (D) and the other demonstrators were convicted under a narrowly drawn statute aimed at one limited kind of conduct, trespass upon the property of another with a malicious intent. The statute does not suffer from overbreadth or vagueness. Secondly, the protesters went to the jail. Jails generally are not open to the public. Finally, they entered the jail through a driveway used only for jail purposes and not generally used by the public. Hence, the jury was authorized to find that the State (P) had proven every element of the crime of trespass. This conviction did not deprive Adderley (D) of any constitutional rights. The state may control the use of its own property for its own lawful nondiscriminatory purpose. There is no evidence that Adderley (D) was arrested because the sheriff objected to what was being sung or said. Rather, he objected to their presence on that part of the jail grounds. The assumption, that demonstrators have a constitutional right to expound their views whenever, wherever, and however they please, was vigorously rejected in *Cox*, and is rejected again here. Adderley's (D) conviction is affirmed.

DISSENT: (Douglas, J.) A trespass law is being used to penalize people for exercising their constitutional right. There was no violence here, nor any threats of violence. The jailhouse routine was uninterrupted. This case gives the sheriff the power to decide in his discretion when public places can be used for demonstrations. It does damage to the First Amendment to allow a trespass statute to bar a person from going onto public property.

▶ ANALYSIS

State statutes cannot be invoked arbitrarily to defeat First Amendment freedoms. State trespass convictions have been reversed where the only acts involved were the peaceable assembly at and refusal to leave a public facility or public place. The "sit-in demonstration" cases state that peaceful presence in a place held open to the public cannot be made a crime. In *Wright v. Georgia*, 373 U.S. 284 (1962), the Court found the distinguishing factor in *Adderley* to be that a jail is not a place held open to the public. In *Logan Valley Plaza*, 391 U.S. 308 (1968), private property that had been held open to public use was treated like a public place meaning that neither state nor private trespass rules could be applied to limit the reasonable exercise of First Amendment rights. There, the Court reversed trespass convictions that arose out of union members' peaceful picketing of a grocery store in a privately owned shopping center.

■▬■

Quicknotes

FIRST AMENDMENT Prohibits Congress from enacting any law respecting an establishment of religion, prohibiting the free exercise of religion, abridging freedom of speech or the press, the right of peaceful assembly and the right to petition for a redress of grievances.

■▬■

Police Department of Chicago v. Mosley

Municipality (D) v. Picketer (P)

408 U.S. 92 (1972).

NATURE OF CASE: Action to enjoin enforcement of a statute.

FACT SUMMARY: An ordinance prohibited all picketing around schools during school hours except for labor disputes.

🏛 RULE OF LAW
A state may not permit or prohibit peaceful picketing based on the content of the sign.

FACTS: Mosley (P) peacefully picketed a high school, claiming it discriminated against blacks. Chicago (D) then enacted an ordinance that prohibited the picketing of schools from one-half hour before school to one-half hour after it had ended. Only those involved in labor disputes were exempted from the ordinance. Mosley (P) brought suit to enjoin enforcement of the statute as applied to him. Mosley (P) alleged that once an exception has been made to a reasonable regulation concerning the time and place of picketing, other picketing may not be prohibited merely because of the content of the sign.

ISSUE: May a state permit or prohibit picketing based on the content of the sign?

HOLDING AND DECISION: (Marshall, J.) No. A state may not permit or prohibit peaceful picketing based on the content of the sign. A state may reasonably regulate the time, place and manner of picketing if necessary to protect a valid interest. Content may not be regulated. A state may not prohibit or permit picketing based on the content of the sign, i.e., the nature of the ideas expressed. The ordinance herein finds that those having labor grievances do not constitute an interference with school operations because of the nature of their message. All other pickets are deemed to interfere with such operations because of the nature of their messages. This is violative of the Equal Protection Clause and First Amendment rights. Once exceptions are made, all must be allowed to express their rights. The statute is unconstitutional. Affirmed.

▶ ANALYSIS

In *Madison School District v. Wisconsin Employment Relations Comm.*, 429 U.S. 167 (1976), the Court held that a state may not enjoin a dissident member of a teacher's union from speaking at a public meeting of the Board of Education while permitting the unit representative to do so. If there are conflicting demands for use of the same place, a state may make a choice among potential users. *Cox v. Louisiana*, 379 U.S. 559 (1965).

Quicknotes

EQUAL PROTECTION CLAUSE A constitutional provision that each person be guaranteed the same protection of the laws enjoyed by other persons in like circumstances.

FIRST AMENDMENT Prohibits Congress from enacting any law respecting an establishment of religion, prohibiting the free exercise of religion, abridging freedom of speech or the press, the right of peaceful assembly and the right to petition for a redress of grievances.

■═■

Lehman v. City of Shaker Heights

Political candidate (P) v. Municipality (D)

418 U.S. 298 (1974).

NATURE OF CASE: On writ of certiorari after denial of declaration and injunctive relief.

FACT SUMMARY: Lehman (P), a political candidate, challenged a City of Shaker Heights (D) policy that does not allow political advertising on its transit vehicles.

🏛 RULE OF LAW
A city that operates a public rapid transit system and sells advertising space on its vehicles is not required by the First and Fourteenth Amendments to accept paid political advertising on behalf of a candidate for public office.

FACTS: Lehman (P), a candidate for state office, sought to promote his candidacy by purchasing advertising space on the City of Shaker Heights' (D) buses. He was refused space because the City (D) had a policy that did not permit political advertising on its transit vehicles.

ISSUE: Is a city that operates a public rapid transit system and sells advertising space on its vehicles required by the First and Fourteenth Amendments to accept paid political advertising on behalf of a candidate for public office?

HOLDING AND DECISION: (Blackmun, J.) No. A city that operates a public rapid transit system and sells advertising space on its vehicles is not required by the First and Fourteenth Amendments to accept paid political advertising on behalf of a candidate for public office. No First Amendment forum is present in a case such as this where a city operates a public transit system and sells advertising space on its vehicles. It's true that because state action exists, the policies and practices governing access to the transit systems advertising space must not be arbitrary, capricious or invidious. Here, the City of Shaker Heights (D) decided only to accept nonpolitical advertising. This decision minimizes chances of abuse, the appearance of favoritism, and the risk of imposing upon a captive audience. A city may reasonably limit access to advertising space, and such a limitation, in this case, did not violate the First Amendment. Affirmed.

CONCURRENCE: (Douglas, J.) The ownership and operation of a bus by a city does not without more make it a forum for communication. The right of commuters to be free from forced intrusions on their privacy precludes the city from transforming its vehicles of public transportation into forums for the dissemination of ideas upon this captive audience.

DISSENT: (Brennan, J.) The City (D) created a forum for the dissemination of information and expression of ideas when it accepted and displayed commercial and public service advertisements on its rapid transit vehicles. Once a public forum is established, both free speech and equal protection principles prohibit discrimination based solely on subject matter or content. That the discrimination is among entire classes of ideas, rather than among points of view within a particular class, does not render it any less odious.

▌ *ANALYSIS*

Justice Blackmun's reluctance to recognize a public forum claim in *Lehman* should be compared with his majority opinion less than a year later in *Southeastern Promotions, Ltd. v. Conrad*, 420 U.S. 546 (1975). There, the Court found that First Amendment rights had been violated by a municipal board managing City Theater's refusal of permission to present the musical "Hair." The refusal was based on the ground that the production would not be in the community's best interest. Blackmun did not reach the issue of "Hair's" alleged obscenity, but found that the refusal constituted a prior restraint imposed without affording the rigorous procedural safeguards required. He noted that municipal theaters were public forums designed for expressive activities, and neither the *Lehman* captive audience nor any other circumstances, qualifying as exceptions to the prior restraint doctrine, were present.

■■■

Quicknotes

PUBLIC FORUM Refers to lands upon which speech may be made.

■■■

United States v. O'Brien

Federal government (P) v. Draft protestor (D)

391 U.S. 367 (1968).

NATURE OF CASE: Appeals from a conviction for burning a draft card.

FACT SUMMARY: O'Brien (D) burned his draft card during a public demonstration and was subsequently convicted of violating the Universal Military Training and Service Act.

🏛 RULE OF LAW
When speech and nonspeech elements are combined in the same course of conduct, a sufficiently important governmental interest in regulating the nonspeech element can justify incidental limitations on First Amendment freedoms.

FACTS: O'Brien (D) burned his Selective Service registration certificate on the steps of a courthouse and was subsequently convicted of violating the Universal Military Training and Service Act of 1948, as amended in 1965. In pertinent part the Act makes it a federal offense to knowingly destroy or mutilate such certificates. O'Brien (D) maintained that he burned his draft card publicly to express his opposition to the Vietnam conflict and to influence others to adopt his antiwar beliefs and that the Act was an unconstitutional abridgement of his free speech rights. The district court rejected this argument, but on appeal the court of appeals held that the 1965 amendment abridged freedom of speech. Nonetheless the court affirmed O'Brien's (D) conviction under that part of the Act that in its view effectively made violation of the nonpossession regulation a crime. Both O'Brien (D) and the Government (P) appealed.

ISSUE: When speech and nonspeech elements are combined in the same course of conduct, can a sufficiently important governmental interest in regulating the nonspeech element justify incidental limitations on First Amendment freedoms?

HOLDING AND DECISION: (Warren, C.J.) Yes. When speech and nonspeech elements are combined in the same course of conduct, a sufficiently important governmental interest in regulating the nonspeech element can justify incidental limitations on First Amendment freedoms. This Court cannot accept the view that an apparently limitless variety of conduct can be labeled speech whenever the person engaging in the conduct intends thereby to express an idea. However, even on the assumption that the alleged communicative element in O'Brien's (D) conduct is sufficient to bring into play the First Amendment, it does not necessarily follow that the destruction of a registration certificate is constitutionally protected activity. A government regulation is sufficiently justified if it is within the constitutional power of the government; if it furthers an important governmental interest; if it is unrelated to the suppression of free expression; and if the incidental

restriction is no greater than is essential to the furtherance of that interest. Congress has the power to raise and support armies. Pursuant to this power, Congress may establish a system of registration for individuals. The issuance of certificates indicating the registration of individuals is a legitimate and substantial administrative aid in the functioning of this system. Reversed.

CONCURRENCE: (Harlan, J.) It is my understanding that the Court does not foreclose consideration of First Amendment claims in those rare instances when the "incidental" restriction imposed on expression by a regulation furthering an "important or substantial" governmental interest has the practical effect of entirely preventing a "speaker" from reaching a significant audience with whom he could not otherwise lawfully communicate. Because O'Brien (D) could have communicated his message in many ways other than burning his draft card, this is not such a case.

DISSENT: (Douglas, J.) The underlying issue in this case is whether conscription is permissible absent a state of war. This case should be reargued to address this point. Further, "symbolic speech" deserves more protection than the Court has given it.

▶ ANALYSIS

Justice Harlan wrote a brief concurring opinion, expressing concern that the Court's rationale might, in a different case, have the effect of entirely preventing a speaker from reaching a significant audience with whom he could not otherwise lawfully communicate. Justice Douglas dissented on the ground that the underlying and basic problem was whether conscription is permissible in the absence of a declaration of war.

Quicknotes

FIRST AMENDMENT Prohibits Congress from enacting any law respecting an establishment of religion, prohibiting the free exercise of religion, abridging freedom of speech or the press, the right of peaceful assembly and the right to petition for a redress of grievances.

Buckley v. Valeo

Senator (P) v. Federal government (D)

424 U.S. 1 (1976).

NATURE OF CASE: Action for declaration of unconstitutionality.

FACT SUMMARY: Senator Buckley (P) and others challenged the Federal Election Campaign Act's contribution and expenditure limitation, reporting and disclosure requirements and public financing of presidential elections.

🏛 RULE OF LAW
Although "the [F]irst [A]mendment protects political association as well as political expression . . . a limitation upon the amount that any one person or group may contribute to (and associate with) a candidate or political committee entails only a marginal restriction on the contributor's ability to engage in free communication (and association)"; but "a restriction on the amount of money a person or group can spend on political communication (as a whole) during a campaign (excessively) reduces the quantity of expression by restricting the number of issues discussed, the depth of their exploration, and the size of the audience reached."

FACTS: In order to curtail political corruption, Congress in the Federal Election Campaign Act of 1971, as amended in 1974, developed an intricate statutory scheme for the regulation of federal political campaigns. Inter alia, Congress imposed a $1,000 limitation on individual contributions "to a single candidate" in § 608(b)(1); a $5,000 limitation on "contributions" to a single candidate by political committees in § 608(b)(2); a $25,000 limitation on total "contributions" by any individual in one year to political candidates in § 608(b)(3); a $1,000 ceiling in "expenditures" relative to a known candidate in § 608(e)(1); and similar ceilings on "expenditures" by the candidate and his family and on overall campaign "expenditures" § 608(a) and (c). In addition, Congress required disclosure by candidates of all "contributions" greater than $10, and by individuals of all "contributions and expenditures" aggregating over $1,000—§ 434(e). In a separate action, Congress provided for federal financing of presidential elections. Senator Buckley (D) and others, pursuant to a special section in the Act of 1971, brought this action to have all the abovementioned sections declared an unconstitutional violation of their First Amendment rights of freedom of expression and association. This appeal followed.

ISSUE: Does the strong governmental interest in preventing election corruption justify imposition of substantial restrictions on the effective ability of any individual to express his political beliefs and engage in political association?

HOLDING AND DECISION: (Per curiam) No. Although "the [F]irst [A]mendment protects political association as well as political expression . . . a limitation upon the amount that any one person or group may contribute to (and associate with) a candidate or a political committee entails only a marginal restriction on the contributor's ability to engage in free communication (and association)"; but "a restriction on the amount of money a person or group can spend on political communication (as a whole) during a campaign (excessively) reduces the quantity of expression by restricting the number of issues discussed, the depth of their exploration, and the size of the audience reached." As such, the so-called "contribution" (i.e., to candidates) limitations here (§ 608(b)1–3) may be upheld as valid means for limiting political corruption by "fat cats." The so-called "expenditure" (on political expression) limitations (§ 608 a,c,e), however, places too broad a restriction on the individual's ability to speak out and must therefore be voided. As for the reporting and disclosure requirements, broad as they are, they are clearly upheld by the "compelling government interest" in deterring corruption by getting important information to the voters and providing records for enforcement of the law. Finally, the challenge to the public financing of presidential elections is simply unfounded since it entails no abridgment of speech whatsoever. Affirmed in part, reversed in part.

CONCURRENCE AND DISSENT: (Burger, C.J.) The disclosure requirements for small contributions are unnecessarily broad intrusions into First Amendment rights since only large contributions are likely to cause the corruption the Act is supposed to remedy. The contribution limitations upheld by the court place just as great a burden on political expression as expenditure limitations. Finally, there is no constitutional justification for the "incestuous" relationship between government and politics that the public financing law, upheld by the court, creates.

CONCURRENCE AND DISSENT: (White, J.) Since the expenditure limitations, struck down by the court, are neutral as to the content of speech, are not motivated by the fear of political expression and reflect the well founded conclusion of Congress that regulation of campaign finances are essential to protect the integrity of the system, the First Amendment is not violated by them.

CONCURRENCE AND DISSENT: (Marshall, J.) A limitation on the amount of personal assets a candidate

Continued on next page.

may use in an election is an important method of insuring that public office does not become a domain of the wealthy only.

CONCURRENCE AND DISSENT: (Blackmun, J.) The Court does not properly distinguish between contribution limitations and expenditure limitations.

▶ ANALYSIS

In this case, the Court has identified one of the few "compelling governmental interests" that may be employed to justify congressional regulation of an area subject to strict judicial scrutiny. That interest is the interest in maintaining the integrity of the political process. Note, however, that even though the interest is held compelling, the Court does not automatically affirm its imposition. Note that the Court's decision left the Federal Election Campaign Act rift with loopholes. Perhaps the most exploited was that which permitted individuals to "expend" (i.e., separately from any candidate or his organization) large sums to endorse a vote for a particular candidate.

■▬■

Quicknotes

FIRST AMENDMENT Prohibits Congress from enacting any law respecting an establishment of religion, prohibiting the free exercise of religion, abridging freedom of speech or the press, the right of peaceful assembly and the right to petition for a redress of grievances.

■▬■

Branzburg v. Hayes

News reporters (D) v. State and federal government (P)

408 U.S. 665 (1972).

NATURE OF CASE: Appeal from contempt citations for failure to testify before state and federal grand juries.

FACT SUMMARY: Newsmen refused to testify before state and federal grand juries, claiming that their news sources were confidential.

RULE OF LAW
The First Amendment's freedom of press does not exempt a news reporter from disclosing to a grand jury information that he has received in confidence.

FACTS: Branzburg (D), who had written articles for a newspaper about drug activities he had observed, refused to testify before a state grand jury regarding his information. [No further facts stated in casebook excerpt.]

ISSUE: Does the First Amendment protect a news reporter from disclosing to a grand jury, information that he has received in confidence?

HOLDING AND DECISION: (White, J.) No. The First Amendment's freedom of press does not exempt a news reporter from disclosing to a grand jury information that he has received in confidence. The First Amendment does not invalidate every incidental burdening of the press that may result from the enforcement of civil or criminal statutes of general applicability. News reporters cannot invoke a testimonial privilege not enjoined by other citizens. The Constitution should not shield criminals who wish to remain anonymous from prosecution through disclosure. Forcing news reporters to testify will not impede the flow of news. The news reporter may never be called. Many political groups will still turn to the reporter because they are dependent on the media for exposure. Grand jury proceedings are secret and the police are experienced in protecting informants. More important, the public's interest in news flow does not override the public's interest in deterring crime. Here, the grand juries were not probing at will without relation to existing need; the information sought was necessary to the respective investigations. A grand jury is not restricted to seeking information from non-newsmen; it may choose the best method for its task. The contempt citations are affirmed.

CONCURRENCE: (Powell, J.) It must be emphasized that the Court's holding is a limited one and that a newsman who is called upon to give information bearing only a remote and tenuous relationship to the subject of the investigation, or who has some other reason to believe that his testimony implicates confidential source relationships without a legitimate need of law enforcement, will have access to the court on a motion to quash the subpoena and an appropriate protective order may be entered. In short, the courts will be available

to newsmen under circumstances where legitimate first amendment interests require protection.

DISSENT: (Douglas, J.) To mandate disclosure of a reporter's confidential sources will seriously impede the dissemination of ideas a free press offers.

DISSENT: (Stewart, J.) A corollary of the right to publish is the right to gather news. The right to gather news implies, in turn, a right to a confidential relationship between a reporter and his or her source. Since informants are necessary to the news-gathering business as we know it today, the promise of confidentiality may be a necessary prerequisite to a productive relationship between a newsperson and their informants. First Amendment rights require special safeguards.

▶ *ANALYSIS*

Guidelines promulgated by the Attorney General for federal officials to follow when subpoenaing members of the press to testify before grand juries or at criminal trials included the following test for information: whether there is "sufficient reason to believe that the information sought is essential to a successful investigation" and cannot be obtained from non-press sources. However, in "emergencies and other unusual situations," "subpoenas which do not conform to the guidelines may be issued."

Quicknotes

FIRST AMENDMENT Prohibits Congress from enacting any law respecting an establishment of religion, prohibiting the free exercise of religion, abridging freedom of speech or the press, the right of peaceful assembly and the right to petition for a redress of grievances.

Red Lion Broadcasting Co. v. FCC

Broadcasting company (P) v. Federal agency (D)

395 U.S. 367 (1969).

NATURE OF CASE: Suit challenging the validity of federal regulations pertaining to broadcasting.

FACT SUMMARY: Red Lion Broadcasting Co. (P) challenged the constitutionality of the Federal Communications Commission's (D) fairness doctrine, which obligates the broadcasting media to make airtime available for rebuttal purposes.

🏛 RULE OF LAW
Reasonable governmental regulations designed to ensure equal access to the airwaves do not violate the first amendment.

FACTS: Red Lion Broadcasting Company (Red Lion) (P) carried a radio program in which Reverend Billy James Hargis made various charges concerning Fred J. Cook, author of an unflattering book about Senator Barry Goldwater. Among other things, Hargis alleged that Cook had once been fired by a newspaper for fabricating charges against city officials and had later worked for a publication that had Communist affiliations. Upon learning of the broadcast, Cook asked Red Lion (P) for free airtime in which to reply, but his request was denied. The Federal Communications Commission (D), however, concluded that the Hargis broadcast had constituted a personal attack upon Cook, and that Red Lion (P) was therefore obligated to make free broadcast time available to him. When the FCC's (D) position was upheld by the lower federal courts, Red Lion (P) appealed to the Supreme Court. During the pendency of the Red Lion (P) litigation, the FCC (D) adopted specific regulations requiring broadcasters to make free airtime available following personal attacks, political endorsements, editorials, etc. The Seventh Circuit Court of Appeals declared the new regulations unconstitutional. The FCC (D) then appealed to the Supreme Court, which joined the *Red Lion* and *U.S. et al. v. Radio Television News Directors Ass'n et al.* (P) cases and proceeded to consider whether or not the regulations and actions of the FCC (D) were repugnant to the First Amendment.

ISSUE: Do reasonable governmental regulations designed to ensure equal access to the airwaves violate the First Amendment?

HOLDING AND DECISION: (White, J.) No. Reasonable governmental regulations designed to ensure equal access to the airwaves do not violate the First Amendment. Broadcasters may not assert their rights of free speech in a way that interferes with the exercise of those rights by others. The opportunity to be heard on radio or television is not universally available. In fact, a license to broadcast is extremely difficult to secure. If those with such licenses were not subject to regulation, they could stifle the First Amendment rights of others by completely controlling the content of all broadcasts. The informational values and opportunity to hear divergent points of view would then be lost. It is conceivable that too much regulation might cause stations to shy away from controversy and from responsible reporting, but this problem can be dealt with when and if it arises.

▶ ANALYSIS

In *Miami Herald Publishing Co. v. Tornille*, 418 U.S. 241 (1974), the Supreme Court refused to burden newspaper publishers with the same opportunity to reply requirements as *Red Lion* seemingly imposes upon members of the broadcasting media. In invalidating, on First Amendment grounds, a Florida statute that obligated newspapers to publish replies by candidates to printed editorials, the Court cited the basic right of every publisher to determine the content of his product. Chief Justice Burger also alluded to the potential expense of publishing replies, and observed that such responses might induce newspapers to omit certain newsworthy or otherwise important items. On the whole, *Tornille* does not seem to establish a convincing basis for distinguishing between newspapers and radio stations for purposes of applying mandatory access laws.

■=■

Quicknotes

FIFTH AMENDMENT Provides that no person shall be compelled to serve as a witness against himself, or be subject to trial for the same offense twice, or be deprived of life, liberty, or property without due process of law.

■=■

The Constitution and Religion

Quick Reference Rules of Law

PAGE

1. **The Anti-coercion Principle.**   Religious invocations and benedictions may not be given at a public primary or secondary school graduation ceremony. (Lee v. Weisman)   *148*

2. **The Nonendorsement Principle and De Facto Establishments.**   The Establishment Clause does not prohibit the inclusion of a nativity scene in a municipal Christmas display. (Lynch v. Donnelly)   *149*

3. **Facially Neutral Statutes That Incidentally Aid Religion: Permissible and Impermissible Effects.**   A state's decision to defray the cost of educational expenses incurred by parents evidences a purpose that is both secular and understandable, and does not violate the Establishment Clause. (Mueller v. Allen)   *150*

4. **The Free Exercise Clause: Required Accommodations.**   A state may proscribe the use of psychoactive substances even in a religious context. (Employment Division, Department of Human Resources v. Smith)   *151*

5. **Permissible Accommodation.**   Where the legislature fashions a law to accommodate religious adherents' concerns, the law must have a primary effect that does not advance their religion so as to comply with the Establishment Clause of the First Amendment. (Corporation of Presiding Bishop of the Church of Jesus Christ of Latter-Day Saints v. Amos)   *152*

Lee v. Weisman

School officials (D) v. Father of student (P)

505 U.S. 577 (1992).

NATURE OF CASE: Appeal of permanent injunction.

FACT SUMMARY: Daniel Weisman (P), father of student Deborah (P), sought a permanent injunction barring the Providence public school officials (D) from inviting clergy to deliver invocations and benedictions at graduation ceremonies.

🏛 RULE OF LAW
Religious invocations and benedictions may not be given at a public primary or secondary school graduation ceremony.

FACTS: As allowed by the Providence School Committee (D), Principal Lee (D) invited Rabbi Gutterman to give the invocation and benediction at Lee's (D) middle school's graduation. Attendance at graduation exercises at Providence public schools is voluntary. Following school procedure, Lee (D) gave Rabbi Gutterman written guidelines for nonsectarian prayers. David Weisman (P), on behalf of himself and his daughter Deborah (P), sought a TRO against school officials (P) to prevent Rabbi Gutterman from delivering prayers at Deborah's (P) graduation. The TRO was denied, and Deborah (P) went through the ceremonies. The students stood for a few minutes while Rabbi Gutterman delivered prayers. The Weismans' (P) suit continued since Deborah (P) was a student at a Providence public high school and would likely face the same situation at high school graduation. Applying the test of *Lemon v. Kurtzman*, 403 U.S. 602 (1971), the district court held the prayers violated the Establishment Clause because they had a primary effect of advancing religion. The district court permanently enjoined the school officials (D) from inviting clergy to give invocations and benedictions at future graduations. The court of appeals affirmed.

ISSUE: May religious invocations and benedictions be given at a public primary or secondary school graduation ceremony?

HOLDING AND DECISION: (Kennedy, J.) No. Religious invocations and benedictions may not be given at a public primary or secondary school graduation ceremony. Here, state officials (D) directed the performance of a formal, explicit religious exercise at public school graduation. Principal Lee (D) decided the prayers should be given, selected the cleric, and gave written guidelines for the prayer. Even for students who object to religious exercise, attendance and participation was in every practical sense obligatory. High school graduation is one of life's most significant occasions. To say that attendance is "voluntary" is formalistic in the extreme. Such prayers in public schools carry a particular risk of coercion. There is public and peer pressure on attending students to stand as a group or maintain respectful silence.

A dissenter is injured by his reasonable perception that others view his standing as approval and that he is being forced by the state to pray. The First Amendment protects the objector from having to take unilateral, private action to avoid compromising religious principles at a state function. The fact that the prayer was "nonsectarian" does not make government involvement acceptable. Affirmed.

CONCURRENCE: (Blackmun, J.) The Establishment Clause not only prohibits government coercion, but also any government engagement in religious practices. The simple issue is whether the state placed a stamp of approval on a religious activity. Here, it did.

DISSENT: (Scalia, J.) The Establishment Clause must be construed in light of government policies of accommodation and support for religion that are an accepted part of our political and cultural heritage. Nonsectarian prayers at graduations and other public celebrations are a long-standing American tradition. From the Framers to our current President, Congress, and Supreme Court, government leaders have opened public functions with prayer. The Establishment Clause only bars state religious activity backed by threat of penalty for nonparticipation. The coercion involved in school prayer cases is that students are compelled to attend school. No coercion exists here.

▶ ANALYSIS

The dissent claimed that the Court's failure to apply the three-part *Lemon* test means the test is no longer good law. However, Justice Kennedy's opinion for the Court expressly declined to reconsider *Lemon*. Justices Kennedy and Souter both cited *Lemon* with approval, though they did not apply the test. Justice Blackmun's concurrence, joined by Justices Stevens and O'Connor, expressed the view that *Lemon* still applies in all Establishment Clause cases.

■■■

Quicknotes

ESTABLISHMENT CLAUSE The constitutional provision prohibiting the government from favoring any one religion over others, or engaging in religious activities or advocacy.

FIRST AMENDMENT Prohibits Congress from enacting any law respecting an establishment of religion, prohibiting the free exercise of religion, abridging freedom of speech or the press, the right of peaceful assembly and the right to petition for a redress of grievances.

■■■

Lynch v. Donnelly

Municipality (D) v. Residents (P)

465 U.S. 668 (1984).

NATURE OF CASE: Appeal from judgment finding a violation of the Establishment Clause.

FACT SUMMARY: The district court held that Pawtucket (D) violated the Establishment Clause by including a nativity scene in its Christmas display.

🏛 RULE OF LAW
The Establishment Clause does not prohibit the inclusion of a nativity scene in a municipal Christmas display.

FACTS: Donnelly (P) and other residents (P) of Pawtucket, Rhode Island sued to enjoin the City (D) from including a nativity scene in its annual Christmas display, as it had done for over 40 years. They contended the inclusion violated the Establishment Clause by bestowing a benefit on the Christian religion. The district court granted a permanent injunction forbidding the City from including the scene in the display. The court of appeals affirmed, and the Supreme Court granted certiorari.

ISSUE: Does the Establishment Clause prohibit the inclusion of a nativity scene in a municipal Christmas display?

HOLDING AND DECISION: (Burger, C.J.) No. The Establishment Clause does not prohibit the inclusion of a nativity scene in a municipal Christmas display. The scene confers no more benefit on religion than other innocuous symbols recognizing the existence of religion in our society. The City's (D) purpose in including the display was to celebrate and depict the origin of the Christmas holiday. This clearly was a legitimate secular purpose. As a result, the inclusion of the scene was not unconstitutional. Reversed.

CONCURRENCE: (O'Connor, J.) Pawtucket (D) did not endorse Christianity by including the scene in its display. Therefore, it did not violate the Establishment Clause.

DISSENT: (Brennan, J.) The nativity scene recreates an event that lies at the heart of the Christian faith. Therefore, its inclusion clearly constituted an impermissible government involvement in religion.

DISSENT: (Blackmun, J.) Use of the religious symbol in a municipally sponsored display compels Christians to acknowledge its symbolic meaning and to alienate non-Christians. This is misuse of a sacred symbol.

▶ ANALYSIS

The Court articulated a three-part test to use in determining whether particular governmental action violates the Establishment Clause in *Lemon v. Kurtzman*, 403 U.S. 602 (1970). The test requires the Court to determine: (1) whether the action has a secular purpose; (2) whether it advances or inhibits religion; and (3) whether it creates an excessive government entanglement in religion. In the present case, the Court stated that such a test is not to be blindly followed, and that ad hoc line-drawing must be performed.

Quicknotes

ESTABLISHMENT CLAUSE The constitutional provision prohibiting the government from favoring any one religion over others, or engaging in religious activities or advocacy.

Mueller v. Allen

Resident (P) v. State (D)

463 U.S. 388 (1983).

NATURE OF CASE: Action challenging the constitutionality of a state tax deduction law.

FACT SUMMARY: Mueller (P) instituted suit challenging the constitutionality of a Minnesota law allowing taxpayers, in computing their state income tax, to deduct certain expenses incurred in providing for their children's education, whether or not the children attended public schools or private parochial schools.

🏛 RULE OF LAW
A state's decision to defray the cost of educational expenses incurred by parents evidences a purpose that is both secular and understandable, and does not violate the Establishment Clause.

FACTS: Minnesota passed a law allowing taxpayers, in figuring their state income tax, to deduct actual expenses incurred for the "tuition, textbooks and transportation" of dependents attending elementary or secondary schools," whether or not the schools were nonsectarian or sectarian. A maximum $500 deduction for each dependent in grades K through six and $700 for each dependent in grades seven through twelve was permitted. Mueller (P) brought suit challenging the validity of the law under the Establishment Clause. The court of appeals held that the statute did not violate the Establishment Clause.

ISSUE: Does a state's decision to defray the cost of educational expenses incurred by parents violate the Establishment Clause?

HOLDING AND DECISION: (Rehnquist, J.) No. A state's decision to defray the cost of educational expenses incurred by parents evidences a purpose that is both secular and understandable, and does not violate the Establishment Clause. A three-part test was laid down in the *Lemon* case, 403 U.S. 602 (1971), and is the means by which it can be ascertained whether a particular program that in some manner aids parochial schools (either directly or indirectly) violates the Establishment Clause. The first part inquires whether the program has a secular purpose. In this case, the answer is yes. The tax deduction attempts to give parents an incentive to educate their children and this serves the secular purpose of ensuring a well-educated citizenry. The second part of the test asks the related question of whether the program has "the primary effect of advancing the sectarian aims of the nonpublic schools." Here, the answer is no. The deduction is available to all parents, including those sending their children to public schools and it channels whatever funds available to such schools only as a result of numerous, private choices of individual parents of school-age children. The third part of the test to which

this program must be put inquires whether or not the program "excessively entangles" the state in religion. It does not. The only decision that might remotely involve state officials in state surveillance of religious type issues would be the decisions state officials have to make in determining whether particular textbooks qualify for the deduction. In making this decision, they must disallow deductions taken from "instructional materials used in the teaching of religious tenets, doctrines or worship, the purpose of which is to inculcate such tenets, doctrines or worship." Making this type of decision does not differ substantially from making the types of decisions approved in early opinions of this Court. Thus, the program at issue here must be considered constitutional, as it has passed the three parts of the appropriate test. Affirmed.

DISSENT: (Marshall, J.) That the statute here makes some small benefit available to all parents does not alter the fact that the most substantial benefit provided is available only to those parents who send their children to schools that charge tuition. The statute is, therefore, little more than a subsidy of tuition masquerading as a subsidy of general educational expenses. The other expenses are de minimis in comparison to tuition expenses.

▎ *ANALYSIS*

In the previously decided *Nyquist* case, 413 U.S. 756 (1973), on which the constitutional challenge to this tax deduction program relied heavily, New York had passed a statute that gave the parents of children attending private schools thinly disguised "tax benefits" that actually amounted to tuition grants. This was found to violate the Establishment Clause. By simply providing in its tax deduction statute that all parents could take such tuition deductions, Minnesota kept its tax deduction scheme from being declared unconstitutional. Yet, it is really a change in form more than in substance, for most public school parents do not have to pay tuition. So, giving them the opportunity to deduct tuition expenses is of little practical consequence and does little to change the effect of the program in providing indirect aid to mostly parochial schools.

■=■

Quicknotes

ESTABLISHMENT CLAUSE The constitutional provision prohibiting the government from favoring any one religion over others, or engaging in religious activities or advocacy.

■=■

Employment Division, Department of Human Resources v. Smith

State agency (D) v. Unemployment benefits applicant (P)

494 U.S. 872 (1990).

NATURE OF CASE: Review of decision reversing denial of unemployment compensation.

FACT SUMMARY: Smith (P) was denied unemployment compensation because he had been terminated for misconduct, this being the religious ingestion of peyote, a controlled substance under state law.

🏛 RULE OF LAW
A state may proscribe the use of psychoactive substances even in a religious context.

FACTS: Smith (P), an American Indian, was a member of a religious sect that included in its worship services the ingestion of peyote, a controlled substance under state law. Smith (P) was fired from his job for using the drug. He (P) was denied unemployment benefits as his termination was for misconduct. Smith (P) filed an action challenging this denial, contending that Oregon's proscription of peyote in all contexts violated the Free Exercise Clause of the First Amendment. The Oregon Supreme Court so held and ordered that Smith (P) be given unemployment compensation. The U.S. Supreme Court granted certiorari.

ISSUE: May a state proscribe the use of psychoactive substances even in a religious context?

HOLDING AND DECISION: (Scalia, J.) Yes. A state may proscribe the use of psychoactive substances even in a religious context. A state may not enact a law that has the effect of specifically burdening a religion; to do so would violate the Free Exercise Clause of the First Amendment. However, there is nothing in the clause to exempt religiously based conduct from the reach of a general law of regulation. If an act is illegal, the fact it is religiously based will not make it otherwise. Where a religious act implicates some other constitutional right, the rule is in some cases to the contrary. Here, however, the ingestion of peyote is certainly not a right and the fact it is religiously based does not make it so. Reversed.

CONCURRENCE: (O'Connor, J.) Any burden on religiously based conduct must be shown by the government to serve a compelling interest. The deferential standard adopted by the Court is a major departure from free exercise jurisprudence.

DISSENT: (Blackmun, J.) A proscription such as that at issue here must be supported by a compelling state interest, something not present here.

▶ ANALYSIS

A few examples exist in the area of free exercise jurisprudence wherein religiously based conduct was held to be exempt from state interference. However, as the opinion states, this was when other rights were also implicated. An example of this is *Pierce v. Society of Sisters*, 268 U.S. 510 (1925), where it was held that a state could not proscribe religious education. The right of parents to direct their children was implicated there.

Quicknotes

FIRST AMENDMENT Prohibits Congress from enacting any law respecting an establishment of religion, prohibiting the free exercise of religion, abridging freedom of speech or the press, the right of peaceful assembly and the right to petition for a redress of grievances.

FREE EXERCISE CLAUSE The guarantee of the First Amendment to the United States Constitution prohibiting Congress from enacting laws regarding the establishment of religion or prohibiting the free exercise thereof.

Corporation of Presiding Bishop of the Church of Jesus Christ of Latter-Day Saints v. Amos

Religious organization (D) v. Employee (P)

483 U.S. 327 (1987).

NATURE OF CASE: Appeal from award of damages for wrongful termination.

FACT SUMMARY: In Amos's (P) suit for damages against Latter-Day Saints (D), the district court ruled that §702 of the 1964 Civil Rights Act, which exempts religious organizations from Title VII's prohibition against discrimination in employment on the basis of religion, violates the Establishment Clause of the First Amendment when applied to the secular nonprofit activities of religious organizations.

🏛 RULE OF LAW
Where the legislature fashions a law to accommodate religious adherents' concerns, the law must have a primary effect that does not advance their religion so as to comply with the Establishment Clause of the First Amendment.

FACTS: Amos (P) was a janitor at the Desert Gymnasium, a nonprofit facility open to the public and run by the Mormon Church. He was fired because he failed to qualify for a certificate stating that he was a member of the Church eligible to attend its temples because he observed the Church's standards involving church attendance, tithing, and abstinence from coffee, tea, alcohol, and tobacco. As a result, Amos (P) brought this action for damages against the Latter-Day Saints (D), contending that §702, as amended, of the 1964 Civil Rights Act, which exempts religious organizations from Title VII's prohibition against discrimination in employment on the basis of religion, violates the Establishment Clause of the First Amendment when applied to the secular nonprofit activities of religious organizations. The district court, in agreement with this contention, awarded Amos (P) damages. Latter-Day Saints (D) appealed.

ISSUE: Where the legislature fashions a law to accommodate religious adherents' concerns, must the law have a primary effect that does not advance their religion so as to comply with the Establishment Clause of the First Amendment?

HOLDING AND DECISION: (White, J.) Yes. Where the legislature fashions a law to accommodate religious adherents' concerns, then the law must have a primary effect that does not advance their religion so as to comply with the Establishment Clause of the First Amendment. This rule was derived from the second prong of the *Lemon v. Kurtzman*, 403 U.S. 602 (1971), three-part analysis regarding the constitutionality of religious legislation. This relevant part of *Lemon's* analysis, in effect, prohibits the legislature

from advancing or inhibiting religion through its own activities and influence. That is, the legislature is prohibited from having as its purpose the advancement or suppression of religion when it creates religious legislation. Moreover, even when legislative purpose isn't clear, if this form of legislation has the primary effect of advancing or inhibiting, then it will be implied that this was the desired effect the legislature intended, thereby making the legislation unconstitutional. Ideally, religious legislation should allow religious organizations to advance religion, in contrast to the legislature directly advancing religion. In the instant case, the purpose of the amendment to §702 is clear. Prior to this amendment, religious organizations were merely allowed to discriminate in employment on the basis of religion with respect to religious activities. However, these activities were difficult to distinguish from secular activities, thereby affecting the way an organization may carry out its religious mission for fear of potential liability. Consequently, the legislature allowed religious organizations to discriminate in employment on the basis of religion with respect to religious or secular activities, for the purpose of limiting governmental interference with the decision-making process in religions. Clearly, then, the legislature intended to remove restraints upon religious organizations' abilities to carry out their religious missions, which is a permissible religious legislative purpose. Aside from this, the 1972 amendment to §702 was merely intended to extend to secular activities that advance a religious organization's mission. In this respect, the nonprofit activity involved here clearly advances a religious mission since it was formed to benefit an organization member's health and spirituality. Hence, applying §702 as amended to the nonprofit activities of the religious employer involved here is rationally related to the legitimate purpose of alleviating significant governmental interference with the ability of religious organizations to define and carry out their religious missions. Reversed.

CONCURRENCE: (Brennan, J.) The cases involved here challenge the application of §702's categorical exemption to the activities of a nonprofit organization. The particular character of nonprofit activity, which is most likely religious, makes inappropriate a case-by-case determination whether its nature is religious or secular.

CONCURRENCE: (O'Connor, J.) The cases here involve a government decision to lift from a nonprofit activity of a religious organization the burden of demonstrating that the particular nonprofit activity is religious, as

Continued on next page.

well as the burden of refraining from discriminating on the basis of religion. Because there is a probability that the nonprofit activity of a religious organization will itself be involved in the organization's religious mission, the objective observer should perceive the government action as an accommodation of the exercise of religion rather than a government endorsement of religion.

▶ *ANALYSIS*

In connection with the above decision, see McConnel, Accommodation of Religion, 1985 Sup. Ct. Rev. 1, 1-3, where McConnel states that the "much discussed 'tension' between the two Religion Clauses largely arises from the Court's substitution of a misleading formula (the three-part *Lemon* [test]) and subsidiary, instrumental values (especially the separation of church and state) in the place of the central value of religious liberty. [Between] the accommodations compelled by the Free Exercise Clause and the benefits to religion prohibited by the Establishment Clause there exists a class of permissible government actions toward religion, which have as their purpose and effects the facilitation of religious liberty. Neither strict neutrality nor separationism can account for the idea of accommodation or define its limits. Only an interpretation of the Religion Clauses based on religious liberty [satisfactorily] distinguishes permissible accommodations from impermissible establishments."

■══■

Quicknotes

ESTABLISHMENT CLAUSE The constitutional provision prohibiting the government from favoring any one religion over others, or engaging in religious activities or advocacy.

FREE EXERCISE CLAUSE The guarantee of the First Amendment to the United States Constitution prohibiting Congress from enacting laws regarding the establishment of religion or prohibiting the free exercise thereof.

■══■

State Action, Baselines, and the Problem of Private Power

Quick Reference Rules of Law

PAGE

1. **Pure Inaction and the Theory of Governmental Neutrality.**   Action of a private party is considered state action where the state has delegated to that party a function traditionally exclusively reserved to the state. (Flagg Brothers v. Brooks) — *156*

2. **Judicial Action and the Theory of Government Neutrality.**   Judicial enforcement of a private racially restrictive covenant is considered state action for Fourteenth Amendment purposes. (Shelley v. Kraemer) — *157*

3. **State Subsidization of Private Conduct.**   Racial discrimination by a business that is located in and constitutes part of a state-owned public facility is considered to be state action and is forbidden by the Fourteenth Amendment. (Burton v. Wilmington Parking Authority) — *159*

4. **State Licensing and Authorization.**   Merely granting a liquor license to a private club that engages in discriminatory practices is not sufficient state action to invoke the Fourteenth Amendment. (Moose Lodge No. 107 v. Irvis) — *161*

5. **State Licensing and Authorization.**   A privately owned utility may cease providing service without raising due process concerns, even if it is highly regulated. (Jackson v. Metropolitan Edison Co.) — *162*

6. **Constitutionally Required Departures from Neutrality? The Public Function Doctrine.**   When private property is the equivalent of a public "business block" it ceases to be strictly private and First Amendment rights may not be arbitrarily curtailed. (Marsh v. Alabama) — *163*

Flagg Brothers v. Brooks

Storage company (D) v. Property owner (P)

436 U.S. 149 (1978).

NATURE OF CASE: Class action seeking damages and an injunction against unconstitutional state action.

FACT SUMMARY: Brooks (P) sought to enjoin the sale of the furnishings that had been picked up and stored with Flagg Brothers (D) pursuant to an eviction from her apartment.

🏛 RULE OF LAW
Action of a private party is considered state action where the state has delegated to that party a function traditionally exclusively reserved to the state.

FACTS: During her eviction, Brooks (P) instructed workmen from Flagg Brothers (D) to proceed to move and store her goods as arranged by the City Marshall even though she felt the cost too high. Eventually, a dispute over payment of the bill resulted in a threat by Flagg (D) to sell Brooks's (P) goods if the bill was not paid. Brooks (P) brought a class action suit for damages, an injunction against such sale, and a declaration that the sale would violate the Due Process and Equal Protection Clauses. The court of appeals reversed a dismissal of the complaint for failure to state a claim for relief. It found there had been state action in that New York had delegated a portion of its sovereign monopoly power over conflict resolution to warehousemen and had, by statutorily acquiescing to their selling stored goods, permitted them to execute a lien and thus perform a function that was traditionally associated with sovereignty (in this case, a sheriff's function).

ISSUE: Are acts of a private party considered state action where they result from the state's delegating to that party a function traditionally exclusively reserved to the state?

HOLDING AND DECISION: (Rehnquist, J.) Yes. Action of a private party is considered state action where the state has delegated to that party a function traditionally exclusively reserved to the state. Settlement of disputes between creditors and debtors is not traditionally an exclusive public function, so the line of sovereign function cases does not support a finding of state action here. Furthermore, the statute at issue simply reflects the state's acquiescence in a private action, which does not convert such action into that of the state. Reversed.

DISSENT: (Stevens, J.) The test of what is a state function for purposes of the Due Process Clause is not whether there has been a delegation of an exclusive sovereign function but whether, as here, there has been a delegation of a function traditionally and historically associated with sovereignty.

▶ ANALYSIS

Prior cases indicate there are few functions that are considered exclusively reserved to the states, although there are many that have been traditionally performed by governments. One area the courts have continually recognized as involving a function exclusively reserved to the states is the conducting of public elections.

■═■

Quicknotes

DUE PROCESS CLAUSE Clauses found in the Fifth and Fourteenth Amendments to the United States Constitution providing that no person shall be deprived of "life, liberty, or property, without due process of law."

EQUAL PROTECTION CLAUSE A constitutional provision that each person be guaranteed the same protection of the laws enjoyed by other persons in like circumstances.

■═■

Shelley v. Kraemer

Buyer of real property (D) v. Covenantee (P)

334 U.S. 1 (1948).

NATURE OF CASE: Action to enforce a restrictive covenant in the sale of real property.

FACT SUMMARY: Kraemer (P) sought to void a sale of real property to Shelley (D) from a Mr. Fitzgerald relying on a racially restrictive covenant.

RULE OF LAW

Judicial enforcement of a private racially restrictive covenant is considered state action for Fourteenth Amendment purposes.

FACTS: On February 16, 1911, 30 out of a total of 39 owners of property fronting both sides of Labadie Avenue between Taylor Avenue and Cora Avenue in St. Louis signed an agreement, which was subsequently recorded, which provided in part that the property could not be used or occupied by anyone of the Negro or Mongolian race for a period of 50 years. This covenant was to be valid whether it was included in future conveyances or not and was to attach to the land as a condition precedent to the sale of the property. On August 11, 1945, Shelley (D), a Negro, purchased a parcel of land subject to the restrictive covenant from a Mr. Fitzgerald. Shelley (D) did not have any actual knowledge of the restrictive agreement at the time of the purchase. On October 9, 1945, Kraemer (P), an owner of other property subject to the terms of the restrictive covenant, brought suit in the Circuit Court of St. Louis to enjoin Shelley (D) from taking possession of the property and to divest title from Shelley (D) and revest title in Fitzgerald or in such person as the court should direct. The trial court held for Shelley (D), but on appeal the Supreme Court of Missouri reversed their decision. Shelley (D) contended that the restrictive covenant violated the Equal Protection Clause of the Fourteenth Amendment. Kraemer (P) contended that no state action was involved in the private restrictive covenant and even if there were state action, the courts would enforce a restrictive covenant barring whites from purchasing certain land and so there was equal protection of the law. He further contended that if he was not allowed to enforce the covenant that he would be denied equal protection of the law.

ISSUE: Does the Equal Protection Clause of the Fourteenth Amendment prevent judicial enforcement by state courts of restrictive covenants based on race or color?

HOLDING AND DECISION: (Vinson, C.J.) Yes. Judicial enforcement of a private racially restrictive covenant is considered state action for Fourteenth Amendment purposes. Because the restrictive covenants did not involve any action by the state legislature or City Council, the restrictive covenant itself did not violate any rights protected by the Fourteenth Amendment, since it was strictly a private covenant. But the judicial enforcement of the covenant did qualify as state action. From the time of the adoption of the Fourteenth Amendment until the present, the court has consistently ruled that the action of the states to which the amendment has reference includes action of state courts and state judicial officers. In this case because there was a willing buyer and seller, Shelley (D) would have been able to enforce the restrictive covenants only with the active intervention of the state courts. The court rejected Kraemer's (P) argument that since the state courts would enforce restrictive covenants excluding white persons from ownership of property that there was no denial of equal protection. The court stated that equal protection of the law is not achieved through indiscriminate imposition of inequalities. As to Kraemer's (P) contention that he was being denied equal protection of the laws because his restrictive covenant was not being enforced, the court stated that the Constitution does not confer the right to demand action by the state that would result in the denial of equal protection of the laws to other individuals. Therefore, in granting judicial enforcement of the restrictive agreement, the state has denied Shelley (D) equal protection of the laws and the action of the state courts cannot stand. The court noted that the enjoyment of property rights, free from discrimination by the states, was among the objectives sought to be effectuated by the framers of the Fourteenth Amendment. Reversed.

▶ ANALYSIS

The Court in its post–*Shelley v. Kraemer* decisions has given this decision a fairly narrow reading. A broad reading of this case requires that whenever a state court enforces a private racial restrictive covenant that such action constitutes state action that is forbidden by the Fourteenth Amendment. In cases where the ruling in this case could have been found to be applicable, the court has used a different rationale. Some of the court's statements suggest that more state involvement than evenhanded enforcement of private biases was necessary to find unconstitutional state action. Justice Black, in a dissenting opinion, stated that the decision in this case only is applicable in cases involving property rights.

■=■

Quicknotes

EQUAL PROTECTION CLAUSE A constitutional provision that each person be guaranteed the same protection of the laws enjoyed by other persons in like circumstances.

Continued on next page.

FOURTEENTH AMENDMENT Declares that no state shall make or enforce any law that shall abridge the privileges and immunities of citizens of the United States. No state shall deny to any person within its jurisdiction the equal protection of the laws.

■≡■

Burton v. Wilmington Parking Authority

Customer (P) v. Lessor public authority (D)

365 U.S. 715 (1961).

NATURE OF CASE: Action seeking declaratory and injunctive relief for racial discrimination.

FACT SUMMARY: Wilmington Parking Authority (D) leased space in a parking facility to Eagle Coffee Shoppe for use as a restaurant and they refused to serve Burton (P), a Negro.

🏛 RULE OF LAW
Racial discrimination by a business that is located in and constitutes part of a state-owned public facility is considered to be state action and is forbidden by the Fourteenth Amendment.

FACTS: Wilmington Parking Authority (D) was going to erect a public parking facility, but before it started construction it was advised that the anticipated revenue from the parking of cars and proceeds from the sale of its bonds would not be sufficient to finance the construction costs of the facility. To secure additional capital, the Authority (D) decided to enter into long-term leases with responsible tenants for commercial use of some of the space available in the projected garage building. A 20-year lease was entered into with Eagle Coffee Shoppe, Inc., for a space to be used as a restaurant. Even though the Authority (D) had the power to adopt rules and regulations requiring that the restaurant services be made available to the general public, the lease contained no such requirement of Eagle Coffee Shoppes. Under a Delaware statute, Eagle Coffee Shoppe was classified as a restaurant and not an inn and, therefore, was not required to serve all persons entering their shop. Burton (P) attempted to enter the restaurant but was refused service because he was a Negro. As a result, Burton (P) filed an action seeking declaratory and injunctive relief against Wilmington Parking Authority (D), claiming that as the restaurant was the Authority's (D) lessee, and the Authority (D) was an agency of the state, that the discrimination was therefore state action. However, the Supreme Court of Delaware held that Eagle was acting in a purely private capacity under its lease and that the action was not that of the Authority (D) and was not, therefore, state action. The court based its conclusion on the fact that only 15% of the total cost of the facility was advanced from public funds and that the revenue from parking was only 30.5% of the total income. Eagle had expended considerable amounts of its own funds on furnishings and there was no public entrance direct from the parking area. The only connection Eagle had with the public facility was the payment of $28,700 in rent annually. The decision was appealed to the Supreme Court.

ISSUE: Is racial discrimination by a business that leases facilities from the state considered to be state action?

HOLDING AND DECISION: (Clark, J.) Yes. Racial discrimination by a business that is located in and constitutes part of a state-owned public facility is considered to be state action and is forbidden by the Fourteenth Amendment. The Court held that the restaurant was so closely tied in with the Parking Authority (D) that the discriminatory action by the restaurant was considered to be state action. The Court pointed out that the land and building were publicly owned and that the costs of land acquisition, construction, and maintenance were defrayed entirely from donations by the City of Wilmington from loans and revenue bonds, and from the proceeds of rentals and parking services out of which the loans and bonds were payable. The Court didn't feel that the figures used by the Delaware Supreme Court were very accurate. The Court also noted that the restaurant operated as an integral part of a public building devoted to a public parking service and that part of the facility was open to the public while in another part Negroes were refused service. The fact that the Parking Authority (D) didn't require in the lease that the restaurant be open to the public doesn't allow the restaurant to discriminate against Negroes with impunity. By its inaction, the Authority (D), and through it the state, made itself a party to the refusal of service. Because of the financial interdependence between the Authority (D) and the restaurant, and because of the physical relation of the facility, the discriminatory action by the restaurant cannot be considered purely private action. The Court also pointed out that it is impossible for the Court to create a formula by which it can be determined what is and is not state action. It is necessary to look at the facts in each case in order to determine if state action is involved. Reversed and remanded.

CONCURRENCE: (Stewart, J.) The Court's decision could have been reached by a more direct route. The statute that permits a restaurant to refuse service to individuals with impunity has been construed by the Delaware Supreme Court to authorize racial discrimination. As such, the statute itself should have been declared unconstitutional.

DISSENT: (Harlan, J.) The majority did not define what the requirements were for a finding of state action other than to piece together various factual tidbits. Beyond that, it is not clear on what basis the Delaware Supreme Court's decision rested. If their decision interpreted the statute as authorizing racial discrimination, it was clearly unconstitutional. If, on the other hand, their decision merely reaffirmed the common-law right of a business to serve only

Continued on next page.

when it pleases, then, and only then, would the "state action" issue be squarely before this court.

▶ *ANALYSIS*

As Justice Stewart pointed out in his dissent, the Court in this case did not clearly define the requirements for a finding of state action. In subsequent cases, however, it became clearer that the critical factor in the *Burton* case was the leasing of public property to a private enterprise for its exclusive use. The City of Montgomery, Alabama, rented or granted the exclusive use of certain public recreation areas to private groups that practiced racial discrimination. The Court found no difficulty in invalidating this practice. But a more troublesome problem was presented by the grant of non-exclusive permits to such groups. A case involving such non-exclusive use was remanded for further findings on how much restriction was placed on free public access by these non-exclusive permits. Finally, in *Moose Lodge No. 107 v. Irvis*, 407 U.S. 163 (1972), the Court found that the granting of a liquor license to a private fraternal organization that discriminated was not sufficient state action to involve the Equal Protection Clause.

■═■

Quicknotes

EQUAL PROTECTION CLAUSE A constitutional provision that each person be guaranteed the same protection of the laws enjoyed by other persons in like circumstances.

FOURTEENTH AMENDMENT Declares that no state shall make or enforce any law that shall abridge the privileges and immunities of citizens of the United States. No state shall deny to any person within its jurisdiction the equal protection of the laws.

■═■

Moose Lodge No. 107 v. Irvis

Private club (D) v. Guest (P)

407 U.S. 163 (1972).

NATURE OF CASE: Constitutional challenge against racial discrimination in a private club.

FACT SUMMARY: The Moose Lodge (D) refused to serve liquor to the black guest of a member solely on the basis of his race.

RULE OF LAW
Merely granting a liquor license to a private club that engages in discriminatory practices is not sufficient state action to invoke the Fourteenth Amendment.

FACTS: Irvis (P), a Negro, was invited to the Moose Lodge (D) by a member. The Lodge (D) refused to serve liquor to Irvis (P) solely because he was black. Irvis (P) brought an action in federal district court alleging that the state was authorizing and furthering discrimination. Irvis (P) requested the Court to enjoin the Lodge's (D) discriminatory practices. Irvis's (P) claim of state action under the Fourteenth Amendment was based solely upon the granting of a liquor license to the Lodge. The district court found state action present based on the state's total control over the granting of licenses.

ISSUE: Is the issuance of a liquor license alone sufficient state action to invoke the Fourteenth Amendment?

HOLDING AND DECISION: (Rehnquist, J.) No. Merely granting a liquor license to a private club that engages in discriminatory practices is not sufficient state action to invoke the Fourteenth Amendment. For state action to be found, it must be shown that the state, through an exercise of its power and authority, encouraged discrimination. Merely granting a permit enabling a private club to serve liquor to its members and their guests is essentially neutral conduct. It cannot be said that such conduct either fosters or encourages discriminatory practices. It also cannot be said that the state is lending either its prestige or support to a discriminatory group. Merely regulating the physical aspects of the club or granting a liquor license is not sufficient state action to invoke the prohibitions of the Fourteenth Amendment. The case might be decided contra if the rules and bylaws of the club required racial discrimination. Here they do not. Reversed and remanded.

DISSENT: (Douglas, J.) Liquor licenses in Pennsylvania are not freely available, and are subject to a complex quota system. The state-enforced scarcity of licenses restricts the ability of blacks to obtain liquor. I would affirm the judgment below.

DISSENT: (Brennan, J.) The state's liquor regulations intertwine the state with the operation of the Lodge (D) in a significant way and lends the state's authority to the sordid business of racial discrimination. When the Lodge (D) obtained its liquor license, the state became an active participant in the operation of the Lodge's (D) bar.

ANALYSIS

Granting a lease in a public facility has been held to be sufficient governmental involvement to invoke the Fourteenth Amendment. *Burton v. Wilmington Parking Authority*, 365 U.S. 715 (1961). Another example of state action is where a private discriminatory facility contracts with the police to hire deputies to enforce the discriminatory practices. *Griffin v. Maryland*, 378 U.S. 130 (1964).

Quicknotes

FOURTEENTH AMENDMENT Declares that no state shall make or enforce any law that shall abridge the privileges and immunities of citizens of the United States. No state shall deny to any person within its jurisdiction the equal protection of the laws.

Jackson v. Metropolitan Edison Co.

Customer (P) v. Power company (D)

419 U.S. 345 (1974).

NATURE OF CASE: Appeal of constitutional challenge to termination of electrical service for non-payment.

FACT SUMMARY: Metropolitan Edison (D), a privately owned, regulated power company, terminated service to Jackson (P) for nonpayment.

🏛 RULE OF LAW
A privately owned utility may cease providing service without raising due process concerns, even if it is highly regulated.

FACTS: Metropolitan Edison (D) was a privately-owned utility company. It was regulated by the State Utility Commission. The evidence tended to show that Metropolitan Edison (D) was a legal monopoly, although this issue was inconclusive. Metropolitan Edison (D) terminated service to Jackson (P) for alleged nonpayment, a practice sanctioned by the utilities commission. Jackson (P) brought suit, alleging a violation of due process. The court of appeals held for Metropolitan Edison (D).

ISSUE: May a privately owned utility cease providing service without raising due process concerns, even if it is highly regulated?

HOLDING AND DECISION: (Rehnquist, J.) Yes. A privately owned utility may cease providing service without raising due process concerns, even if it is highly regulated. A decision made by a business that is highly regulated involves state action only if the state was actively involved in the decision or otherwise coerced it. The mere fact of regulation or approval does not give rise to state action. Here all the state did was regulate Metropolitan Edison (D) and approve its procedures. The state did not actively involve itself in decision-making. Therefore, no state action existed. Affirmed.

DISSENT: (Marshall, J.) Where a state confers a monopoly on an organization, that organization assumes many obligations of the state. That, coupled with procedural approval, gives rise to state action here.

▶ ANALYSIS

It would seem that the key concept in this area is governmental neutrality. As long as the government takes a passive role in decision-making, no state action is involved. Of course, there are those, such as Justice Marshall in dissent here, who believe that licensing and regulation is more than neutrality, but rather is imprimatur necessary for state action.

Quicknotes

DUE PROCESS The constitutional mandate requiring the courts to protect and enforce individuals' rights and liberties consistent with prevailing principles of fairness and justice and prohibiting the federal and state governments from such activities that deprive its citizens of life, liberty, or property interest.

Marsh v. Alabama

Distributor of literature (P) v. State (D)

326 U.S. 501 (1946).

NATURE OF CASE: Appeal from a criminal conviction.

FACT SUMMARY: Marsh (D) attempted to distribute religious literature in a company-owned town.

RULE OF LAW
When private property is the equivalent of a public "business block" it ceases to be strictly private and First Amendment rights may not be arbitrarily curtailed.

FACTS: Chickasaw was a company-owned town in Alabama (D). Its business district was open to the public and public highways ran through it. The company prohibited all solicitation or distribution of literature without a permit. Marsh (P), a Jehovah's Witness, attempted to pass out religious literature on the sidewalks of the business district. Marsh (D) was arrested and convicted of a misdemeanor for remaining on private property after being asked to leave. Marsh (D) alleged that this violated her First and Fourteenth Amendment rights and the sidewalks in the business block were quasi-public.

ISSUE: Where private property has taken on the public character of a public business block, may First Amendment rights be arbitrarily curtailed?

HOLDING AND DECISION: (Black, J.) No. When private property is the equivalent of a public "business block" it ceases to be strictly private and First Amendment rights may not be arbitrarily curtailed. Certain property becomes quasi-public as it becomes opened to the general public. The greater the access to and encouragement of public use, the less arbitrary freedom is granted to the owner as to the use and condition of his property. Where the property becomes the equivalent of a public business block, private ownership will not excuse arbitrary curtailment of First Amendment rights. The public's right to free access to information and Marsh's (D) right to practice her First Amendment rights cannot be arbitrarily interfered with by the company. It cannot allow the distribution of certain material and arbitrarily deny access to others. Those living in company towns have a right to receive free access to divergent views. When the company's right to the free use of its quasi-public property is balanced against these other rights, the company's rights must give way. Reversed and remanded.

DISSENT: (Reed, J.) We permit company towns and there is no compelling reason to accommodate trespasses. Absent public dedication there is no reason to treat company towns any differently than other private property.

ANALYSIS

Marsh has subsequently been limited to cases involving company towns and public dedications. Private property rights are still deemed superior to First Amendment rights in other situations. The rationale in *Marsh* is basically that the inhabitants of the town or those interested in influencing them have no other means to reasonably do so since the company can restrict newspapers, etc. In other situations, many public areas are available for distribution to the citizens of a community without requiring private property owners to suffer unwanted intrusions.

Quicknotes

FIRST AMENDMENT Prohibits Congress from enacting any law respecting an establishment of religion, prohibiting the free exercise of religion, abridging freedom of speech or the press, the right of peaceful assembly and the right to petition for a redress of grievances.

Glossary

Common Latin Words and Phrases Encountered in the Law

A FORTIORI: Because one fact exists or has been proven, therefore a second fact that is related to the first fact must also exist.

A PRIORI: From the cause to the effect. A term of logic used to denote that when one generally accepted truth is shown to be a cause, another particular effect must necessarily follow.

AB INITIO: From the beginning; a condition which has existed throughout, as in a marriage which was void ab initio.

ACTUS REUS: The wrongful act; in criminal law, such action sufficient to trigger criminal liability.

AD VALOREM: According to value; an ad valorem tax is imposed upon an item located within the taxing jurisdiction calculated by the value of such item.

AMICUS CURIAE: Friend of the court. Its most common usage takes the form of an amicus curiae brief, filed by a person who is not a party to an action but is nonetheless allowed to offer an argument supporting his legal interests.

ARGUENDO: In arguing. A statement, possibly hypothetical, made for the purpose of argument, is one made arguendo.

BILL QUIA TIMET: A bill to quiet title (establish ownership) to real property.

BONA FIDE: True, honest, or genuine. May refer to a person's legal position based on good faith or lacking notice of fraud (such as a bona fide purchaser for value) or to the authenticity of a particular document (such as a bona fide last will and testament).

CAUSA MORTIS: With approaching death in mind. A gift causa mortis is a gift given by a party who feels certain that death is imminent.

CAVEAT EMPTOR: Let the buyer beware. This maxim is reflected in the rule of law that a buyer purchases at his own risk because it is his responsibility to examine, judge, test, and otherwise inspect what he is buying.

CERTIORARI: A writ of review. Petitions for review of a case by the United States Supreme Court are most often done by means of a writ of certiorari.

CONTRA: On the other hand. Opposite. Contrary to.

CORAM NOBIS: Before us; writs of error directed to the court that originally rendered the judgment.

CORAM VOBIS: Before you; writs of error directed by an appellate court to a lower court to correct a factual error.

CORPUS DELICTI: The body of the crime; the requisite elements of a crime amounting to objective proof that a crime has been committed.

CUM TESTAMENTO ANNEXO, ADMINISTRATOR (ADMINISTRATOR C.T.A.): With will annexed; an administrator c.t.a. settles an estate pursuant to a will in which he is not appointed.

DE BONIS NON, ADMINISTRATOR (ADMINISTRATOR D.B.N.): Of goods not administered; an administrator d.b.n. settles a partially settled estate.

DE FACTO: In fact; in reality; actually. Existing in fact but not officially approved or engendered.

DE JURE: By right; lawful. Describes a condition that is legitimate "as a matter of law," in contrast to the term "de facto," which connotes something existing in fact but not legally sanctioned or authorized. For example, de facto segregation refers to segregation brought about by housing patterns, etc., whereas de jure segregation refers to segregation created by law.

DE MINIMIS: Of minimal importance; insignificant; a trifle; not worth bothering about.

DE NOVO: Anew; a second time; afresh. A trial de novo is a new trial held at the appellate level as if the case originated there and the trial at a lower level had not taken place.

DICTA: Generally used as an abbreviated form of obiter dicta, a term describing those portions of a judicial opinion incidental or not necessary to resolution of the specific question before the court. Such nonessential statements and remarks are not considered to be binding precedent.

DUCES TECUM: Refers to a particular type of writ or subpoena requesting a party or organization to produce certain documents in their possession.

EN BANC: Full bench. Where a court sits with all justices present rather than the usual quorum.

EX PARTE: For one side or one party only. An ex parte proceeding is one undertaken for the benefit of only one party, without notice to, or an appearance by, an adverse party.

EX POST FACTO: After the fact. An ex post facto law is a law that retroactively changes the consequences of a prior act.

EX REL.: Abbreviated form of the term "ex relatione," meaning upon relation or information. When the state brings an action in which it has no interest against an individual at the instigation of one who has a private interest in the matter.

FORUM NON CONVENIENS: Inconvenient forum. Although a court may have jurisdiction over the case, the action should be tried in a more conveniently located court, one to which parties and witnesses may more easily travel, for example.

GUARDIAN AD LITEM: A guardian of an infant as to litigation, appointed to represent the infant and pursue his/her rights.

HABEAS CORPUS: You have the body. The modern writ of habeas corpus is a writ directing that a person (body) being detained (such as a prisoner) be brought before the court so that the legality of his detention can be judicially ascertained.

IN CAMERA: In private, in chambers. When a hearing is held before a judge in his chambers or when all spectators are excluded from the courtroom.

IN FORMA PAUPERIS: In the manner of a pauper. A party who proceeds in forma pauperis because of his poverty is one who is allowed to bring suit without liability for costs.

INFRA: Below, under. A word referring the reader to a later part of a book. (The opposite of supra.)

IN LOCO PARENTIS: In the place of a parent.

IN PARI DELICTO: Equally wrong; a court of equity will not grant requested relief to an applicant who is in pari delicto, or as much at fault in the transactions giving rise to the controversy as is the opponent of the applicant.

IN PARI MATERIA: On like subject matter or upon the same matter. Statutes relating to the same person or things are said to be in pari materia. It is a general rule of statutory construction that such statutes should be construed together, i.e., looked at as if they together constituted one law.

IN PERSONAM: Against the person. Jurisdiction over the person of an individual.

IN RE: In the matter of. Used to designate a proceeding involving an estate or other property.

IN REM: A term that signifies an action against the res, or thing. An action in rem is basically one that is taken directly against property, as distinguished from an action in personam, i.e., against the person.

INTER ALIA: Among other things. Used to show that the whole of a statement, pleading, list, statute, etc., has not been set forth in its entirety.

INTER PARTES: Between the parties. May refer to contracts, conveyances or other transactions having legal significance.

INTER VIVOS: Between the living. An inter vivos gift is a gift made by a living grantor, as distinguished from bequests contained in a will, which pass upon the death of the testator.

IPSO FACTO: By the mere fact itself.

JUS: Law or the entire body of law.

LEX LOCI: The law of the place; the notion that the rights of parties to a legal proceeding are governed by the law of the place where those rights arose.

MALUM IN SE: Evil or wrong in and of itself; inherently wrong. This term describes an act that is wrong by its very nature, as opposed to one which would not be wrong but for the fact that there is a specific legal prohibition against it (malum prohibitum).

MALUM PROHIBITUM: Wrong because prohibited, but not inherently evil. Used to describe something that is wrong because it is expressly forbidden by law but that is not in and of itself evil, e.g., speeding.

MANDAMUS: We command. A writ directing an official to take a certain action.

MENS REA: A guilty mind; a criminal intent. A term used to signify the mental state that accompanies a crime or other prohibited act. Some crimes require only a general mens rea (general intent to do the prohibited act), but others, like assault with intent to murder, require the existence of a specific mens rea.

MODUS OPERANDI: Method of operating; generally refers to the manner or style of a criminal in committing crimes, admissible in appropriate cases as evidence of the identity of a defendant.

NEXUS: A connection to.

NISI PRIUS: A court of first impression. A nisi prius court is one where issues of fact are tried before a judge or jury.

N.O.V. (NON OBSTANTE VEREDICTO): Notwithstanding the verdict. A judgment n.o.v. is a judgment given in favor of one party despite the fact that a verdict was returned in favor of the other party, the justification being that the verdict either had no reasonable support in fact or was contrary to law.

NUNC PRO TUNC: Now for then. This phrase refers to actions that may be taken and will then have full retroactive effect.

PENDENTE LITE: Pending the suit; pending litigation under way.

PER CAPITA: By head; beneficiaries of an estate, if they take in equal shares, take per capita.

PER CURIAM: By the court; signifies an opinion ostensibly written "by the whole court" and with no identified author.

PER SE: By itself, in itself; inherently.

PER STIRPES: By representation. Used primarily in the law of wills to describe the method of distribution where a person, generally because of death, is unable to take that which is left to him by the will of another, and therefore his heirs divide such property between them rather than take under the will individually.

PRIMA FACIE: On its face, at first sight. A prima facie case is one that is sufficient on its face, meaning that the evidence supporting it is adequate to establish the case until contradicted or overcome by other evidence.

PRO TANTO: For so much; as far as it goes. Often used in eminent domain cases when a property owner receives partial payment for his land without prejudice to his right to bring suit for the full amount he claims his land to be worth.

QUANTUM MERUIT: As much as he deserves. Refers to recovery based on the doctrine of unjust enrichment in those cases in which a party has rendered valuable services or furnished materials that were accepted and enjoyed by another under circumstances that would reasonably notify the recipient that the rendering party expected to be paid. In essence, the law implies a contract to pay the reasonable value of the services or materials furnished.

QUASI: Almost like; as if; nearly. This term is essentially used to signify that one subject or thing is almost analogous to another but that material differences between them do exist. For example, a quasi-criminal proceeding is one that is not strictly criminal but shares enough of the same characteristics to require some of the same safeguards (e.g., procedural due process must be followed in a parole hearing).

QUID PRO QUO: Something for something. In contract law, the consideration, something of value, passed between the parties to render the contract binding.

RES GESTAE: Things done; in evidence law, this principle justifies the admission of a statement that would otherwise be hearsay when it is made so closely to the event in question as to be said to be a part of it, or with such spontaneity as not to have the possibility of falsehood.

RES IPSA LOQUITUR: The thing speaks for itself. This doctrine gives rise to a rebuttable presumption of negligence when the instrumentality causing the injury was within the exclusive control of the defendant, and the injury was one that does not normally occur unless a person has been negligent.

RES JUDICATA: A matter adjudged. Doctrine which provides that once a court of competent jurisdiction has rendered a final judgment or decree on the merits, that judgment or decree is conclusive upon the parties to the case and prevents them from engaging in any other litigation on the points and issues determined therein.

RESPONDEAT SUPERIOR: Let the master reply. This doctrine holds the master liable for the wrongful acts of his servant (or the principal for his agent) in those cases in which the servant (or agent) was acting within the scope of his authority at the time of the injury.

STARE DECISIS: To stand by or adhere to that which has been decided. The common law doctrine of stare decisis attempts to give security and certainty to the law by following the policy that once a principle of law as applicable to a certain set of facts has been set forth in a decision, it forms a precedent which will subsequently be followed, even though a different decision might be made were it the first time the question had arisen. Of course, stare decisis is not an inviolable principle and is departed from in instances where there is good cause (e.g., considerations of public policy led the Supreme Court to disregard prior decisions sanctioning segregation).

SUPRA: Above. A word referring a reader to an earlier part of a book.

ULTRA VIRES: Beyond the power. This phrase is most commonly used to refer to actions taken by a corporation that are beyond the power or legal authority of the corporation.

Addendum of French Derivatives

IN PAIS: Not pursuant to legal proceedings.

CHATTEL: Tangible personal property.

CY PRES: Doctrine permitting courts to apply trust funds to purposes not expressed in the trust but necessary to carry out the settlor's intent.

PER AUTRE VIE: For another's life; during another's life. In property law, an estate may be granted that will terminate upon the death of someone other than the grantee.

PROFIT A PRENDRE: A license to remove minerals or other produce from land.

VOIR DIRE: Process of questioning jurors as to their predispositions about the case or parties to a proceeding in order to identify those jurors displaying bias or prejudice.

Casenote Legal Briefs

Administrative Law .... Breyer, Stewart, Sunstein & Vermeule
Administrative Law .... Cass, Diver & Beermann
Administrative Law .... Funk, Shapiro & Weaver
Administrative Law .... Mashaw, Merrill & Shane
Administrative Law .... Strauss, Rakoff, & Farina
    (Gellhorn & Byse)
Agency & Partnership .... Hynes & Loewenstein
Antitrust .... Pitofsky, Goldschmid & Wood
Antitrust .... Sullivan & Hovenkamp
Bankruptcy .... Warren & Bussel
Business Organizations .... Allen, Kraakman & Subramanian
Business Organizations .... Bauman, Weiss & Palmiter
Business Organizations .... Hamilton & Macey
Business Organizations .... Klein, Ramseyer & Bainbridge
Business Organizations .... O'Kelley & Thompson
Business Organizations .... Soderquist, Smiddy & Cunningham
Civil Procedure .... Field, Kaplan & Clermont
Civil Procedure .... Freer & Perdue
Civil Procedure .... Friedenthal, Miller, Sexton & Hershkoff
Civil Procedure .... Hazard, Tait, Fletcher & Bundy
Civil Procedure .... Marcus, Redish & Sherman
Civil Procedure .... Subrin, Minow, Brodin & Main
Civil Procedure .... Yeazell
Commercial Law .... LoPucki, Warren, Keating & Mann
Commercial Law .... Warren & Walt
Commercial Law .... Whaley
Community Property .... Bird
Community Property .... Blumberg
Conflicts .... Brilmayer & Goldsmith
Conflicts .... Currie, Kay, Kramer & Roosevelt
Constitutional Law .... Brest, Levinson, Balkin & Amar
Constitutional Law .... Chemerinsky
Constitutional Law .... Choper, Fallon, Kamisar & Shiffrin (Lockhart)
Constitutional Law .... Cohen, Varat & Amar
Constitutional Law .... Farber, Eskridge & Frickey
Constitutional Law .... Rotunda
Constitutional Law .... Sullivan & Gunther
Constitutional Law .... Stone, Seidman, Sunstein, Tushnet & Karlan
Contracts .... Barnett
Contracts .... Burton
Contracts .... Calamari, Perillo & Bender
Contracts .... Crandall & Whaley
Contracts .... Dawson, Harvey, Henderson & Baird
Contracts .... Farnsworth, Young, Sanger, Cohen & Brooks
Contracts .... Fuller & Eisenberg
Contracts .... Knapp, Crystal & Prince
Contracts .... Murphy, Speidel & Ayres
Copyright .... Cohen, Loren, Okediji & O'Rourke
Copyright .... Goldstein & Reese
Criminal Law .... Bonnie, Coughlin, Jeffries & Low
Criminal Law .... Boyce, Dripps & Perkins
Criminal Law .... Dressler
Criminal Law .... Johnson & Cloud
Criminal Law .... Kadish, Schulhofer & Steiker
Criminal Law .... Kaplan, Weisberg & Binder
Criminal Procedure .... Allen, Hoffmann, Livingston & Stuntz
Criminal Procedure .... Dressler & Thomas
Criminal Procedure .... Haddad, Marsh, Zagel, Meyer,
    Starkman & Bauer
Criminal Procedure .... Kamisar, LaFave, Israel, King & Kerr
Criminal Procedure .... Saltzburg & Capra
Debtors and Creditors .... Warren & Westbrook
Employment Discrimination .... Friedman
Employment Discrimination .... Zimmer, Sullivan & White
Employment Law .... Rothstein & Liebman
Environmental Law .... Menell & Stewart

Environmental Law .... Percival, Schroder, Miller & Leape
Environmental Law .... Plater, Abrams, Goldfarb, Graham,
    Heinzerling & Wirth
Evidence .... Broun, Mosteller & Giannelli
Evidence .... Fisher
Evidence .... Mueller & Kirkpatrick
Evidence .... Sklansky
Evidence .... Waltz, Park & Friedman
Family Law .... Areen & Regan
Family Law .... Ellman, Kurtz & Scott
Family Law .... Harris, Teitelbaum & Carbone
Family Law .... Wadlington & O'Brien
Family Law .... Weisberg & Appleton
Federal Courts .... Fallon, Meltzer & Shapiro (Hart & Wechsler)
Federal Courts .... Low & Jeffries
Health Law .... Furrow, Greaney, Johnson,
    Jost & Schwartz
Immigration Law .... Aleinikoff, Martin & Motomura
Immigration Law .... Legomsky
Insurance Law .... Abraham
Intellectual Property .... Merges, Menell & Lemley
International Business Transactions .... Folsom, Gordon,
    Spanogle & Fitzgerald
International Law .... Blakesley, Firmage, Scott & Williams
International Law .... Carter, Trimble & Weiner
International Law .... Damrosch, Henkin, Pugh, Schachter &
    Smit
International Law .... Dunoff, Ratner & Wippman
Labor Law .... Cox, Bok, Gorman & Finkin
Land Use .... Callies, Freilich & Roberts
Legislation .... Eskridge, Frickey & Garrett
Oil & Gas .... Lowe, Anderson, Smith & Pierce
Patent Law .... Adelman, Radner, Thomas & Wegner
Products Liability .... Owen, Montgomery & Davis
Professional Responsibility .... Gillers
Professional Responsibility .... Hazard, Koniak, Cramton & Cohen
Property .... Casner, Leach, French, Korngold
    & VanderVelde
Property .... Cribbet, Johnson, Findley & Smith
Property .... Donahue, Kauper & Martin
Property .... Dukeminier, Krier, Alexander & Schill
Property .... Haar & Liebman
Property .... Kurtz & Hovenkamp
Property .... Nelson, Stoebuck & Whitman
Property .... Rabin, Kwall & Kwall
Property .... Singer
Real Estate .... Korngold & Goldstein
Real Estate Transactions .... Nelson & Whitman
Remedies .... Laycock
Remedies .... Shoben, Tabb & Janutis
Securities Regulation .... Coffee, Seligman & Sale
Securities Regulation .... Cox, Hillman & Langevoort
Sports Law .... Weiler & Roberts
Taxation (Corporate) .... Lind, Schwartz, Lathrope & Rosenberg
Taxation (Individual) .... Burke & Friel
Taxation (Individual) .... Freeland, Lathrope, Lind & Stephens
Taxation (Individual) .... Klein, Bankman, Shaviro, & Stark
Torts .... Dobbs & Hayden
Torts .... Epstein
Torts .... Franklin & Rabin
Torts .... Henderson, Pearson, Kysar & Siliciano
Torts .... Schwartz, Kelly & Partlett (Prosser)
Wills, Trusts & Estates .... Dukeminier, Johanson, Lindgren & Sitkoff
Wills, Trusts & Estates .... Dobris, Sterk & Leslie
Wills, Trusts & Estates .... Scoles, Halbach, Roberts & Begleiter